Art
and the
Religious Experience:
The "Language" of the Sacred

Mark Rothko: *Earth Greens* (1955). Oil on canvas, 91½″ x 73½″. Courtesy Galerie Beyeler, Basel, Switzerland.

Art
and the
Religious Experience:
The "Language" of the Sacred

F. David Martin

Lewisburg
Bucknell University Press

NX
6 50
C 5
M3

Associated University Presses, Inc.
Cranbury, New Jersey 08512

ISBN: 0-8387-7935-2
Printed in the United States of America

The author wishes to thank The Viking Press,
Inc., for permission to quote from *The Bell* by
Iris Murdoch. Copyright © 1958 by Iris Murdoch.
Reprinted by permission of The Viking Press, Inc.

To Doady

Contents

List of Illustrations

Color Plates

The following appear after page 144.

Musical Examples

Foreword

If ours is an apocalyptic time, it is a time of radical transition, a time in which we are not only entering a new age, but also abandoning or losing the cosmos and history of our past. An apocalyptic time is by necessity revolutionary, for it can envision and enact a new creation only by bringing to an end that old creation which stands immediately before it as the given reality which it can know or name. Two primary symbolic words have become paradigmatic in our time, the "primordial" and the "eschatological," and each stands for a world lying beyond the actual horizon of both our history and our present. The primordial is not simply the original or the beginning, it is also a beginning or an original which is lost; it is absent from the active expressions of our consciousness and experience, and appears or is real only in those moments when our historical or given identities are active or silent. We may, perhaps, return to a primordial meaning or identity, but we may do so only by a radical act of disengagement or reversal, an act which must, if only momentarily, bring our history to an end.

In an apocalyptic situation there is an inevitable tendency to identify the primordial and the eschatological, *Urzeit* and *Endzeit,* the original Adam and the final Adam. Accordingly, Protestant dialectical theology, arising in the apocalyptic situation following the First World War, identified

13

eschatological with primordial time. We may also observe the modern or the post-modern imagination engaged in a radical quest for a primordial time as the eschatological time for us, and this quest dominates not only the manifestly archaic symbolic imagery of Yeats and Joyce, but also the Christian imagery of Eliot. With the disintegration or collapse of the previously dominant expressions of our tradition, primordial meanings and identities became comprehensively manifest, and not only in religion and the arts, but also in politics, psychoanalysis, and philosophy. The philosophers who most fully embodied this quest for primordial meaning are Whitehead and Heidegger, and perhaps we have only just reached the point where it is possible to bring their quests for ultimate meaning into a common focus or perspective.

F. David Martin has not only performed the valuable service of bringing Whiteheadian and Heideggerian aesthetics together, but he effects this synthesis in the context of a rich and exciting investigation of all the major Western art forms, and it is just this context which releases and enriches the meaning which he discovers. Martin's is also a religious or theological quest, and it can be identified theologically as a quest for primordial meaning in our historical and apocalyptic situation. In his conception of participative experience, Martin not only attempts a synthesis of Heidegger and Whitehead, but he also attempts to conjoin the "I" with the "thing" in such a way as to expose an original selfhood and an original creation, thereby unveiling an exposed self-abandonment as the way to a primordial world and identity. It is essential to this quest to establish and maintain a mediating correlation between *Being-as-transcendental* and *Being-as-immanent*. Neither manifestation of *Being* appears in any obvious way in what we can know and experience as our given present or our mediated past. But either *Being-as-transcendental* or *Being-as-immanent* does clearly appear in the fullest expressions of art, and it is just in these concrete expressions or embodiments of Being that the face of God is manifest.

It is not accidental that Martin so fully employs Tillich's theological method of correlation. Thus depth becomes Martin's primary religious image, and he follows Tillich in identifying the depth dimension with *Being*. Yet Martin's own quest must carry him beyond Tillich by leading him more deeply into the primordial, and, as the thinking of Whitehead and Heidegger makes clear, the fullness of primordial meaning radically challenges our inherited symbols and categories of depth and transcendence. Is *Being-as-transcendental* always manifest "awe-fully"? Is the depth dimension necessarily redemptive in a traditional sense? Are only the Judaic-Christian symbols of transcendence and immanence true or living symbols in the West? Or for us today? And, if so, must they continue to bear their traditional symbolic form and identity? For example, Martin's analysis leads to the inevitable conclusion that abstract painting is a triumph of the secular. And he would have it as a religious triumph. Yet no way lies present of establishing this truth apart from a radical and comprehensive reconstruction of our inherited religious meaning and symbolism.

We cannot legitimately expect so rich a book to also succeed in this enterprise. Yet Martin's religious aesthetics does point in a new theological direction, and it does so by posing the fundamental question of the possibility for us of a fully primordial imagery and symbolism. One possible weakness of Martin's analysis is that it seems to subordinate *Being-as-immanent* to *Being-as-transcendental*. Or, at least, it is *Being-as-transcendental* which actually dominates his analysis. But we might expect that a fully primordial imagery would transcend or lie beyond our inherited imagery of transcendence and immanence, and, indeed, would initiate us into a region where everything which we know as God-language would dissolve. It might also be noted that our inherited God-language dissolves in fully eschatological or apocalyptic imagery, and this is true not only in the apocalyptic vision of Blake, but also in the eschatological vision of Teilhard de Chardin. What, then, is the relation between primordial and eschatological vision, or primordial and eschatological imagery? Are they finally or fundamentally identical? Is a quest for an apocalyptic End finally a quest for a primordial Beginning? Is the *Being* which Heidegger names finally identical with the Kingdom of God? Or is Whitehead's idea of the consequent nature of God a metaphysical conceptualization of the Kingdom of God? Does a fundamental, a consistent, and a comprehensive uprooting and transformation of our inherited religious symbolism and imagery inevitably lead to a meaning and identity which are simultaneously primordial and eschatological? Or totally primordial and hence wholly noneschatological? Or totally eschatological and hence wholly nonprimordial?

These questions are not idle questions, and apart from their resolution we will find no way into full or genuine religious or theological meaning in our apocalyptic situation. Or should we say our primordial situation? Is our crisis finally leading us to an original human and cosmic identity? Surely there is no arena which more fully offers a possibility of resolving these ultimate questions than the arts. In this book the reader will discover not only a comprehensive philosophical and religious analysis of the arts, but also an analysis which carries ultimate questions into the actual context of concrete works of art, and in such a manner as to unveil hitherto unsuspected meanings. While the book will not resolve our religious questions, it succeeds in posing them in a new manner and mode, and it richly illustrates how a full religious quest in our time can lead beyond the boundaries of what has been given to us as the religiously nameable.

Thomas J. J. Altizer

Preface

Charles Hartshorne and Eliseo Vivas, my old friends and teachers, who shared the same office at The University of Chicago many years ago, first aroused my curiosity about the role of the aesthetic in religions. But it was the encouragement and suggestions of Paul Tillich that provided the direct impetus of this project. And then later there were many provocative discussions with Theodore M. Greene. Carrol C. Pratt of Princeton University generously assisted with the chapter on music. Harry R. Garvin and Joseph P. Fell, III, of Bucknell University read the entire manuscript and contributed richly with their counsel. But I reserve for myself the inadequacies, especially since in several instances I stubbornly refused to heed the advice of my friends and critics. I wish gratefully to acknowledge the financial aid of The Lilly Foundation and Bucknell University which made it possible for me to take a year's leave of absence. Bibliographical and technical assistance was given by Mrs. Iva Weaver and Miss Jill Lindberg. And I owe special gratitude to my family, who protected the many hours that are essential to any serious work.

The motif of this study is the participative experience with the arts as the principal path into the depth or religious dimension. The first chapter sketches in broad strokes the participative experience and the religious experience. As the base for this analysis, I use the philosophy of Martin Heidegger. However, I am not attempting an exegesis of Heidegger. I am attempting to go my own way in directions suggested especially by the later writings of Heidegger. In chapter 2, Whitehead's theory of perception is used to help make more precise the detailed operations of the participative experience. In the following chapters, music, painting, literature, and architecture are examined with reference to how they not only lure us into participation with the religious dimension but interpret that dimension.

At the end of the last century, Matthew Arnold intimated that the aesthetic experience, especially of the arts, would become the religious experience. This transformation will not happen because the aesthetic or participative experience lacks the outward expressions that fulfill and, in turn, distinguish the religious experience. But Arnold was prophetic, I believe, in the sense that increasingly the arts would provide the most direct access to the sacred.

Acknowledgments

For permission to quote from copyrighted material, I should like to thank the following publishers:

Art Journal and the College Art Association, New York City, for permission to quote from my "Naming Paintings," 1966.

Associated Music Publishers, Inc., New York City, for permission to reproduce a few bars from Bach's *St. Matthew Passion* and *The Art of Fugue.*

Books for Libraries Press, Freeport, New York, for permission to quote from Gabriel Marcel's *The Philosophy of Existence,* 1948.

Boosey and Hawks Music Publishers, Ltd., New York City, for permission to reproduce a few bars from Benjamin Britten's *War Requiem,* 1962. Reprinted by permission of Boosey and Hawkes, Inc. Text from the *Missa Pro Defunctis* and the poems of Wilfred Owen.

Bucknell Review, Lewisburg, Pa., for permission to quote from my "Heidegger's Thinking Being and Whitehead's Theory of Perception," 1969.

19

Sound and The Fury, 1946, and the *Essays by Thomas Mann,* 1965.

Religious Studies, London, England, for permission to quote from my "The Aesthetic in Religious Experience," 1968.

The Viking Press, New York City, for permission to quote from Iris Murdoch's *The Bell,* 1958.

Art
and the
Religious Experience:
The "Language" of the Sacred

Man is estranged from that with which he is most familiar, and he must continuously seek to discover it.

Heraclitus

1

The Aesthetic in the Religious Experience

I

William James catalogued an amazing diversity of religious experiences. Yet even the pluralistic James was able to find a nucleus: an uneasiness and its solution. "1. The uneasiness," he writes, "reduced to its simplest terms, is a sense that there is *something wrong about us* as we naturally stand. 2. The solution is a sense that *we are saved from the wrongness* by making proper connection with the higher powers."[1] But because of his moralistic predilections, James does not account for those religious experiences that center on the sense of mystery stemming from man's theoretical limitations. Consider Einstein, for example: "The most beautiful thing we can experience is the mysterious side of life. It is the deep feeling which is at the cradle of all true art and science. . . . In this sense, and only in this sense, I count myself amongst the most deeply religious people."[2] For Einstein

---

1. *The Varieties of Religious Experience* (New York: Random House, 1936), p. 498.
2. *Comment je vois le monde,* traduit par le Colonel Cros (Paris: E. Flammamarion, 1934), p. 7.

as for Pascal (*Pensées*, Fr. 267), "the last proceeding of reason is to recognize that there is an infinity of things which are beyond it." Or as Peirce put it: "Our science is altogether middle-sized and mediocre. Its insignificance compared with the universe cannot be exaggerated."[3] Or as Saul Bellow has Herzog say: "Go through what is comprehensible and you conclude that only the incomprehensible gives any light." Thus I propose the following revision of James's conception of the nucleus of the religious experience: 1) uneasy aware-ness of the limitations of man's moral or theoretical powers, especially when reality is restricted to what can be known primarily by means of sensation; 2) awe-full awareness of a further reality—beyond or behind or within; 3) conviction that participation with this further reality is of supreme im-portance.

These three elements seem to be universally present in all religious experiences, but apparently they are not the only ones. For example, religious conviction seems to be always accompanied by feelings of ultimate concern, reverence, and peace, or feelings closely allied. Joachim Wach maintains, furthermore, that religious experiences invariably include three fundamental forms of expression: theoretical, practical, and sociological.[4] Except in passing I shall not be concerned with these religious feelings and the three fundamental forms of religious expression, for I wish rather to focus attention upon the empirical grounds from which these feelings and forms arise. I hope to show that the awareness of these em-pirical grounds is made possible through a particular kind of aesthetic experience—what I shall call a "participative experience." In the participative experience self-conscious-ness is lost and we become completely absorbed in the empirical grounds. Through this participation we have our only direct access to "a further reality." Indeed, without the

---

3. *Collected Papers of Charles Sanders Peirce*, ed. Charles Hartshorne and
   Paul Weiss (Cambridge, Mass.: Harvard University Press, 1931–35), I: 119.
4. *Types of Religious Experience* (Chicago: University of Chicago Press,
   1951), chap. 2. See also Wach's *The Comparative Study of Religions*, ed.
   Joseph M. Kitagawa (New York: Columbia University Press, 1958).

participative experience the religious experience is impossible. A deeply felt participative experience, furthermore, is an awe-full awareness of this further reality, and such awareness inevitably is accompanied by belief in the supreme importance of participating with this further reality and by such feelings as ultimate concern, reverence, and peace. The complete religious experience, nevertheless, is broader than the participative experience—granting that a fine line cannot be drawn between them—because the complete religious experience more explicitly includes theoretical, practical, and sociological forms of expression. Or, to put it another way, a deeply felt participative experience without the fusion of theoretical, practical, and sociological forms of expression is a narrow or incomplete religious experience. Conversely, a deeply felt participative experience wedded to some explicit cognitive understanding of the sacred and an ultimate moral commitment and a community of worship would be a complete religious experience.

My revision of James's formulation is not an attempt to describe a nucleus of necessary and sufficient properties based on either the traditional or the current uses of the term *religious experience*. There simply is no consensus about the meaning of this term. Thus my conception of the nucleus is a proposal or a stipulative definition that attempts to be clear about my meaning for the term. Since the justification for this proposal depends on its usefulness, the proposal will function as a hypothesis to be tested by its power to clarify the phenomena of the religious experience and its relationships to other experiences, especially the aesthetic and the artistic.

The nonreligious experience may also involve an awareness of the limitations of our powers, but not to the uneasy point of challenging the assumption that anything can be cognitively and justifiably asserted about reality that goes beyond evidence based upon sensation. The sense data of a table, for example, include everything about the table that can stimulate our sense organs, such as its colors. However, the table as an object is an enduring and unified complex of sense data. And some epistemologists therefore claim that the table, or any object, is not sensed but rather is a logical construction inferred from sense data. Even if this claim is justified, the awareness of the table is not of a further reality because it rests solely upon the evidence of sensation. And in the nonreligious experience, insofar as the basis for any truth claim is relevant, there is no explicit awareness of anything further than sense data and objects, nor is such a possibility seriously considered. Thus the logical positivists, to take an extreme but clear example of a sense-bound epistemology, are generally quite aware of man's limitations, but they refuse to entertain even the possibility of any further reality beyond the evidence of sensation. The "unknowns" are problems; *i.e.,* at least in principle scientifically verifiable solutions are possible. If not, as A. J. Ayer in his early work so tenaciously repeats, sentences that articulate these so-called problems are simply meaningless.[5] Thus any uneasiness about the limitations of our powers is easily dismissed. Insofar as empirical knowledge is the aim of an experience, what can be known are sense data or objects, that which can be touched or controlled. And insofar as this aim is guided by methods that are now considered the most reliable, all claims to knowledge must be verified through scientific procedures. All such claims must be reducible to statements that are in principle verifiable. The statements must propose assertions that directly or indirectly refer to sense data or objects. The verification of these statements depends ultimately upon the accurate and common observations of sense data by "normal or standard observers," although in some cases these observers may have to be highly trained. Ideally these observations are repeatable under specifiable conditions and approach precise mathematical quantification. In any case, sentences that propose assertions about reality but are not subject to the veri-

---

5. *Language, Truth and Logic* (London: V. Gollancz, 1936). In the later work of Ayer and logical positivism generally, the sharpness of this position has been modified.

fiability principle have no cognitive significance. Such sentences are the product of a kind of mental cramp produced by linguistic confusion. Underlying this one-dimensional scientism is a basic and very useful assumption: the occurrences of sense data and objects are predictable because they are determined by or are the product of a certain given set of conditions composed also of sense data and objects. The possibility of the religious experience begins when we decide that this assumption is not enough—when we face the fact that what we are able to touch or control is not the only reality we are searching for, that in some sense claims about this further reality are justifiable.

Following the distinctions of Heidegger, especially as modified after *Being and Time* (1927), I shall call sense data and objects "beings" or "things,"[6] and the world of beings or things "ontical reality." This reality can be subjected to the procedures and uses of science, the technological and practical disciplines as well as the theoretical sciences. "Ontological reality," on the other hand, is composed of *Being* which reveals itself, if at all, not as a thing but as a "presence" in our experience. *Being* is that temporal and yet permanent reality, a continual coming and an endless origin, that is the source or ground of objects, and yet *Being* is not an object. Nor is *Being* a sense datum or data, for *Being* is that intangible matrix and power that makes possible the existence of any sense datum. Nor is *Being* the common denominator of all

---

6. This is a free following at this point, for "sense data" and "objects" for Heidegger are abstractions from beings or things: "We never really first perceive a throng of sensations, *e.g.*, tones and noises, in the appearance of things. . . . We hear the door shut in the house and never hear acoustical sensations or even mere sounds. In order to hear a bare sound we have to listen-away from things, divert our ear from them, *i.e.*, listen abstractly." "The Origin of The Work of Art," trans. Albert Hofstadter, *Philosophies of Art and Beauty*, ed. Albert Hofstadter and Richard Kuhns (New York: Random House, The Modern Library, 1964), p. 656. Terms such as "sense data," "objects," and "revealed by sensation" are alien to Heidegger's terminology, a heritage of the Humean tradition that Heidegger rejects. For my purposes, however, such terms are useful because they help bring out more precisely the relationships between the ontical and ontological dimensions of reality and the way these dimensions come into our experience.

beings. Rather, *Being* refers to the to-be of whatever is,
whereas being refers to anything that is as revealed by sensation. *Being* is that which renders possible all "is," that
familiar copula asserting or implying existence. *Being* gives
beings their "is." *Being* is the primordial power that conditions and makes beings possible. *Being* is the depth dimension of all beings that both includes and transcends them.
Thus *Being* is a further reality, and beings get their enduring value, their ultimate significance, from *Being*. That is
one of the reasons why *Being* is sometimes described, though
rarely by Heidegger, as the "Wholly Other." Heidegger
usually avoids such terms, because for him, unlike Plato and
most philosophers in his tradition, beings and *Being* although distinguishable are inseparable and completely interdependent. A being is in-*Being*. A being is never without
Being because *Being* makes the existence of beings possible,
makes them manifest. On the other hand, *Being* is never
without beings because *Being* reveals itself only in beings.
Being is nothing apart from beings, and so *Being* is not some
"thing-in-itself" or some kind of invisible world lurking
behind beings. Thus *Being* is always embodied; *Being* as
absolute—as "ab-solved" from all beings—is an empty negative
concept. *Being* is the lighting process by which beings are
illumined as beings. Yet the light does not appear by itself
as a being but only in the beings it enlightens. *Being* con-
tracts in the beings it makes manifest and thus hides as it
reveals. The lighting of *Being* is a hidden light, immersed in
darkness. *Being* always conceals something of itself in making
possible any disclosure. This is the mystery of *Being*.

The awareness of beings, the surface of reality, includes
the explicit awareness of *Being*, the depth of reality—provided that we are ontologically sensitive. Then in the ontical
experience there is included *plus ultra*, "an otherness," a
direct acquaintance or encounter with the presence of *Being*.
For example, when we are cognizant of a person as a mere
means to our ends, as an "it" in Buber's terms, we take

account of him only as a being. But if we are aware of him as a "Thou," as being something more than an object to be manipulated, some aspect of his *Being* dimension has come to presence explicitly in our experience. Similarly, if we treat nonhuman beings merely for their usefulness, we miss their *Being* dimension. Since assertions about beings can be verified through scientific procedures, at least in principle, beings are a subject of knowledge. Such beings are a scattering of the unity of *Being,* and the scientist, in order to know such beings better, dissects and scatters this unity even further. *Being* as such, conversely, cannot be dissected and scattered. Thus *Being* cannot be verified through scientific procedures, and thus *Being* is not a subject of "knowledge."[7] *Being* cannot be observed, nor can we form a mental image of *Being,* nor can *Being* be strictly defined or even described. *Being* eludes every category applicable to beings. Whereas the reality of beings is enclosed, the reality of *Being* is open. *Being* overflows the dichotomy between the subject and predicate of a proposition. To force *Being* into precise concepts is to lose *Being. Being* is a subject matter that defies strict determination and thus can never be fully grasped in thought. Yet since *Being* can come to presence in our experience, *Being* is subject to clarification. For although *Being* is neither observable nor inferable from observation, *Being* is encounterable because *Being* participates in beings. *Being* is manifest not as alongside beings or in addition to them, but in and through them. *Being* is the background or depth dimension from which all beings stand out as observable, and that background can be felt as a presence. In fact we always have at least an implicit awareness of *Being,* no matter how much we ignore or deny it. Whereas we sense beings, we are aware, either implicitly or explicitly, of *Being.* Thus *Being* can be recognized even though *Being* cannot be cognized.

---

7. For a sharply opposed position that claims that *Being* (God) is an object revealed by sensation, and therefore is subject to the scientific method, see Henry Nelson Wieman, *Religious Experience and Scientific Method* (New York: The Macmillan Co., 1926) , esp. chap. 1.

Whereas beings are a subject of knowledge, *Being* is a subject of understanding. Both beings and *Being* are subjects of comprehension.

I find these Heideggerian distinctions useful because they help focus attention upon the line I am trying to draw between the religious and the nonreligious experience. However, since the study of the religious experience has not been a systematic concern of Heidegger's, further distinctions are necessary. Whether Heidegger would agree with these further distinctions and the analyses based upon them is, of course, problematical.

If in an experience only beings or ontical reality come into explicit awareness, then that experience is nonreligious or one-dimensional. If in an experience *Being* or ontological reality also comes into explicit awareness, then that experience begins to take on a religious or two-dimensional character.[8] For example, Iris Murdoch in *The Bell* describes a transition from an ontical to an ontological experience:

> Dora had been in the National Gallery a thousand times and the pictures were almost as familiar to her as her own face. Passing between them now, as through a well-loved grove, she felt a calm descending on her. She wandered a little, watching with compassion the poor visitors armed with guide books who were peering anxiously at the masterpieces. Dora did not need to peer. She could look, as one can at last when one knows a great thing very well, confronting it with a dignity which it has itself conferred. She felt that the pictures belonged to her, and reflected ruefully that they were about the only thing that did. Vaguely, consoled by the presence of something welcoming and responding in the place, her footsteps took her to various shrines at which she had worshipped so often before.[9]

The religious character of the experience deepens as the

---

8. Paul Weiss makes essentially the same point when he maintains that those who fail to insist on the presence of the ontological in the religious experience, for example Dewey in *A Common Faith,* "have no way of distinguishing a supposed religious experience from similarly toned but quite different occurrences." *The God We Seek* (Carbondale, Ill.: Southern Illinois University Press, 1964), p. 53.

9. *The Bell* (New York: Viking Press, 1966), p. 182.

ontological awareness brings with it awe-full awareness and
the conviction or belief that participation with ontological
reality is of supreme importance.[10] Then what I shall refer
to as *Being-as-transcendental* comes to awareness. Whereas
Being-as-immanent refers only to the depth of dimension as
embodied in some being or beings, *Being-as-transcendental*
also refers to the depth dimension as a unity that somehow
is more than its embodiment in beings. This unity of *Being*,
however, does not exist without its embodiments. Beings,
Being-as-immanent, and *Being-as-transcendental* are a continuum. *Being-as-transcendental*, unlike the disembodied
Being of the mystics, is *Being-as-immanent-as-transcendental*,
but this awkward neologism mercifully will be avoided. *Being* as disembodied, a conception that along with Heidegger
I consider a misconception, will be referred to as *Being-as-
absolute*. The more or less orthodox Christian conception of
Being, as formulated by Kierkegaard for example, is not
quite *Being-as-absolute*. Through special revelation, *Being*
or God incarnates itself in *some* beings. On the other hand,
Kierkegaard would reject the conception of *Being-as-transcendental*, as I have formulated it, because this conception
asserts the immanence of *Being* in *all* beings. Therefore
revelation is general. The immanency and transcendency of
Being are inseparable, but *Being-as-transcendental* will come
into awareness only if the experience of *Being-as-immanent*
is strongly coercive. Dora, as she continues through the museum, apparently is having, or is very close to having, such
an experience:

> Dora was always moved by the pictures. Today she was
> moved, but in a new way. She marvelled, with a kind of grati-
> tude, that they were all still here, and her heart was filled with
> love for the pictures, their authority, their marvellous generos-
> ity, their splendour. It occurred to her that here at last was

10. On the question of the value function of *Being*—for example, the relationship between the subjective value of *Being* to us and the objective
value in *Being* that claims our homage—see Rudolf Otto, *The Idea of
The Holy*, trans. John W. Harvey (London: Oxford University Press,
1928) , esp. pp. 52ff.

something real and something perfect. Who had said that, about perfection and reality being in the same place? Here was something which her consciousness could not wretchedly devour, and by making it part of her fantasy make it worthless. . . . The pictures were something real outside herself, which spoke kindly, and yet in sovereign tones, something superior and good whose presence destroyed the dreary trance-like solipsism of her earlier mood. When the world had seemed to be subjective it had seemed to be without interest or value. But now there was something else in it after all.

These thoughts, not clearly articulated, flitted through Dora's mind. She had never thought about the pictures in this way before; nor did she draw now any very explicit moral. Yet she felt that she had had a revelation. She looked at the radiant, sombre, tender, powerful canvas of Gainsborough and felt a sudden desire to go down on her knees before it, embracing it, shedding tears.[11]

The stronger the awareness of *Being-as-immanent*, the stronger the awareness of *Being-as-transcendental*. Then the awareness becomes awe-full. Then the belief in the supreme importance of our relation to *Being* follows, as well as such feelings as ultimate concern, reverence, and peace. This belief and its accompanying feelings, in turn, lead to an irresistible need for theoretical, practical, and sociological forms to express the supreme importance of *Being*. The coerciveness of *Being* culminates in commitment.

An experience in which only beings come to explicit consciousness is ontical or secular. An experience in which *Being-as-immanent* also comes to explicit awareness enters the ontological or religious dimension, but it is not religious. When there is an awe-full awareness of *Being-as-immanent*, then *Being-as-transcendental* is more or less vaguely suggested as the source of this experience. This experience is implicitly religious. When, furthermore, there is an explicit awareness of *Being-as-transcendental*, the experience is explicitly religious in the narrow sense. If, finally, theoretical, practical, and sociological forms of expression are involved with this

11. *The Bell,* p. 183.

explicit awareness of *Being-as-transcendental,* then this experience is explicitly religious in the broad sense. On the other hand, the experience of *Being-as-absolute* is not religious in either the narrow or broad sense. The experience of *Being-as-absolute* is purely illusory, a mist of make-believe, for there are no empirical grounds for this so-called further reality.

An awareness of *Being-as-transcendental,* whether implicit or explicit, is always accompanied by awe, the wonder of wonders. When the awareness is explicit, the awe deepens and our participation with *Being* is believed to be supremely important. To be cognizant of a person as an "it" is an ontical experience. To be aware of him as a "Thou" is an ontological experience, an awareness of *Being-as-immanent.* To be vaguely aware of the "Thou" as a part of *Being-as-transcendental* is an experience that is implicitly religious. To be explicitly aware of the "Thou" as part of *Being-as-transcendental* is a religious experience, at least in the narrow sense, for example the way Alyosha and Father Zossima in Dostoevski's *The Brothers Karamazov* are aware of others. In an experience that is implicitly religious, the awareness of the immanence of *Being* dominates the awareness of *Being's* transcendency. In an experience that is explicitly religious, the awareness of the transcendency of *Being* dominates the awareness of *Being's* immanence. Only when the transcendency of *Being* comes to explicit awareness does the experience become explicitly religious. Otherwise, although *Being* might arouse our awe, more or less, *Being* would not convince us of its supreme importance. *Being* would lack ultimate coerciveness. When *Being* is experienced as *Being-as-transcendental, Being* becomes holy or sacred. Then—usually but not necessarily, and depending upon the personality and the cultural situation—theoretical, practical, and sociological forms of expression may fuse with the experience of *Being* and the religious experience becomes not only explicit but complete. *Being* is worshiped.

Usually with optimistic naturalists like John Dewey, there

is a fundamental belief in the essential stoutness and relia-
bility of the ontical world and its plasticity to man's purposes.
While this belief is lacking in atheistic existentialists such as
Sartre, their comfortless awareness of man's limitations in the
faceless hostility of the world also stops short of belief in
Being as here interpreted. On the other hand, existentialists
such as Marcel and Jaspers, while inheriting like Sartre the
world of Nietzsche rather than the world of Dewey, find
comfort and hope in their belief in *Being*. Heidegger also
believes in *Being*, of course; and insofar as this includes belief in *Being's* supreme importance, as is so apparent in
Marcel and Jaspers, Heidegger is religious. In his writings
since *Being and Time*, *Being-as-transcendental* rather than
Being-as-immanent has perhaps become his basic concern,[12]
but Heidegger has remained strangely neutral on the question of the relation or identification of *Being* and God.
Whatever the explanation for his hesitancy, the facts clearly
indicate that when *Being-as-transcendental* is experienced,
there is both awe-full awareness and belief in the supreme
importance of our participation with *Being*. *Being* is experienced as holy. Therefore it seems appropriate to me to
name *Being* as holy—God.

A problem can be solved by scientific means, at least in
principle. A mystery cannot be solved even in principle by
scientific means. Whereas a problem is subject to an appropriate technique because it can be isolated and marked off,
a mystery eludes every possible technique because it is inexhaustible. A mystery is permanently enigmatic. However
much "explained," there is a character or quality about a
mystery that transcends every possible explanation. For an
experience to have a religious dimension, there must be not
only an awareness of mystery but also belief—or at least the
possibility must be seriously entertained and not rejected—

---

12. This is one of the most lively issues in current theology. See, for example, *The Later Heidegger and Theology*, ed. James M. Robinson and
John B. Cobb, Jr. (New York: Harper and Row, 1963). The distinction
between *Being-as-immanent* and *Being-as-transcendental* is, of course,
foreign to Heidegger's terminology.

that this awareness of mystery originates from ontological reality. It is believed that the ontical depends somehow upon the ontological, named as the Holy by Otto, *Being* by Heidegger, *Being-itself* by Tillich, the Encompassing by Jaspers, and simply God, usually mythically conceived, by the less sophisticated. Often there are sharp differences in the interpretation of the ontological; for example, the ontological transcends the ontical for Kierkegaard, is mainly immanent for the early Heidegger, and is both immanent and transcendental for Marcel, Whitehead, and the late Heidegger. Yet those who believe *religiously* in ontological reality are in general agreement on three basic claims. First, ontological reality cannot be verified or disproved by scientific means because its inexhaustible complexity cannot be thinned out into a problem. Second, ontological reality, nevertheless, can be encountered and understood. Third, this ontological understanding as related to *Being-as-transcendental* is of supreme importance. Thus the religious experience is a love that is a fidelity to *Being*, however named, that fundamentally influences the way of our lives. For among other reasons, this fidelity unites us with our world.

It is perfectly possible to be aware of mystery and yet dismiss the possibility of its ontological origin. Thus Wittgenstein, unlike Ayer, is conscious of mystery: "Feeling the world as a limited whole—it is this that is mystical." "There are, indeed, things that cannot be put into words. *They make themselves manifest*. They are what is mystical."[13] But Wittgenstein never, at least in his writings, suggests that the cause of our awareness of mystery is anything more than a lack in our ontical powers. There is no indication that the cause of this awareness might be in the inexhaustibility of an ontological reality that even unlimited ontical powers could not encompass. For Wittgenstein mystery is neither degraded into meaninglessness, as with Ayer and most of the analysts and positivists, nor "upgraded" into an aspect of

---

13. *Tractatus Logico-Philosophicus* (London: K. Paul, Trench, Trubner and Co., 1922), 6.45 and 6.522.

ultimate reality, as with Heidegger, Marcel, and Jaspers.

Knowledge of the ontological or *Being* is not possible, for if it were, the inexhaustibility of the ontological would be reduced to the exhaustibility of the ontical. Mystery would be reduced to something unknown about beings, a problem subject in the future to scientific procedures, and that is the same as reducing the ontological to the ontical, to the outward show. Whereas with beings it is possible to come to a "nothing but," with *Being* there is always "something more." As Heidegger puts it, "Calculative thought places itself under compulsion to master everything in the logical terms of its procedure. It has no notion that in calculation everything calculable is already a whole before it starts working out its sums and products, a whole whose unity naturally belongs to the incalculable which, with its mystery, ever eludes the clutches of calculation."[14] The power of *Being* is the "whole" which provides the preconceptual context that makes calculative thought or knowledge possible. *Being* is primary; knowledge is secondary and cannot prove *Being*, for knowledge works within a more or less vague prejudicative affirmation of *Being* and cannot but presuppose it. *Being* is the point of departure from which any proof becomes possible. *Being* is the giver of givens, *i.e.*, beings. *Being* is a giver, however, that is also a given, but *Being* as given is always present as a presence and never as a sense datum or object. That is why *Being* is not describable, for any type of description is an objectification, a reduction of what is described to a thing. Nevertheless, a primordial and implicit understanding of *Being* is presupposed. Thus Jaspers insists that "*Being* is not the sum of objects; rather objects

14. "What is Metaphysics?" trans. R. F. C. Hull and Alan Crick, *Existence and Being* (Chicago: H. Regnery Co., 1949), p. 388. Something of the same point is made more metaphorically by Heidegger in his essay on Hölderlin, "Remembrance of the Poet," trans. Douglas Scott, *ibid.*, p. 279: "But now if homecoming means becoming at home in proximity to the source, then must not the return home consist chiefly, and perhaps for a long time, in getting to know this mystery, or even first of all in learning how to get to know it. But we never get to know a mystery by . . . analysing it; we only get to know it by carefully guarding the mystery *as* mystery."

extend, as it were, towards our intellect in the subject-object division, from the Encompassing of *Being* itself, which is beyond objective comprehension, but from which nevertheless all separate, determinate objective knowledge derives its limits and its meaning and from which it derives the mood that comes out of the totality in which it has significance."[15] Merleau-Ponty makes essentially the same point less abstractly: "to return to things themselves is to return to that world which precedes knowledge, of which knowledge always *speaks*, and in relation to which every scientific schematization is an abstract and derivative sign-language, as is geography in relation to the countryside in which we have learnt beforehand what a forest, a prairie or a river is."[16] In short, ontical knowledge is rendered possible by ontological understanding.

Being is not unintelligible, despite the fact that anyone who believes in *Being*, however interpreted, can neither prove nor describe *Being*. Even to recognize *Being* as a mystery and not as a problem is a step toward understanding. Moreover, since *Being* can be encountered, *Being* can be indicated, attested to, witnessed for; and *Being* can be thought about in a more primal mode of thinking than is possible in the abstract mode of calculative thought. Thus one can use reasons that try to support his belief in *Being* and make it plausible.[17] The long history of "justifying

15. "On My Philosophy," trans. Felix Kaufmann in *Existentialism from Dostoevsky to Sartre,* ed. Walter Kaufmann (Cleveland: The World Publishing Co., Meridian Books, 1964) , p. 151.
16. *Phenomenology of Perception,* trans. Colin Smith (London: Humanities Press, 1962) , p. ix. Cf. Michael Polanyi, *Personal Knowledge* (Chicago: University of Chicago Press, 1958) , p. 286: "Objectivism [positivism] has totally falsified our conception of truth, by exalting what we can know and prove, while covering up with ambiguous utterances all that we *cannot* prove, even though the latter knowledge underlies, and must ultimately set its seal to, all that we *can* prove."
17. For a discussion of the principal distinctions between "proof" and "plausibility" see Joseph Margolis, *The Language of Art and Art Criticism* (Detroit: Wayne State University Press, 1965) , pp. 85–94. Plausibility, furthermore, is a species of verifiability, as Tillich points out:

> The verifying test belongs to the nature of truth; in this positivism is right. . . . The safest test is the repeatable experiment. A cognitive

reasons" has divided religions, theologies, religious philosophies, and ontologies. Yet in most cases the source of the
ultimate reason—and thus the origin of the "family resem-
blances," in Wittgenstein's sense, that all religious experiences, religions, theologies, religious philosophies, and ontologies share—is the coercive convictional power of the presence
of *Being* in the ontological experience itself. When the
coercive quality of this experience is strong, we have an awe-
full awareness and this may lead, in turn, to belief in *Being-
as-transcendental.* Although we contact *Being-as-transcendental* only as the depth dimensions of beings, and then only
explicitly as we participate with these beings in their distinctive individuality, this further reality is felt as the source
of all enduring values. The participation with this depth
reality as immanent in surface reality is believed to be of
supreme importance. Thus the ontological experience is "the
Good" for the religious. The nonreligious also have contact
with *Being,* for any experience of surface reality involves a
depth that makes it possible. But since there is little or no
feeling of the coercive quality of the depth dimension, there
is no awe-full awareness, no sense of mystery as marvelous.
The nonreligious even may be explicitly aware of a depth
dimension—as many high-minded humanists are, especially
in personal relationships; but the nonreligious dismiss belief
in the transcendency and ultimacy of the depth dimension, of

---

realm in which it can be used has the advantage of methodological
strictness and the possibility of testing an assertion in every moment.
But it is not permissible to make the experimental method of verification the exclusive pattern of all verification. Verification can occur
within the life-process itself. Verification of this type (experiential in
contradistinction to experimental) has the advantage that it need not
halt and disrupt the totality of a life-process in order to distil calculable elements out of it (which experimental verification must do). The
verifying experiences of a non-experimental character are truer to life,
though less exact and definite.

Systematic Theology (Chicago: University of Chicago Press, 1951), 1: 102.
The thinking that attempts to make plausible our understanding of
Being is aptly described by William J. Richardson as "foundational
thought." *Heidegger: Through Phenomenology to Thought* (The Hague:
M. Nijhoff, 1963). See also the distinction between "verification" and
"validation" as used by Polanyi, *Personal Knowledge,* p. 202.

Being-as-transcendental or Holy *Being*. And rightly so from their point of view, for they lack the empirical foundation— the coerciveness—that would ground such an affirmation. Whereas the truth about beings is demonstrated truth, the truth about *Being* is "felt truth." Whereas demonstrated truth produces belief *that* or belief *about,* felt truth is belief *in.* The ontological experience must be its own assurance. No reason can supplant this ultimate precognitional intimacy and affirmation. There is, as Marcel has tried to explain in so many different ways, an irreducible "isness" in certain experiences that eludes sense perception and inferences based on sense perception. That is why *Being* cannot be exhausted by any finite set of concepts, or flattened into the computers, or locked into the equations of science. That is also why the basic statements about *Being* are symbolical or metaphorical. For as W. M. Urban points out: ". . . an aspect of reality [*Being*] is given which cannot be adequately expressed otherwise. It is not true that whatever is expressed symbolically can be better expressed otherwise. It is not true that whatever is expressed symbolically can be better expressed literally. For there *is* no literal expression, but only another kind of symbol. It is not true that we should seek the blunt truth, for the so-called blunt truth has a way of becoming an untruth."[18] Thus the language of the sacred necessarily uses somewhat different means than the language of the secular. Because literal statements are expressions of the thought patterns and language structures geared to beings, literal statements leave behind all or most of the "is," the *Being* dimension. Compare the disparity which exists between "lived experience," with its always implicit and sometimes explicit contact with *Being,* and life as it is presented clearly and distinctly in psychiatric and sociological texts after being dismembered, filtered, and sterilized through the techniques of abstract thinking divorced from experiences of *Being.*

---

18. *Language and Reality* (London: George Allen and Unwin, 1951), p. 500.

According to Marcel, "Being is what withstands—or what would withstand—an exhaustive analysis bearing on the data of experience and aiming to reduce them step by step to elements increasingly devoid of intrinsic or significant value."[19] *Being* in sensible reality is experienced as a presence rather than being inferred and reified from sense data,[20] for *Being*, although making objects possible, is not an object. Its "presence is a reality; it is a kind of influx; it depends upon us to be permeable to this influx, but not . . . to call it forth."[21] We control things, for, as Francis Bacon remarked at the dawn of our technological age, we put nature to the rack in order to wring out the answers to our questions; but *Being* controls us, for *Being* cannot be coerced. Whereas we are, at least in principle, the masters of ontical reality; *Being* is the master of us. Thus *Being* reveals itself to the humble, to

---

19. "On the Ontological Mystery," *The Philosophy of Existence*, trans. Manya Harari (Freeport, New York: Books for Libraries Press, 1948), p. 5.
20. Schleiermacher, for example, in some of his works infers the existence of God (*Being-as-transcendental*) from introspective sense data, his feeling of "absolute dependence." He reasons that if this feeling is present, then there must be a cause that accounts for this feeling; and because of the absolute character of this feeling, it must have an ontological origin. See Otto's criticisms of Schleiermacher on this point, *The Idea of The Holy*, pp. 10 and 20f. This is not the whole story, however, for there are passages in Schleiermacher that affirm a direct awareness of God. See, for example, *On Religion*, trans. John Oman (New York: Harper and Brothers, 1958), pp. 41ff. It is surely futile to attempt to infer and reify *Being*, for then *Being* is reduced to a being. Thus theodicy is atheism. This is one of the points of Tillich's insistent reminder that God is "the God beyond gods." Max Scheler, one of the first to apply the phenomenological method to the religious experience, came to the following fundamental conclusion: "This is therefore the *first sure truth* of all religious phenomenology: on whatever level of his *religious development* he may be, the human being is *invariably* looking into the realm of being and value which is in basis and origin utterly different from the whole remaining empirical world; it is not inferred from that other world, neither won from it by idealization, and access to it is possible solely in the religious act. This is the proposition of the *originality and non-derivation of religious experience*." *On the Eternal in Man*, tr. Bernard Noble (London: SCM Press, 1960), p. 173.
21. "On the Ontological Mystery," p. 24. Cf. Jaspers "On My Philosophy," p. 149: "Everything that becomes an *object* to me approaches me, as it were, from the dark background of Being. Every object is a determinate being (as *this* confronting me in a subject-object division), but never all Being. No being known as an object is *the* Being. . . . This Being . . . is that which always makes its presence known, which does not appear itself, but from which everything comes to us."

those capable of piety toward reality, to those who have a responsive receptivity, a creative hospitality that lets what *is* be as it is. We must let *Being* be. Then we "undergo" *Being*—it affects, overpowers, and transforms us. Since *Being* is constitutive of ontical reality, the influx of *Being* can come through any ontical experience. Probably love, as Marcel points out, is the most apparent path to presence:

> There are some people who reveal themselves as "present"—that is to say, at our disposal—when we are in pain or in need to confide in someone, while there are other people who do not give us this feeling, however great is their goodwill. It should be noted at once that the distinction between presence and absence is not at all the same as that between attention and distraction. The most attentive and the most conscientious listener may give me the impression of not being present; he gives me nothing, he cannot make room for me in himself, whatever the material favours which he is prepared to grant me. The truth is that there is a way of listening which is a way of giving, and another way of listening which is a way of refusing, of refusing *oneself;* the material gift, the visible action, do not necessarily witness to presence. We must not speak of proof in this connection; the word would be out of place. Presence is something which reveals itself immediately and unmistakably in a look, a smile, an intonation or a handshake.
>
> It will perhaps make it clearer if I say that the person who is at my disposal is the one who is capable of being with me with the whole of himself when I am in need; while the one who is not at my disposal seems merely to offer me a temporary loan raised on his resources. For the one I am a presence; for the other I am an object.[22]

In "presence" I am linked *with* another person by means of the intersubjectivity of *Being*. There is nothing between us because "presence" has removed the between. I am with the other person like the coexistence of a tone with its harmony. In the absence of "presence," I am no more than *alongside* or *beside* the other person.

The experience of *Being* is always an awareness of

---

22. "On the Ontological Mystery," pp. 25f.

presence, but not all experiences of presence include an awareness of *Being*. Thus self-consciousness, consciousness cognizant of itself in operation, is the consciousness of the presence of nonreflective consciousness. For example, although nonreflective consciousness is perceiving some sense data, that perceiving consciousness cannot, in turn, be perceived— it is wholly inaccessible to observation.[23] Consciousness, as described by Husserl in great detail, is inherently intentional and projective. Consciousness always transcends things, in flight between the past and the future. Consciousness is not an object with properties. Or as Sartre puts it: "Consciousness is a being, the nature of which is to be conscious of the nothingness of its being."[24] My nonreflective consciousness is not an "it" for me but "I am" my nonreflective consciousness. But by means of our reflective consciousness we can become cognizant of the presence of our nonreflective consciousness. For when we reflect, our reflection bears upon an unreflective experience, and in that process there is a consciousness of the presence of the consciousness that is making that unreflective experience possible. Yet this very self-consciousness precludes—as the following analysis will attempt to show—the awareness of *Being*.

The transparency to *Being* in others reveals itself, as Lionel Trilling remarks, "not in doctrine, not in systems, ethics, and creeds, but in manner and style. We know whether or not a person is in touch with the sources of life not by what he says, by its doctrinal correctness, but by the way he says it, by the tone of his voice, the look in his eyes, by his manner and style."[25] For example, Albert Schweitzer, although I met him only once, unmistakably made me aware of his transparency to *Being* by the way he "listened" to

23. This is the point behind Heidegger's criticism of Kant's characterization of self-consciousness as something substantial, the "I" or the "I think." *Being and Time,* trans. John Macquarrie and Edward Robinson (New York: Harper and Row, 1962), pp. 366–68.
24. *Being and Nothingness,* trans. Hazel E. Barnes (New York: Philosophical Library, Inc., 1956), p. 47.
25. "The Two Environments," *Encounter* 25 (July 1965): 9.

others. Our transparency to *Being,* on the other hand, reveals itself when the cogency of the rapport between our ontological sensitivity and *Being* convinces us that our experience is not illusory. In both cases there are sympathy and empathy, an intimate and unique affinity, a rightness and necessity, a certain "clicking-into-place" of sensitiveness to *Being.* In the perceptual world there may be ontical deficiency, as in color blindness and the lack of a musical ear. We may fail to see the color design of Mark Rothko's *Earth Greens* (Frontispiece), just as we may fail to hear the structure of Bach's *The Art of Fugue.* Yet both *Gestalten* can be perceived if we can overcome our ontical shortcomings, for in both works the *Gestalten* are there. Similarly, although *Being* is there, we may fail to recognize its presence if we are ontologically obtuse. If by intuition is meant the immediate conscious encounter with something, then, in the final analysis, to understand *Being* we must intuit *Being,* just as to know yellow requires the intuition of yellow. Both experiences require direct acquaintance with irreducible ultimates (*Being* and yellow respectively) issuing into affective union between subject and object; both are *sui generis;* both are corrigible, and very little can be communicated about either *Being* or yellow to anyone who has no firsthand experience of them. Both experiences have an empirical anchorage or a "given"; but the experience of *Being* involves a deeper level of consciousness than the experience of yellow, and the modes of receptivity in which the "given" is apprehended differ fundamentally.[26] Therefore I shall avoid the term *intuition* with reference to the immediate encounter with *Being* and use rather the term *awareness,* reserving *intuition* for the immediate encounter with anything ontical. Since *Being* comes to awareness only through some being, there is always an intuitive element included in that awareness. But unlike a

---

26. Émile Durkheim comes to the similar conclusion that "religious beliefs rest upon a specific experience whose demonstrative value is, in one sense, not one bit inferior to that of scientific experiments, though different from them." *The Elementary Forms of the Religious Life,* trans. J. W. Swain (Glencoe, Ill.: Free Press, 1947), p. 417.

mere intuition, the awareness of *Being*, as will be described shortly, includes the involvement not only of sense organs and intellect but of the self as a totality. Furthermore, the *Being* dimension of a being has a peculiar power that anything experienced as merely ontical lacks. In this sense the surface of a being is static and thus can be intuited, whereas the depth dimension of a being is dynamic and thus escapes intuition. *Being* "comes forth" into awareness as self-revealing. In an intuition we do the grasping, whereas in an awareness we are grasped. For the person who is insensitive to *Being*, as Rudolf Otto points out, there is only one way to help:

> He must be guided and led on by consideration and discussion . . . until he reaches the point at which "the numinous" [*Being*] in him perforce begins to stir . . . into consciousness. We can cooperate in this process by bringing before his notice all that can be found in other regions of the mind, already known and familiar, to resemble, or again to afford some special contrast to, the particular experience we wish to elucidate. Then we must add: "This X of ours is not precisely *this* experience, but akin to this one and the opposite of that other. Cannot you now realize for yourself what it is?"[27]

This does not mean that we become aware of *Being* free from beings. Mystics such as Meister Eckhart and St. John of the Cross claim to have encountered *Being* as disembodied, *i.e.*, *Being-as-absolute*, but it is very doubtful that this claim can be justified.[28] In any case, for those of us who are not mystics, *Being* breaks into our experience by dis-

---

27. *The Idea of The Holy*, p. 7.
28. Concerning the many confusions involved in the claim that *Being* can be encountered without mediation, see H. D. Lewis, *Morals and Revelation* (London: George Allen and Unwin, 1951), chap. 8. "Mystic" and "mysticism" are highly ambiguous terms. Zen Buddhists and Wordsworth, for example, are often classified as mystics, and yet they make no claim of encountering *Being-as-absolute*. Restricting the term "mystic" to the type of Meister Eckhardt is closer to conventional usage concerning mysticism, and it helps avoid confusion. See Gerardus van der Leeuw, *Religion in Essence and Manifestation*, trans. J. E. Turner (London: George Allen and Unwin, 1938), chap. 75. Also W. T. Stace, *Mysticism and Philosophy* (Philadelphia: J. B. Lippincott Co., 1960).

rupting but never eliminating our modes of ontical experience. And if we are ontologically sensitive, the presence of *Being* will be experienced in this disruption. The following example of Sartre's—although he interprets it in such a way that the presence of Being would be denied—illustrates the point:

> I am in a public park. Not far away there is a lawn and along the edge of that lawn there are benches. A man passes by those benches. I see this man; I apprehend him as an object and at the same time as a man. What does this signify? What do I mean when I assert that this object is a man [that the presence of *Being* is experienced]?
>
> If I were to think of him as being only a puppet, I should apply to him the categories which I ordinarily use to group temporal-spatial "things." That is, I should apprehend him as being "beside" the benches, two yards and twenty inches from the lawn, as exercising a certain pressure on the ground, etc. His relation with other objects would be of the purely additive type; this means that I could have him disappear without the relations of the other objects around him being perceptibly changed. In short, no new relation would appear through him between those things in my universe: grouped and synthesized from my point of view into instrumental complexes. . . . Perceiving him as a man, on the other hand, is not to apprehend an additive relation between the chair and him; it is to register an organization without distance of the things in my universe around that privileged object. To be sure, the lawn remains two yards and twenty inches away from him, but it is also as a lawn bound to him in a relation which at once both transcends and contains it. Instead of the two terms of the distance being indifferent, interchangeable, and in reciprocal relation, the distance is unfolded starting from the man whom I see and extending up to the lawn as the synthetic upsurge of a univocal relation. We are dealing with a relation which is without parts, given at one stroke, inside of which there unfolds a spatiality which is not my spatiality; for instead of a grouping toward me of the objects, there is now an orientation which flees from me. . . . Thus the appearance among the objects of my universe of an element of disintegration in that universe is what I mean by the appearance of a man in my universe.[29]

29. *Being and Nothingness*, pp. 254f.

Because of the disintegration but not the disappearance of the ontical modes of experience, our observation of objects seen from the outside becomes interlaced with an awareness of *plus ultra* in the inside.[30] *Being* has an explosive quality that can crack the conventions of our ontical experience. Through those cracks we become aware of *Being*. In such experiences we become aware of *Being* as more than a construction of a Sartrean consciousness—for in Sartre's system there is *Being-for-itself* and *Being-in-itself* but no place for *Being* as I have been using the term—and this awareness of *Being* is accomplished by means of a creative receptivity in addition to observation and inference. Such experiences are two-dimensional, for *Being* is present as the depth dimension of beings. We encounter *Being* in the glance through beings. Although the ontical and the ontological are distinguishable, they are not separable. That is why we never can be quite certain where the ontical ends and the ontological begins.

Ontical obtuseness is caused by some organic deficiency or lack of training. Ontological obtuseness, on the other hand, is caused mainly by the exaltation of technical intelligence, *homo faber,* resulting in an ontical over-involvement that becomes a kind of intoxication. Everyone must possess ontical sensitivity to some degree in order to survive in the world of things. Ontological sensitivity seems to be possessed by everyone, also, and it is usually easily noticeable in children, but this sensitivity can be destroyed by the sound and the fury of things.[31] This loss usually does not interfere with biological survival and practical success. Indeed it seems to be becoming a prerequisite in a positivistic society. But in that process, the value of a man progressively becomes re-

---

30. From an entirely different point of view and in very different terms, Eliade comes to a similar conclusion. "Methodological Remarks on the Study of Religious Symbolism," *The History of Religions,* ed. Mircea Eliade and Joseph M. Kitagawa (Chicago: University of Chicago Press, 1959), p. 103.

31. See, for example, the description by Ruskin of how the ontological experiences of his childhood and youth faded away as his "reflective and practical power increased and the 'cares of the world' gained upon me." Quoted by Otto, *The Idea of The Holy,* p. 221.

duced to man power, to the functions he performs in the world of goods and services. For since another individual can also perform these functions, the given man has no distinctive worth. He is a value of a variable for which someone else may be substituted. In the technological world of things he feels that his claim to uniqueness and indispensability is denied, with the result that he may accept this abstraction of himself as a bundle of functions as his whole self. Then he loses his sense of identity because he is no longer open to his own or to another person's *Being*, the "I" and "Thou." To handle another person as no more than a means to some end, as the technologically obsessed do, is to also handle ourselves as puppets. Even the idiot Benjy in Faulkner's *The Sound and the Fury* is more human than his brother, Jason, for despite Benjy's pathetic organic deficiencies he is sensitive to *Being* and thus has, however dimly discerned, a spiritual center. Although "normal," Jason has lost his humanity, except for his sardonic sense of humor and his ability to suffer, in his greed for things. At the end of William Alfred's *Hogan's Goat*, the Mayor, after destroying Matt in order to protect his function as mayor, pathetically explains to Matt that he had to do it: if he isn't the Mayor he is nothing, just nothing. A technologist I know insists that life is meaningless without his research. Authentic identity and autonomy have been lost or almost lost in such men because the will to dominate things and reduce them to manageable proportions, to functions, has become their supreme value and stifled their sense of *Being*. Spiritual achievement has been sacrificed to practical success.

Whereas science is the search for knowledge about ontical reality, technology is the application of scientific knowledge. The scientific experience—as so many scientists such as Einstein attest, and Jaspers has systematically explained—can bring us to awareness of *Being*. Without technology, furthermore, civilization would be impossible, as C. P. Snow in *The Two Cultures and the Scientific Revolution* correctly insists; but along with technology's obvious blessings—even

sometimes its splendor—have come fast-pressing demands
that increasingly threaten us all with an Inferno of onticity.
Through the exercise of our "technical reason," as Tillich
names it, man

> became increasingly able to control physical nature. Through
> the tools placed at his disposal by technical reason, he created a
> world-wide mechanism of large-scale production and competitive
> economy which began to take shape as a kind of "second na-
> ture," a Frankenstein, above physical nature and subjecting
> man to itself. While he was increasingly able to control and
> manipulate physical nature, man became less and less able to
> control this "second nature." He was swallowed up by his own
> creation. Step by step the whole of human life was subordinated
> to the demands of the new world-wide economy.[32]

To the degree that we succumb to, rather than dominate,
this Frankenstein, our lives become scheduled by-products of
the power plants of society, driven like machines into the
dubious safety zones of the herd. Then technology becomes
the systematic organization of our departure from *Being*.
Then the childlike ability to love, to recognize and have
concern even for the *Being* in other persons becomes "adult-
erated" or lost. Then beings and *Being*, although not strange
to each other, become estranged. This technological point of
view, as Kierkegaard insists, has "no understanding of the
narrowness and meanness of mind which is exemplified in
having lost one's self—not by evaporation in the infinite, but
by being entirely finitized, by having become, instead of a
self, a number, just one man more, one more repetition of
this everlasting *Einerlei*."[33] Thus in ontical obsession we
become marauders of *Being*, yet oblivious of our guilt.

Technology tends to arrange reality so that we do not have
to participate with it. Thus technology can so externalize
our lives that we become alienated from ourselves and others,

---

32. "The World Situation," *The Christian Answer*, ed. Henry P. Van Dusen
(New York: Scribner, 1945), p. 5.
33. *The Sickness unto Death*, trans. Walter Lowrie (Princeton: Princeton
University Press, 1941), p. 50.

our artifacts, and nature.[34] Technology not only stiffens the
yoke of custom and convention and the stuffed-shirtedness
of bureaucracy, but the arid, asphyxiating atmosphere of a
technological society can fragment us into "bits of paper,
whirled by the cold wind" (T. S. Eliot, "Burnt Norton").
Swept into the vortex of onticity, we can become so busy
and fatigued with deadlines and becoming what other people
want us to be that we lose the passion for our personal
existence. "The crowd," cries Kierkegaard, "is untruth."
And then, as Garcin exclaims in Sartre's *No Exit:* "Hell
is—other people!" The driving instrumental demands of
technical mentality, furthermore, may exile us from our
artifacts, even works of art. For example, in the Acton
Collection in a private villa in Florence there is a late
thirteenth-century *Madonna and Child,* its artist unknown,
which is exceptionally lovely because, among other reasons,
of the exquisite blue of the Madonna's mantle. I happened
to see this painting some years ago in the company of a
historian of art who was working on a monograph about
early Renaissance haloes. He carefully measured the sizes
of the haloes in this *Madonna and Child* and then did likewise with some other paintings in the room. While talking
to my companion about the *Madonna and Child,* I began
to realize that this expert had "missed" the painting. Art,
at least temporarily, had been reduced to the problem of the
evolving sizes of haloes. To measure and count is, in a sense,
not to see.

The wear and tear of the routines of technology can also
exile us from nature, transforming the natural into something anti-natural. Thus Mark Twain tells how, as he
learned the functions of a steamboat pilot, the Mississippi
River became like a book.

> Now when I had mastered the language of this water, and had
> come to know every trifling feature that bordered the great river

---

34. No one has documented more thoroughly the depersonalizing forces of
technology than Jaspers. See especially *Man in the Modern Age,* trans.
Eden and Cedar Paul (London: Routledge and K. Paul, 1951).

as familiarly as I knew the letters of the alphabet, I had made
a valuable acquisition. But I had lost something, too. I had
lost something which could never be restored to me while I
lived. All the grace, and beauty, the poetry, had gone out of the
majestic river! . . . . All the value any feature of it had for me
now was the amount of usefulness it could furnish toward com-
passing the safe piloting of a steamboat.[35]

The technologically obsessed mind sees nature as an insen-
sate empty space containing "persons" as units to be controlled, and all other beings as raw material to be hammered
into useful shape. When we and artifacts and nature are reduced to such abstractions—however useful these abstractions
may be in providing objects for exploitation—*Being* no
longer can come to presence.[36]

II

Yet ontological reality, always hauntingly there on the
threshold of our awareness, also has its demands. And sometimes—except for the total escapist, if such a human being is
possible—*Being* breaks through our insular self-sufficiency.
Although this may occur in almost any kind of situation,
there are certain experiences that are favorable for returning us to *Being*. For example, with Kierkegaard it is silence.
With Dostoevski it is suffering and sin. With Jaspers it is
failure. With Heidegger it is boredom, despair, and the
consciousness of death. With Buber it is solitude. With
Einstein it is the limitations of man's theoretical comprehen-

---

35. "Life on the Mississippi," in *The Favorite Works of Mark Twain* (Garden
City, N.Y.: Garden City Publishing Co., 1939) , pp. 46f.
36. In this denial of *Being*, as Henry G. Bugbee, Jr. sorrowfully observes, is
the root denial of the possibility of philosophy. Isn't this denial in its
clearest form just the point to which so much of Positivism has come?
That our thought can be responsible only to empirical [ontical] dis-
coveries, or to the elements of an abstract system, and that thought in
any other mode would be vague and irresponsible, devoid of any
authentic purchase: This is "scientism," the antiphilosophical persuasion so evident in our time. *The Inward Morning* (State College, Pa.:
Bald Eagle Press, 1958) , pp. 77f.

sion. With Croce it is the aesthetic experience. Among these many different kinds of experiences there are, furthermore, two basic types that are *especially* favorable for returning us to *Being*. First, there are the experiences of the tragic and the dreadful, what fittingly may be called, to use Sartre's expression, "extreme situations." Second, there is the aesthetic experience.[37]

In the tragic experience something is felt as drastically lacking in our relation to things—a void opens between our recognition of what is and what might be. In the dreadful experience our faith that the void can be filled by our will to power over things fails. When this happens we not only feel ontical reality becoming empty of value, despite the manifoldness of its things, but we also feel an erosion of pride in our powers. The more the feelings of the tragic or the dreadful are felt deeply, leading to what Camus calls "supernatural anxiety" and what, more positively, Peter Bertocci calls "creative insecurity," the more accessible we are to *Being*. This is one of the points of Eliot's lines in "East Coker": "The only wisdom we can hope to acquire is the / wisdom of humility. . . ."

According to Kierkegaard, we must renounce things without reservation. "The infinite resignation is the last stage prior to faith, so that one who has not made this movement has not faith; for only in the infinite resignation do I become clear to myself with respect to my eternal validity, and only then can there be any question of grasping existence by virtue of faith."[38] Most of us cannot or do not want to be the "Knight of Infinite Renunciation" that Kierkegaard demanded of himself. But insofar as we cast in doubt ontical reality as the Alpha and Omega of existence, we become more receptive to *Being*. Almost any kind of unhappy ex-

---

37. Heidegger's career is an interesting exemplification of these main approaches to *Being*. In *Being and Time* (1927) it is the tragic and especially the dreadful experience that is stressed, but in most of his writings since then it is a kind of aesthetic experience.

38. *Fear and Trembling*, trans. Walter Lowrie (Princeton: Princeton University Press, 1941) , pp. 65f.

perience, such as illness, bad luck, poverty, monotony, or old age, is capable of depreciating ontical reality. But it is especially the experiences of the tragic[39] and the dreadful that are most likely to break up the *hybris* and complacency that block us from *Being*.

Suffering, injustice, and guilt are at the center of the tragic vision, and no sedative except death can hide them all. In this age of agony with its cremation ovens and the bomb powerful enough to return us to the Stone Age, the point needs no elaboration. Yet the *full* horror of the tragic, especially its fatal inevitability, can be more or less missed or dismissed by many ways of escape, some demonic and all ultimately unsuccessful. There is animalism, the way of Tennessee Williams's Stanley Kowalski. There is the way of the *Brave New World* and soma, as portrayed by Huxley. There is the way of Sade, sick with sex. There is the way of the scientific humanists, like some of more naïve followers of Dewey, who proclaim that if man's intelligence is put to the proper use of promoting good works, something of Utopia will come. There is the lyrically intoxicated way of so many revolutionaries: "Better a day as a lion," as Pietro Spina exclaims in Silone's *Bread and Wine*, "than a hundred days as a sheep." There is the "perfect moment," the way of Proust. There is pride and defiance, the way of Camus's Sisyphus. There is Stoical aloofness, the way that looks on the world as "much ado about nothing" ("Such a life, what a relief to have understood it"). There is the creation of art for art's sake, the way of Sartre's Roquentin. There is the construction of elaborate rational systems, the way, among others, of many idealists, whistling in the dark as if all were light (The Real is the Rational, says Hegel, and the Rational is the Real). There is dogmatic religion, the way of the fanatic, making faith a castle enclosed by walls of authority which no doubt can pierce. There is fantasy, the way of Albee's Martha and George. There is inertia, the way

---

39. "Tragedy," as I shall use the term, is the interpretation in the arts of the tragic and thus is a species of the tragic.

of Beckett's Vladimir and Estragon. There is nihilism, the way of Dostoevski's possessed. There is suicide, the way of Faulkner's Quentin and Miller's Willy Loman. And, finally, and far more frequently, there is the way of functions, the will to power over things which, even when successful, is a happiness that is a kind of sleep.

Tragic vision, however, neither misses nor dismisses the agony. Moreover, tragic vision wears bifocal lenses. On the lower side, there is sight of the broken world. On the upper side, there is sight of what might be. These two perspectives must be kept in close apposition if the full vista of the tragic is to be taken in. If the perspective of what is dominates too much, then despairing resignation and escapism are the likely results. If the "what might be" dominates too much, then the misery of what is becomes inconsequential. When, however, both perspectives are kept in sight in tense relation, a void opens between real and ideal, fact and wish. In our time this void is vaster than in earlier times, not because the what is is so much worse but rather because the scientific humanism and idealism of the eighteenth and nineteenth centuries pegged our aspirations so high. When, finally, we feel impotent in making significant progress in closing the gap between wish and fact—"the division between the mind that desires and the world that disappoints" (Camus) —the tragic feeling burrows in and undermines the props of ontical reality. The tragic vision reveals the brutal disharmony of human existence.

The vision of the dreadful differs from the tragic to the degree that is sees only meaninglessness, a void of value. Why are there things at all? The very givenness of things is sensed as utterly contingent and aimless. Whereas the tragic experience always involves the fear of, or suffering related to, a specific something, the experience of the dreadful reduces us to such total insignificance that existence appears valueless. All is vanity. Dread—closely related to the *Angst* of Heidegger and the *nausée* of Sartre—is the feeling that accompanies our awareness of losing grip on ontical reality.

Dread is the horror, as Kierkegaard knew, "of everything disappearing before a sick brooding over the tale of one's own miserable self." Beings, including my own being, are seen as depending somehow on my consciousness, and yet my consciousness is so porous that it has no "thingness," nothing substantial, nothing that can be observed. "I think therefore I am" no longer suffices. "A well gone dry," cries Kafka, "water at an unattainable depth and no certainty that it is there. Nothing, nothing." Dread drains one's dignity.

It is the dreadful rather than the tragic that drove Pascal, potentially one of the greatest of scientists, from beings to *Being*. No one, except perhaps Kierkegaard, has expressed the dreadful more eloquently: "For in fact what is man in nature? A nothing in comparison with the Infinite, an All in comparison with the Nothing, a mean between nothing and everything. Since he is infinitely removed from comprehending the extremes, the end of things and their beginning are hopelessly hidden from him in an impenetrable secret; he is equally incapable of seeing the Nothing from which he was made, and the Infinite in which he is swallowed up" (*Pensées,* Fr. 72) . Pascal could find no surcease from the feeling of dread in functions, even in those of the highest cognitive achievement. "Men seek rest in a struggle against difficulties; and when they have conquered these, rest becomes insufferable. For we think either of the misfortunes we have or of those which threaten us. And even if we should see ourselves sufficiently sheltered on all sides, weariness of its own accord would not fail to arise from the depths of the heart wherein it has its natural roots, and to fill the mind with its poison" (Fr. 139) .

The spring of dread is wound in us so tightly that it uncoils of itself. Even little things can get it going more rapidly: the slightest discomfort or a seeming snub or one question too many or a clog in our practical pursuits. But if Heidegger is correct, the tightness of that coil depends above all on our awareness, however vague and however much we try to escape it, of the ultimate seal of our finitude—the absolute unavoidability of death. This abiding menace confronts us with the nothingness of our existence, and the importance of things sinks away.

> The closest closeness which one may have in Being towards death as a possibility, is as far as possible from anything actual. The more unveiledly this possibility gets understood, the more purely does the understanding penetrate into it *as the possibility of the impossibility of any existence at all. . . .* It [Death] is the possibility of the impossibility of every way of comporting oneself towards anything, of every way of existing. In the anticipation of this possibility it becomes "greater and greater"; that is to say, the possibility reveals itself to be such that it knows no measure at all, no more or less, but signifies the possibility of the measureless impossibility of existence.[40]

To know that we will die means that we might not have existed. We are cast into the world, through no choice of our own, in order to die. Thus our existence is launched between nothingness and nothingness, and our recognition of this absolute contingency devalues everything to insignificance. "Crammed between two nothings," Nietzsche noted, we are "a question mark." We are left with the feelings of the uncanny, *unheimlich,* literally meaning unhomely, and a "sickness unto death." The supports of everyday ontical reality, the public world of the anonymous They, inexorably escape our grasp and the earth yawns as an abyss.

The experiences of the tragic and the dreadful are extremely painful and shocking, disillusioning our faith in the beneficence of ontical reality and thrusting us into the dark night of the soul. This recoil from the ontical opens a void. In the case of Heidegger the void is filled by *Being* that remains something less than personal. In the case of Buber, perhaps because his recoil was felt more deeply, the void is filled by *Being* that becomes personal. ("utter / Terror and loneliness. . . . / drive a man to address the Void

---

40. *Being and Time*, pp. 306f.

as 'Thou' "; Edna St. Vincent Millay, "Conversation at Midnight"). Like Buber, William James claimed that "the universe is no longer a mere *It* to us, but a *Thou,* if we are religious. . . ."[41] In the case of Sartre—most of the time—the void remains meaningless, and so he remains an exile in a desacralized cosmos. For many of us, however, unlike Sartre, a severe recoil from the ontical is likely to release our onto-logical powers, although not necessarily, of course, along the lines of Heidegger or Buber. On the periphery of the void the possibility of *Being* comes into awareness, for it may be, as Meister Eckhart said, that we have only to be empty to be filled. In any event, anyone who has felt deeply the vertigo of the void is likely to be more sensitive to the presence of *Being.*

The aesthetic experience is the second major mode of ex-perience that may liberate our ontological sensitivity. Unlike the experiences of extreme situations, the aesthetic experi-ence does not necessarily or usually turn ontical reality into a wasteland. The aesthetic experience, however, always dis-engages us from the ontical treadmill, liberates us from the frenzy of functions. Thus the ontical is seen from a detached angle that may bring *Being* into awareness.

The aesthetic experience in its pure mode is rapt or in-transitive attention to a presented thing, the "given," whether that thing be a color, a cup of coffee, wallpaper, a pretty girl, or a work of art. When the "given" attracts and holds our attention because of its intrinsic value, not for its utility in serving some end, it becomes an aesthetic object. Thus the red in the evening sky is enjoyed for its own sake, for its qualities such as brilliancy and texture, not as a sign of good weather tomorrow. The recognition of this sign function, however, can become a contributing factor in the aesthetic experience, provided that this recognition adds to the interest in the qualities of the red. The aesthetic experi-ence accents the present tense, the here and now. References to the past and future may be involved, of course, but they are

41. *The Will to Believe* (New York: Longmans, Green, and Co., 1921), p. 27.

subordinated to making the present experience more complete and satisfactory. There is "the present tense with the whole emphasis upon the present" (Kierkegaard), and "the primordial empirical given" (C. I. Lewis) is perceived for its own rather than its instrumental value. Thus the aesthetic experience is an intense ontical experience, and this very intensity suspends us from functions.

Aesthetic experiences obviously are among the great joys of the world. Satisfaction is the *sine qua non* of the aesthetic experience, for without it we are not likely to keep our attention rapt for long. Surely the aesthetic experience, perhaps more than any other kind of experience, renews our faith in ontical reality, as Dewey saw quite clearly in *Art as Experience*. Thus the aesthetic experience would seem, like functions, fit to further bury our ontological sensitivities. But this by no means is always the case.

In the first place, in the aesthetic experience we look at things for their intrinsic rather than for their extrinsic values. A rapport between ourselves and the "given" releases us from the drive of functions. Thus scientists like Einstein, who are much more than technologists,[42] relax at

---

42. Such scientists usually find the one-dimensional scientism of Ayer and the positivists at best only partially descriptive of their work and at worst a travesty. Pierre Duhem, for example:

> If he wishes to be nothing but a physicist, and if, as an intransigent positivist, he regards everything not determinable by the method proper to the positive sciences as unknowable, he will notice this tendency powerfully inciting his own research as it has guided those of all times, but he will not look for its origin, because the only method of discovery which he trusts will not be able to reveal it to him. If, on the other hand, he yields to the nature of the human mind, which is repugnant to the extreme demands of positivism, he will want to know the reason for, or explanation of, what carries him along; he will break through the wall at which the procedures of physics stop, helpless, and he will make an affirmation which these procedures do not justify; he will be metaphysical [ontological]. What is this metaphysical affirmation that the physicist will make, despite the nearly forced restraint imposed on the method he customarily uses? He will affirm that underneath the observable data, the only data accessible to his methods of study, are hidden realities whose essence cannot be grasped by these same methods.

The Aim and Structure of Physical Theory, trans. Philip P. Wiener (New York: Atheneum Publishers, 1962), pp. 296f.

times and sit still long enough to view their science as an aesthetic object and a "silence" sets in. Noise—that permeating monstrous prodigy of our age that bores in even at night without respite—is shut out. Then the *Being* dimension of that object, or what Einstein calls "the mysterious side," has a chance to be heard, the "ringing silence" that Heidegger speaks about in his lectures on *Das Wesen der Sprache*. This is the basic point of Whitehead's oft-repeated remark that "religion is what the individual does with his own solitariness." For those of us who have not learned the ways of Eastern meditation, increasingly difficult even if superficially popular in the West, the aesthetic experience is probably the best way to calm our noisy souls and achieve aloneness. Then in solitude and serenity the silent force of *Being* may have resonance in our inward listening. "The times of spiritual history," says Buber, "in which anthropological thought has so far found its depth of experience have been those very times in which a feeling of strict and inescapable solitude took possession of man."[43] Without privacy we cannot commune with *Being*.

In the second place, the aesthetic experience of works of art usually is very different from the aesthetic experience of nonartistic artifacts and natural objects. In the latter cases, there is usually spectator enjoyment without insight, especially for those of us who are not artists. In the case of the aesthetic experience of works of art, however, there is much more likely to be participative enjoyment with insight. Spectator enjoyment, however refreshing, is of passing moment, a holiday from ontological reality except as it may be a preface to privacy, conducive to the silence that rings. Moreover, the ringing sounds *after*, not *during*, that kind of aesthetic experience. The spectator is dominated by curiosity for the show of things. The "given" is a playground, not to be taken seriously except as an object of pleasure. The aesthetic object, including the work of art, is treated as decora-

---

43. *Between Man and Man*, trans. Ronald Gregor Smith (Boston: Beacon Press, 1955), p. 126.

tion. There may be form, the relationships of part to part and part to whole, but the form is not experienced as informing.

The form of a work of art, nevertheless, does inform, provided that we are capable of participation. Every work of art has a "subject matter," any aspect of human experience that is fundamentally related to man as a purposive and normative agent. A subject matter may be anything that involves a value dimension—that which is worth depicting because it is related to some basic human interest—on the condition that this value dimension is susceptible or "subject" to interpretation by an artist.

> If the true artist seeks to express in his art an interpretation of some aspect of the real world of human experience, every genuine work of art, however slight and in whatever medium must have *some* subject matter. It is not *merely* an aesthetically satisfying organization of sensuous particulars. The entire history of the fine arts and literature, from the earliest times on record down to the present, offers overwhelming evidence that art in the various media has arisen from the artist's desire to express and communicate to his fellows some pervasive human emotion, some insight felt by him to have a wider relevancy, some interpretation of a reality other than the work of art itself in all its specificity.[44]

Whereas a subject matter is a value before artistic interpretation, the "content" is the significantly interpreted subject matter as revealed by the form. Form is the means whereby values are threshed from the husks of irrelevancies. Whereas decorative form merely pleases, artistic form also informs, and it informs about neither the arbitrary nor the unimportant. Rather, it draws from the chaotic state of life which, as Van Gogh describes it, is like "a sketch that didn't come off," a distillation, an economy that produces a lucidity which enables us better to understand and cope with what matters most. Thus the informing is about subject matter

---

44. Theodore Meyer Greene, *The Arts and The Art of Criticism* (Princeton: Princeton University Press, 1940) , p. 231.

with value dimensions that go beyond the artist's idiosyn-
cracies and perversities.

A partial or spectator enjoyment of aesthetic objects, including works of art, floats on their surface, for it never gets
to any content. This kind of aesthetic experience makes no
lasting impact, for little has been learned. We brush off such
experiences rather like dust off a coat. A complete or "participative aesthetic experience" of a work of art, on the
other hand, involves the awareness of content, an insight
that is life-enhancing because it sees something of the depth
of reality. Anyone who has fully experienced one of
Cézanne's interpretations of Mte. Ste. Victoire (Plate 15;
see also Plate 14 for photograph of same scene), for example,
cannot help seeing the rhythm and massiveness of mountains
with, in Berenson's phrase, a "higher coefficient of meaning." Our enjoyment is participative because we cannot stay
aloof from that which is seriously important to us. In turn
the participative aesthetic experience (or simply the "participative experience") is transobjective, personal, dramatic,
full of feeling and of wonder deepening into gratitude.
"Gray cold eyes," noted Nietzsche, "do not know the value
of things." The participative experience is not exclusively
intellectual, emotional, volitional, or intuitional, but rather
integral, uniting all these with the additional element of the
awareness of *Being,* which can occur only within this totally
integrated experience. Whereas the aesthetic object remains
apart from the spectator and he scans it objectively as an on-
looker or observer, the participator is an impassioned intelligence—a "quickened, multiplied consciousness," as Pater
put it—opening and committing the whole of himself to the
significance of the object. In Edward Bullough's well-used
terms: psychical distance is maximized by the spectator,
whereas psychical distance is minimized by the participator.
The spectator remains clearly conscious of himself as distinct from the aesthetic object, whereas the participator becomes so absorbed in receiving and retaining the aesthetic
object that in this profound intimacy he tends to lose any

sense of subject-object duality. There is a similar difference between my *knowing* about the love of another, and my own loving, which I *understand* because I participate in that love.

For the participator the object completely commands the foreground of his attention, thus pushing self-consciousness deeply into the background. Whatever has no relevance to the individuality of the absorbing object ceases to exist for consciousness. As Mircea Eliade describes this kind of experience:

> thought is freed from the presence of "I," for the cognitive act ("I know this object," or "This object is mine") is no longer produced; it is thought that *is* (becomes) the given object. The object is no longer known through associations—that is to say, included in a series of previous representations, localized by extrinsic relations (name, dimensions, use, class), and, so to speak, impoverished by the habitual process of abstraction characteristic of secular [ontical] thought—it is grasped directly, in its existential nakedness, as a concrete and irreducible datum.[45]

When, for example, we have a participative experience of or rather *with* a flower, we are not making a botanical observation or thinking of it as an object. For if we did, the flower would pale into a mere instance of the appropriate ontical categories. The vivid impact of the flower would dim as the focus of our attention shifted in the direction of generality. In the participative experience, however, the "concrete suchness" of the object penetrates and permeates the participator's consciousness to the point that consciousness loses almost all of its self-consciousness, until there is nothing but the object. The subjective side of experience "becomes" the object, the subjective and objective poles of experience melting into a unitary phenomenon. However, self-con-

---

45. *Yoga: Immortality and Freedom*, trans. Willard R. Trask (New York: Pantheon Books, 1958), p. 82. Cf. Bernard Berenson's description of what he calls "the aesthetic moment." *Aesthetics and History* (Garden City, N.Y.: Doubleday and Co., 1953), p. 93.

sciousness is never totally abolished even in the most intense participative experiences, for, as Sartre's analysis shows,[46] human consciousness requires some degree of self-conciousness. But the participator ceases to be his ordinary self in his fascinated self-surrender to the unfolding of the aesthetic object unto its fullness.[47] Perhaps that is what D. H. Lawrence was getting at in his description of the way Cézanne saw and painted:

> For the intuitive perception of the apple is so *tangibly* aware of the apple that it is aware of it *all around,* not only just of the front. The eye sees only fronts, and the mind, on the whole, is satisfied with fronts. But intuition needs all-roundedness, and instinct needs insideness. The true imagination is for ever curving round to the other side, to the back of presented appearance.[48]

Thus the participator is able to commune with the great simplicities of nature. This is the point of Henry Bugbee's insistence that "the existence of things, the standing out of the distinct, can only make sense, as we stand forth ourselves, as we are made to stand forth. In *ecstasis* (literally a "being made to stand forth") the meaning of the existent becomes clear, and the infinite importance of existent things becomes clear. . . . How apt are those Chinese scrolls which show men in harmony with all nature, men and things emerging *together* and not as over against one another."[49] The space

---

46. *Being and Nothingness,* esp. pp. 177ff. See also my "On the Supposed Incompatibility of Expressionism and Formalism," *The Journal of Aesthetics and Art Criticism* 15 (Sept. 1956) : 98.
47. Such unity is also a characteristic of the mystic experience; but the mystic experience, unlike the participative experience, is an awareness of *Being-as-absolute,* the ontological free from the ontical.
48. *Paintings of D. H. Lawrence,* ed. Mervyn Levy (New York: The Viking Press, 1964), p. 39.
49. *The Inward Morning,* p. 106. The Zen Buddhists put it this way:

   The unreal life is a life forever unconsummated. The man who stands apart from things, unable to give himself to them, receives payment in kind; because his relation to things is an external one, these things, in turn, withhold their full reality from him. When life is contemplated objectively, nowhere is there to be found anything that is free of limitations, nothing that fully satisfies the yearning of the human

between the aesthetic object and the participator is eliminated. And then, as Schopenhauer saw, it is "all one whether
we see the sun set from the prison or the palace." The spectator perceives and enjoys the aesthetic object, and then
more or less forgets. The participator also perceives and enjoys; but since the content forces him below the surface,
his perception and enjoyment are extraordinary, ecstatic,
and he is unlikely to forget. Whereas the spectator experience is a kind of windowshopping, "stand-offish" and ephem-
eral,[50] the communion of the participative experience has a
fascination and finality that allows some thing to come into
full radiance transporting us to lasting enrichment. As
Whitehead has written:

> Great art is the arrangement of the environment so as to provide
> for the soul vivid, but transient, values. Human beings require
> something which absorbs them for a time, something out of the
> routine which they can stare at. But you cannot subdivide life,
> except in the abstract analysis of thought. Accordingly, the great
> art is more than a transient refreshment. It is something which
> adds to the permanent richness of the soul's self-attainment. It
> justifies itself both by its immediate enjoyment, and also by its
> discipline of the inmost being. Its discipline is not distinct from
> enjoyment, but by reason of it. It transforms the soul into the
> permanent realisation of values extending beyond its former
> self.[51]

In the participative experience values have an ontological
aspect because they expand within and beyond the ontically
given and the passing moment. We find an importance that

---

heart. It is only when man's experience of life is integral that it
"means everything" to him; only when the subject is not outside the
object, where each lives in the other as well as in itself—only then is
life complete from moment to moment.
Daisetz T. Suzuki, *The Essentials of Zen Buddhism,* ed. Bernard Phillips
(London: Rider and Co., 1962), p. xiv.

50. The spectator sensibility taken to its ultimate extreme is a cult now
called "Camp." See Susan Sontag, "Notes on 'camp,'" *Partisan Review* 21
(Fall 1964): 515–30. For a denial that the complete aesthetic experience
is participative, see Ortega y Gasset, "The Dehumanization of Art," *Symposium,* ed. J. Burnham and P. Wheelwright (April 1930), 1: 194–205.

51. *Science and the Modern World* (New York: The Macmillan Co., 1925),
pp. 290f.

supports and transcends the ontically given and yet, for that very reason, deepens our participation with that given. Thus we become co-participants with the ontically given, both embraced in the power of *Being*. Thus ontical reality is not undermined, as in our experience of the tragic, or voided, as in our experience of the dreadful. And especially in a participative experience of a work of art, we feel the beauty of the sensuous as celebrated in the very use and structuring of the artistic media. But within the rhapsody of sensations there is insight. The work of art carries us through the surface of things. *Being* comes into explicit awareness because something of the depth dimension, the enduring value of the ontical subject matter is revealed by the informing form.[52] The work of art never interprets all of *Being*, of course; for since *Being* is inexhaustible and therefore *essentially* mysterious, *Being* stretches beyond every interpretation. "The artist," Schelling noted in *System of Transcendental Idealism,* "seems to have presented in his work, as if instinctively, apart from what he has put into it with obvious intent, an infinity which no finite understanding can unfold." Thus works of art, despite the creed that Nietzsche called "esthetic Socratism," can never be completely intelligible. *Being* as revealed is always inseparably mixed with concealment. Nevertheless, the work of art corners and illuminates *Being*. And so our rapt gaze is held upon both the unveiled and the veiled.

The artist is, in that wonderful phrase of Heidegger's, "The Shepherd of *Being*." By means of a participative ex-

---

52. Cf. Heidegger's description in "Vom Ursprung des Kunstwerkes," *Holzwege,* of a painting by Van Gogh: "The painting is of a pair of peasant's shoes–and nothing else. Just a pair of shoes; yet around and through them emerges the world in which the peasant traces his furrows, watches patiently for the wheat to bloom, or trudges tiredly at evening back from the fields. The cycles of time–Spring, Summer, Autumn, Winter–enfold these simple boots, which, as serviceable and dependable, find their place in a world. Being, as presence, emerges through the painting of the shoes; yet in such a way that it enfolds them in their concrete thingness–just a pair of shoes, and nothing else–as the simple, serviceable gear that they are." Translation by William Barrett in "Art and Being," *Art and Philosophy,* ed. Sidney Hook (New York: New York University Press, 1966), p. 172.

perience with some area of ontical reality, the artist discovers the depth dimension of that area. This discovery requires a receptive creativity, a nonresistant consciousness, a letting *Being* be. Through his constructive creativity, in turn, the artist interprets and preserves his discovery, the unveiling of *Being,* in his art. These two kinds of creativity are not necessarily chronologically distinct. With most artists it seems that the two creativities are inextricably combined. Cézanne told Emile Bernard that "the landscape thinks itself in me and I am its consciousness." In any case, the artist shelters and tends to *Being* as *Being* emerges in things. The artist lets the "is" of some thing shine forth. Creativity depends upon reverence to things.

Art is a gift of *Being.* That is why art, despite its autonomy, has always served as the principal sacred bridge—although, admittedly, very narrowly framed in the Puritan tradition—to the religious experience, and continues to do so even in these apparently post-religious times. And that is why the participative experience of art is more than just a way back to *Being,* as in the tragic, dreadful, and spectator experiences. The participative experience of art consummates these preparatory experiences, for it always includes the presence and articulation of *Being.* And the participative experience of anything that is not a work of art is also an experience of consummation, as in, for example, intense sensuousness, or love for a river, or a person, or something brought forth from our memories, or even a function.[53]

---

53. If Mark Twain is correct (see p. 38) , it would seem that functions could never be experienced participatively. Bugbee has convinced me otherwise. See especially the moving description of how his absorption in the functions of the life of a ship at sea became participative experiences. *The Inward Morning,* pp. 176–93. See also Antoine de Saint-Exupéry, *Wind, Sand and Stars,* trans. Lewis Galantière (New York: Reynal and Hitchcock, 1939) . Functions directly dependent upon the vagaries of nature, such as farming, sea-faring, and space-exploration, are more likely, I believe, to involve us participatively than such functions as business and machine technology. For how technical objects can become aesthetic objects, see Mikel Dufrenne, "The Aesthetic Object and The Technical Object," *Aesthetic Inquiry: Essays on Art Criticism and the Philosophy of Art,* ed. Monroe C. Beardsley and Herbert M. Schueller (Belmont, California: Dickenson Publishing Co., 1967) .

The participative experience requires for those of us who are not artists a receptive creativity that differs only in degree from the receptive creativity of the artist. To the degree that we are less ontologically sensitive than the artist, to that degree our understanding of *Being* in the participative experience is less adequate. And the enlightenment of our ontological sensitivity is beholden above all to the gifts of the artist. These gifts generate the growth of our humanity. The artist shows us the way "to abide with *Being*," as Heidegger puts it in his essays on the poetry of Hölderlin, "to be at home in the homeland." The artist focuses to a fine point that aboriginal light of *Being*, present to us all but usually as concealed or confused, that illuminates our world. Insofar as our ontological sensitivities are enlightened, we are saved from ontical slavery.[54] To be is to participate, to be creatively absorbed with the presence of *Being*. Then we have a spiritual center, a still point around which the broken fragments of experience fold into meaningful patterns. Then we may be at one with sun and stone, as Nabokov writes somewhere. And then the corroding acids of technology can be contained, and even functions may partake of the beauty of *Being*. Every object and event, no matter how mundane, is potentially sacramental.[55]

Both the participative experience and the religious ex-

---

54. According to Berdyaev, unless the duality of subject and object is transcended to some significant degree through participative experiences, this slavery is of two basic kinds: "The 'objective' either entirely engulfs and enslaves human subjectivity or it arouses repulsion and disgust and so isolates human subjectivity and shuts it up in itself. . . . Engulfed entirely by his own ego the subject is a slave, just as a subject which is wholly ejected into an object is a slave. Both in the one case and in the other personality is disintegrated or else it has not yet taken shape." *Slavery and Freedom*, trans. R. M. French (London: Geoffrey Bles: The Centenary Press, 1944), p. 138.

55. "Either all occurrences are in some degree revelation of God [*Being-as-transcendental*], or else there is no such revelation at all; for the conditions of the possibility of any revelation require that there should be nothing which is not revelation." William Temple, *Nature, Man and God* (London: Macmillan and Co., 1935), p. 306. Everything in ontical reality is a "cipher" of *Being*, in Jaspers' terminology, whose secret text can be deciphered not by scientific codes or keys but only through the participative experience.

perience spring from the same empirical grounds; both involve love for *Being;* both are intimate and ultimate; both are attuned to the call of *Being;* both are reverential in attitude to things; both step beyond the confines of the self; both give a man a sense of being reunited with "that with which he is most familiar"; both give enduring value and serenity to existence; and thus both are profoundly regenerative. The participative experience, then, always has a religious quality, for the participative experience penetrates the religious dimension. How deeply into this dimension the experience reaches is revealed by how seriously the participation with *Being* is believed to be of supreme importance; and this in turn, insofar as it is not a groundless belief, depends upon the convictional power of the participative experience itself, the pressure of the presence of *Being.*[56] Thus the secular artist as well as the religious artist reveals *Being,* but not *Being-as-transcendental* because the pressure of *Being* is not powerful enough. Only the "language"—the means of communication—of the religious artist is the language of the sacred. Awe-full awareness occurs only with strongly coercive participative experiences. Then *Being* becomes *Holy Being* or God, accompanied by religious feelings and the need for the various theoretical, practical, and sociological forms of religious expression. The tragic, the dreadful, and the spectator experiences open us to *Being* by freeing us from ontical obsession. But it is only in the participative experience that *Being* begins to grace our destinies.

---

56. Without this convictional power, as Bugbee points out, religious belief or faith is groundless and thus a deception. "I have encountered no attempt to accord the idea of faith a 'sympathetic' interpretation, 'a defence,' more misleading than the kind suggested by Pascal's 'wager' or William James' 'forced option': that faith means tipping the scale in favor of a set of beliefs which can be neither established nor disproven conclusively, because we have everything to gain and nothing to lose a) if they are true, by believing so, and b) by believing they are true even if they are not." *The Inward Morning,* p. 59. It seems to me, however, that secondhand religious belief or faith based entirely on traditional authority, even when that tradition is based on participative experiences, is equally misleading.

2

The Participative Experience

In the participative experience consciousness is released to a thing in such a way that "the thing thinks in me." This is a thinking that listens, as distinct from the busy-ness of calculative thinking. When a thing begins to think in me, the thing becomes dynamic and uncanny. The thing forces me to move out of my self-consciousness to become a part of I know not what. Instead of my dominating a thing, it dominates me. I *wait upon* rather than *wait for* the thing. Instead of placing, classifying, and using a thing as one among many, I am captured by the concrete suchness of the thing and it controls my experience so that the many are subordinated or forgotten. Rather than being *set over against* the thing, I am in sympathetic relation *with* the thing. My consciousness is run through and saturated with the singularity of the thing ("We become what we behold" [McLuhan], the refrain that Blake so beautifully weaves through *Jerusalem*). Thus my self-consciousness, that barrier that keeps me aloof from things, is pushed to the background. My consciousness becomes so immersed in the thing that there is no conscious energy left for explicit reflective consciousness. In the absence of that barrier the individuality of the thing pours through. In this exposed self-abandonment the space between me and the thing disappears. In steadfast intimate concentration, I allow the thing to abide as a thing. The anaesthetic of self-consciousness no longer prevents the complete aesthetic or participative experience. I open myself to the *Being* of the thing.

But the statement that "the thing thinks in me" is a metaphor. What are the conditions and the detailed operations of the participative experience? Without some knowledge of these conditions and operations the role of art in the religious experience can be described only in very general terms, as usually has been the case. For four decades now since the publication of *Being and Time,* Heidegger has wrestled with the question of the "how" of the participative experience, or what he calls "essential" or "meditative" as contrasted with "calculative thinking." Progressively abandoning systematic language, he has turned to a poetic use of language, richly suggestive about *Being* but often extremely baffling about how *Being* is experienced.[1] Heidegger is surely correct in this turn to a poetic way of thinking about *Being;* to use systematic language to describe *Being* is futile because such language inevitably reduces *Being* to a being. Only the arts can describe *Being* in the sense of interpretation or articulation, unveiling *Being* as *Being* and thus giving us understanding though not knowledge of *Being.* Nonetheless systematic language, granting its limitations, is not so ineffective in explaining the conditions and the operations of the participative experience as Heidegger contends. Although systematic language is a useless tool for describing *Being,* it can be a useful tool for describing how *Being* is experienced.

Systematic theories of perception can be helpful here, and Whitehead's theory is especially helpful. (I use this theory

---

1. See, for example, "Conversation on a Country Path about Thinking," in *Discourse on Thinking,* trans. John M. Anderson and E. Hans Freund (New York: Harper and Row, 1966).

of perception without accepting or using Whitehead's complete metaphysical system.) To be sure, Whitehead does not distinguish between ontical and ontological reality. Indeed the differences between the philosophies of Heidegger and Whitehead are profound and in many respects irreconcilable. Nevertheless there are many significant and illuminating convergences. For example, in both, positivism is sharply rejected. Both insist that sense data are abstractions—from beings in the case of Heidegger, from actual entities in the case of Whitehead. Both are philosophers of process. Indeed, Heidegger puts as much emphasis on temporality as Whitehead, although this has not been generally recognized. For both, any actual thing is not self-defined but is its relationships. The "external" enters into the essence of the "internal," and vice versa, and these relationships occur through process. Both find value as something more than a human projection. Both find in art a revelation of the depth dimension of reality. Both are sensitive to the mystery and holiness of existence. Both find an eternal factor in reality.

The interpretations of these convergences differ, of course, often drastically. Possibilities play a pivotal role in both philosophies, for example, but Heidegger would utterly reject the quasi-Platonic status of Whitehead's eternal objects. Whereas Heidegger presents a phenomenological account of possibilities and process in human experience, Whitehead presents a metaphysical account of possibilities and process as having cosmological actuality. Furthermore, neither Heidegger nor Whitehead, two of the most influential philosophers of the twentieth century, seems to have directly influenced the other. Nevertheless Whitehead's theory of perception, especially with respect to the insights it suggests about the conformation of human experience to things, provides a remarkable clarification of Heidegger's crucial claim that in the experience of *Being* "the thing thinks in me." In the first section of this chapter, Whitehead's theory of perception will be briefly summarized.

In the second section, insights based on this theory will be used to clarify the conditions and operations of the participative experience. Hopefully this use of Whitehead's theory, inevitably a part to some extent of his metaphysical system, in conjunction with Heidegger's phenomenological ontology will not commit great violence upon either. My aim, in any case, is not to provide an exegesis of either Whitehead or Heidegger, but rather to use their philosophies as a base from which, in my own way, to explore and clarify the phenomena of the participative experience. Then the problems of how the language of art symbolizes *Being* and the role of art in the religious experience can be studied in the following chapters with more precision.

I

To be an actual entity, Whitehead holds, is to be an occasion of experience, and experience is not an undifferentiated flow but rather a rhythmic transition from one occasion to another. An occasion of experience is a process of integration by a subject of objects, the fusion being so tightly unified that its beginning, middle, and end can be distinguished only after the completion of the process. The movement by which each novel occasion as a subject takes account selectively of past occasions or objects and then passes into an object in the past of new occasions is the creative process. Although a past occasion in which I was the subject has perished, I may remember that occasion and thus the subject that I was becomes an object. In this process the subject has physical feelings or prehensions of objects from the settled past, the past thus becoming efficacious in the present. Feelings have a magnetic quality, for they reach out to what is *there* and transform it into what is *here*. The physical feeling is analyzed into the initial datum, which is the object as it exists independently of the subject; into the objective datum, which is the datum as it actually enters into the subject, involving elimination of factors in the initial datum; and into the subjective form, which is how the subject feels that datum. Thus my past experience as it actually was is the initial datum; what I remember, inevitably involving an emphasis on some factors and a deemphasis on others, is the objective datum; and how I remember, involving perhaps nostalgia, for example, is the subjective form.

From every physical feeling one always derives a conceptual feeling of a possibility of eternal object. As I physically feel the brown grass of my lawn, I conceptually feel the possibility of applying the sprinkler. Whereas a physical feeling takes account of an object from the past, a conceptual feeling takes account of a possibility which may or may not be exemplified in the future. Eternal objects are potential forms of definiteness that act as lures in the coming to be or concrescence of an actual entity. Any form of definiteness (quality or relationship) that can characterize an indefinite number of occasions, as greenness may be exemplified in this or that occasion, is an eternal object. The green that has ingressed into a particular actual entity or society of entities, such as my lawn, is an instance or exemplification of an eternal object, an actualized rather than an abstract possibility. Although eternal objects as abstract possibilities are not actual, they have the power to influence actual entities. The possibility that my lawn may again turn brown compels my continued use of the sprinkler. Both physical and conceptual feelings as such are unconscious, although both involve subjective forms. Consciousness arises only as a factor in the subjective form of an integrated feeling involving a contrast felt between fact and possibility.

Occasions of experience are the smallest units that compose the realm of actuality. Actual occasions group together in societies, of less or more structured complexity. In complexly structured societies or high-grade organisms two pure modes of perception may occur: causal efficacy and presentational immediacy. All actual occasions undergo the mode

of causal efficacy or process, but only occasions in sub-so-
cieties such as brains—within highly structured societies such
as animal bodies—are capable of also experiencing in the
mode of presentational immediacy.

The mode of causal efficacy is vague, haunting, and un-
manageable, heavy with the contact of things gone by which
lay their grip on our present experience. Perception in the
mode of causal efficacy feels the conformation of the present to the past and the future to the present, whereby what is
already made becomes a determinant of what is in the making. Causal efficacy

> produces percepta which are vague, not to be controlled, heavy
> with emotion: it produces the sense of derivation from an im-
> mediate past, and of passage to an immediate future; a sense of
> emotional feeling, belonging to oneself in the past, passing into
> oneself in the present, and passing from oneself in the present
> towards oneself in the future; a sense of influx of influence
> from other vaguer presences in the past, localized and yet evad-
> ing local definition, such influence modifying, enhancing, in-
> hibiting, diverting, the stream of feeling which we are receiving,
> unifying, enjoying, and transmitting. This is our general sense
> of existence, as one item among others, in an efficacious actual
> world.[2]

Perception of causal efficacy is the perception of process.

Every actual entity is a concrescing subject physically feeling objects from the past, conceptually feeling possibilities,
and integrating its physical and conceptual feelings into
propositional feelings. A propositional feeling, unlike a
conceptual feeling, relates its eternal object to a physical
feeling. For example, I relate the possible use of the sprinkler to my lawn. Thus a propositional feeling is always an
integrative feeling. In this synthesizing process or duration
the self-determining subject creatively becomes as it integrates its feelings and reaches a decision that realizes certain
possibilities and rejects others. Whereas the subjective forms
of the physical feelings involve a sense of the past, the sub-

---

2. *Process and Reality* (New York: The Macmillan Co., 1929), p. 271.

jective forms of the propositional feelings involve a sense of the future, and thus both feelings of past and future are felt in the immediacy of the present concrescing duration. Moreover, when the integration into a complex unified feeling is completed and the actual entity's subjective aim or purpose is satisfied, for better or for worse, the subject perishes and becomes an object available for physical feeling by succeeding actual entities. Once fully become, the actual entity is no longer a subject that feels. It has become an object, for its creativity has become absorbed into the becoming of future occasions. Thus perishing is not annihilation, but a transformation of private subjective feeling into what now can be objectively felt. This necessity for transformation from subject to object is also felt in the concrescence of the actual entity. Thus the influence of past and future on the present is always effective, always unified, in any actual occasion.

Perception in the mode of causal efficacy cannot be avoided. In high-grade organisms, however, perception in the pure mode of causal efficacy, i.e., unmixed with presentational immediacy, is consciously experienced very rarely. And even then, as in human experience, the feeling of causal efficacy as a pure mode of perception is on the border of unconsciousness. There is lacking a clear recognition of sensa or actualized forms of definiteness which would locate and discriminate the various objects prehended. In this twilight zone of consciousness the subject feels little more than the contact of objects dimly discerned, and its predominantly passive reaction to this contact, as in the impressions of undiscriminated phenomena unrolling in blind succession and impinging on the mind when we arouse ourselves from a deep sleep. Our bodies are barely felt. Orientation is so confused that even body and bed are not spatially situated. And although there is consciousness of process, of "on-goingness," of the tumultuous motion of the heart and the sound of its beating, there is no consciousness of time, *i.e.,* process dated and delineated by measurable units. We are so imprisoned in process that for the moment we are unable to sense time and place. However, perception in the mode of causal efficacy—the feeling of confused temporal togetherness of immediate past and immediate future in the present—underlies and makes possible all higher forms of consciousness. Our feeling of causal efficacy, furthermore, is permeated with emotion originating from those things whose relevance is given. In this rise of affective tone the percepta are felt as dynamic, as interdependent and interconnected, as involved in past-present-future.

Perception in the mode of presentational immediacy, conversely, "halts at the present, and indulges in a manageable self-enjoyment derived from the immediacy of the show of things."[3] The vivid perception of sensa inhibits apprehension of causal connections, past and future, as when the striking hue of that patch of green so arrests our attention that we ignore the reference of the green to that particular society of occasions called grass. Yet presentational immediacy or sense perception presupposes the primitive mode of causal efficacy, for what is given in sense perception is given by reason of objectifications of actual entities from the settled past. The society or thing called grass characterized by greenness must have been an object "there-then" causally influencing and felt by us before we could discriminate that green "here-now."[4] The grass is more than just green, of course, and as felt in the mode of causal efficacy other details than green are part of the vague totality of experienced content. But in presentational immediacy these other details are omitted, and by a process of selection and emphasis the

3. *Symbolism, Its Meaning and Effect* (New York: The Macmillan Co., 1927), p. 44.
4. Unless error has occurred. It may be, for instance, that occasions in the optic nerve have produced for the brain, by a process Whitehead calls "conceptual reversion," green as a datum instead of brown which in fact is the color of the grass. See *Process and Reality*, p. 40 and *passim*. In any case, however, the sensa perceived in the mode of presentational immediacy must be given to it through the mode of causal efficacy.

green sensa are elicited into clarity and projected[5] upon a contemporaneous society of actual entities in the directly relevant spatiotemporal continuum. We feel the green out there in a specific location, and as contemporary with us. In fact, however, the green is derived from occasions in the immediate past. If in that projection of the green the process of derivation is not consciously felt, the perception is in the pure mode of presentational immediacy, the vivid solipsism of the present moment cut off from an explicit awareness of past and future. Thus the percepta in the pure mode of presentational immediacy are perceived as static entities.

Conscious perception in either of the two "pure modes" is rare. The sensa of presentational immediacy normally call forth other components, for example, refer to the objects or situations from which they have been abstracted. That green then is felt as a stimulus that refers to that grass. Conversely, the sensa given in causal efficacy normally elicit definitive localization. As we awake from a deep sleep, we begin to orient ourselves by discriminating and projecting sensa onto the spatiotemporal continuum. Thus we locate our bodies, the bed, and the room. Sensa are the common forms of definiteness that serve as a link between the two pure modes of perception. When this linkage is felt by a subject, perception occurs in the "mixed mode" of reference.[6]

II

With perception in the pure mode of causal efficacy, the object or physically given dominates the subject. But at best there is only a very low degree of consciousness in the pure mode of causal efficacy. The participative experience, on the other hand, involves a very high degree of consciousness.

5. This projection is accomplished by the highly complex function called "transmutation." See *ibid.*
6. All the more sophisticated or conventional kinds of reference, such as the meanings of words, are based on this perceptual reference. See *Symbolism, Its Meaning and Effect,* and *Process and Reality,* Part II, chap. 8.

With perception in the pure mode of presentational immediacy, there is a mere "staring" at sensa without reference
to the physically given from which the sensa have been abstracted. Although this is a highly conscious experience, it
is not participative because the given is not felt as dominating the subject. Participative experiences, therefore, necessarily involve reference, and of course the vast majority of
conscious experiences are in the mixed mode. Why then is
the participative experience such a rare occurrence for most
of us? Although Whitehead does not discuss this most important question directly, his theory suggests three fundamental operations in experience that tend to prevent participation.

In the first place, no subject can be sensitive to the totality of the physically given that is being prehended. The individuality of the subject would be destroyed if it were
totally dominated by its object, as is almost the case with
simple societies such as electrons. That is why such societies
are almost but not quite completely predictable in their
activities, for their low-grade creativity condemns them to
a very passive reception of their causal influences. The physically given must be harmonized by the subject with its subjective aim, for otherwise the subject's creativity could not
function, which is to say that the subject could not be. This
harmonizing requires the subject negatively to prehend or
ignore those factors in the object incompatible with its subjective aim, thus preserving the unity of the subject. That
is why Whitehead distinguishes between the initial datum,
the physically given as it exists independently of the subject, and the objective datum, the physically given as it actually enters into the subject. When the separation between
the initial and the objective datum becomes significant, a
participative experience is impossible because the subject
by means of its negative prehensions dominates the object.
For example, suppose a farmer is looking at his fields of
wheat and his subjective aim is concentrated upon the profit
this wheat will bring in the market. He ignores all those

factors that are irrelevant to helping him measure the economic value of the wheat. Even the color and the texture, although positively prehended, are taken into his experience only with reference to their extrinsic or instrumental value. Since the gap between the initial datum and the objective datum is significant, there is no opportunity for the full dimensionality of the object to dominate the subject, and thus one of the necessary conditions for a participative experience is unfulfilled.

In the second place, even when the initial datum and objective datum are closely allied because of a minimum of negative prehensions, "conceptual reversion" may occur in a secondary phase of the concrescence of the subject in such a way that the object is not allowed to dominate. For example, suppose I have a physical feeling of the tone C as played on the piano. This will necessarily be followed by a conceptual feeling of the potential form of definiteness or eternal object C-ness. This must occur, according to Whitehead's categories, because every actual entity is "dipolar," *i.e.*, it has a physical or receptive pole that takes account of other actual entities by means of physical feelings, positive or negative, and a mental or active pole which takes account of eternal objects or possibilities by means of conceptual feelings. Since these two poles are inseparable, a physical feeling always has its conceptual counterpart. From each positive physical feeling there is the derivation of a purely conceptual feeling whose datum is the possibility exemplified by the physical datum. This first activity of the mental pole is mere conceptual conformation or registration of the feelings of the physical pole.

There may be, however, by a further process called "conceptual reversion,"

secondary origination of conceptual feelings with data which are partially identical with, and partially diverse from, the eternal objects forming the data in the primary phase of the mental pole; the determination of identity and diversity depending on the subjective aim at attaining depth of intensity by reason of contrast. . . . In this second phase the proximate novelties [secondary origination of eternal objects] are conceptually felt. This is the process by which the subsequent enrichment of subjective forms, both in qualitative patterns, and in intensity through contrast, is made possible by the positive conceptual prehension of relevant alternatives.[7]

Thus the conceptual feeling of C-ness may give rise through reversion to the conceptual feeling, for example, of G-ness.

A propositional feeling or prehension is the process by which an actual entity takes account of a possibility applying in some assigned way to some concrete datum. Whereas a conceptual feeling is the feeling of an unqualified negation, *i.e.,* it is the feeling of a definite eternal object with definite extrusion from any particular realization, a propositional feeling is a hybrid between pure possibility and actuality. In this synthesis the possibility has suffered the elimination of its absolute generality of reference. Thus in a propositional feeling possibility is no longer pure because it is now tied to some assigned entity. If, for instance, I feel the pitch C-ness or G-ness as a possibility related to a specific tonal C, the possibility is not completely pure or abstract because it is felt in relation not to *any* but rather to a specific datum. Propositions are "the tales that perhaps might be told about particular actualities."[8] Fact is confronted with alternatives.

Physical, conceptual, and propositional feelings occur on the nonconscious level. They are raised to the conscious level by a further process which contrasts and integrates the physical with the propositional feeling. All higher experience depends upon the contrast between what is *in fact* and what *might be*. The integration of the two factors into the conscious perception thus confronts the fact or the physical feeling with the potentiality or propositional feeling. For example, there is the particular C felt physically, and a prop-

---

7. *Process and Reality,* pp. 380f.
8. *Ibid.,* p. 392. This uncommon usage of "proposition" is, of course, peculiar to Whitehead's system.

ositional feeling that connects the eternal object C-ness (or
say G-ness, if there is reversion) with this C. Now if the
physical feeling is contrasted and thus integrated with the
propositional feeling, then we will be conscious of the given
C and C-ness (or G-ness, if there is reversion).

Whitehead claims that the subjective aim of all experience is satisfaction, and this is achieved by intensifying
(depth) the largest possible number of factors in experience
(width) within the limits of harmony (balance). Intensification depends upon contrast, and the ability to conceive of
possibilities relevant to and yet contrasting with the physically given factors in experience makes the higher grades
of satisfaction possible. As a condition for intensity of experience, reversions are the conceptions which arise by
reason of the lure of contrast. Experience can be saved from
monotony and triviality only by this contrast. "What might
be" has the capability of relevant contrast with "what is."
If possibilities are dismissed from relevance to fact, experience is trivial. However, the power of reversions to intensify
experience has to be considered in connection with the category of aesthetic harmony, for the contrasts produced by
reversion are contrasts required for the fulfillment of the
aesthetic ideal. If the reversions and their contrasts fail to be
unified, chaos of experience results, as unsatisfactory as the
boredom of triviality. To have to listen simultaneously to
the *Concerto for Orchestra* by Bartok and a reading of
Hamlet would be as frustrating as to have to listen to a
"poem" by Edgar Guest repeated. Consciousness of the maxi-
mum number of possibilities is subject to the restraint that
they must be under conditions allowing for unification or
harmony.

When reversions are contrasted and kept relevant to the
physical given from which they were originally although indirectly derived, they will intensify the feeling of the physically given and thus help keep that given in dominance.
In this case reversions help make the participative experience
possible. But where the reversions are not contrasted with the

physically given, participation becomes impossible. Although the subjective aim always strives for satisfaction, it may be uninterested in the full dimensionality of the physically given. For instance, the physically given may not be worth the trouble, as usually would be true in the case of the tone C disconnected from some musical form. Or when the physically given is painful, we normally try to distract ourselves from that given by concentrating upon reversions. Or practical demands may have priority, as in the example of the farmer and his wheat. For one reason or another we may not contrast our reversions in any significant way with the physically given. Thus I physically feel the C, conceptually feel C-ness and then the reversion G-ness. Now suppose this feeling of G-ness is not significantly contrasted with the physical feeling of C. Instead of intensification and balance there is a separation of factors in the experience that results in a withdrawal from the physically given. The creativity manifested by the reversion leads away from the physically given and the opportunity for a participative experience is lost. This, of course, may be for the best when the physical datum is trivial or painful or dangerously impractical or disharmonious with more valuable data.

In the third place, finally, imaginative feelings or prehensions may operate in our experience in a way that blocks us from the participative experience. In the imaginative feeling a possibility is always contrasted with the physically given, but the genesis of this possibility is not tied even indirectly, as in the case of reversion, to that given. Suppose, for example, that as I am reacting to the C of a piano, I also am reacting to a bodily pain. Now if I contrast the conceptual feeling of this pain with the physical feeling of the C, I will be relating a possibility to the physical feeling of C that is irrelevant and distracting. Once again the subject completely dominates the physically given. On the other hand, suppose that I am hearing an orchestra playing the chord G simultaneously with the piano playing C. I will have a conceptual feeling of G-ness derived from the physi-

cal feeling of the orchestra. Now if I contrast that feeling
of G-ness with the sound of the piano, I will be experiencing
an imaginative feeling. And it is quite likely that this contrast will intensify the feeling of the piano tone. In this case
the possibility of a participative experience is enhanced.

In the participative experience "the thing thinks in me"
in the sense that the possibilities felt in that experience are
controlled by the physically given thing. The possibilities are
contrasted and integrated with the thing in such a way that
the feelings of the physically given are intensified. The possibilities are kept subordinated to this end because the physically given completely dominates our attention. In this
possession by the thing, our consciousness of the subject-
object duality is thrust to the background. The physically
grounded coordination of all factors produces an intensified
satisfaction no other experience can achieve. Our awareness
becomes a thinking that is a thanking.

We could not survive, of course, if things continually dominated us. The exigencies of existence force us most of the
time to dominate things. And so we become, as Samuel
Beckett observes, creatures of custom and convention.

> Habit is the ballast that chains the dog to his vomit. Breathing
> is habit. Life is habit. Or rather life is a succession of habits,
> since the individual is a succession of individuals. . . . Habit
> then is the generic term for the countless treaties concluded be-
> tween the countless subjects that constitute the individual and
> their countless correlative objects. The periods of transition that
> separate consecutive adaptations . . . represent the perilous
> zones in the life of the individual, dangerous, precarious, pain-
> ful, mysterious and fertile, when for a moment the boredom of
> living is replaced by the suffering of being. . . . The suffering of
> being: that is the free play of every faculty.[9]

This free play rarely occurs because our pernicious devotion
to habit paralyzes our perceptive faculties, closes them off
from being receptive to things. But participative experiences

9. *Proust* (New York: Grove Press, 1931), pp. 8f.

are still possible, despite our habits, and the survival of our humanity, if not of our bodies, depends upon their realization some of the time. There are, moreover, two fundamental factors suggested by Whitehead's theory that favor our breaking through the habits of nonparticipative experiences.

In the first place, the subjective aim of every experience ultimately is beauty, for beauty is the only ultimate satisfaction. Without beauty, sooner or later, nothing would be justified. Beauty is a quality which finds its exemplification in actual occasions to the degree that the subjective forms of the various prehensions, physical and conceptual, are successfully interwoven in patterned contrasts. Beauty is the mean between the boredom of unity and the chaos of variety. The synthesis that maximizes variety and still maintains unity, *i.e.*, beauty, is best exemplified in the participative experience. For in participation the power of the physically given not only stimulates the prehension of a wide variety of possibilities, but also this variety is unified by patterned contrasts because of the dominance of the physically given. In this process the subjective forms of self-consciousness are weakened to the point of unconsciousness by being completely subordinated to the physically given. This is the most intense, coherent, and self-justifying of all experiences. Often, of course, we fall short of beauty, due to some failure of sensitivity or concentration on our part. Or the discords of reality may force us, even habituate us, to live with ugliness now for the possibility of beauty tomorrow. Or practical exigencies may require us to ignore beauty. The farmer who only contemplates his wheat will let it spoil. Nevertheless, since beauty is the value that justifies all other values, the lack of beauty in our lives, although the fundamental evil, acts as an unremitting spur for something better. The ideal of beauty, however vaguely comprehended, lures us on because no other ideal when actualized gives complete satisfaction.

In the second place, the lure of beauty is embedded in

reality as the persuasion of God. Possibilities are not only grounded in the primordial nature of God but structured in relevance to our creative process. The many possibilities conceived in their bare isolated multiplicity lack influence. They require the transition to the conception of them as efficacious in actuality by reason of God's conceptual realization of them. God's propositional feelings of possibilities exemplify in their subjective forms mutual sensitivity and valuation which make these possibilities relevant alternatives for us. Unordered and thus unavailable possibility becomes ordered and thus available possibility acting as the primordial lure for our conceptual feeling. "We must conceive the Divine Eros as the active entertainment of all ideals, with the urge to their finite realization, each in its due season."[10] We aim for beauty because this is the ideal to which all other ideals are subordinated. And we do not invent but rather discover this hierarchy because "the teleology of the Universe is directed to the production of Beauty."[11]

This claim by Whitehead is highly interpretative and speculative, dependent upon his metaphysical system for its elaboration and defense. Heidegger rejects all metaphysical systems in favor of a phenomenological ontology. Yet Heidegger, especially in his later work, also points to two basic factors—remarkably similar to Whitehead's although developed very differently—that favor our breaking through the habits of nonparticipative experiences. In the first place, if we persistently fail to explicitly experience *Being* through participation with beings, such emotions as *Angst* and guilt will be deeply felt no matter how much we try to escape them. To be closed off from *Being* is to be inauthentic, to fail to have the courage to be, and this state inevitably will report itself. Then, provided we have the "resolve" to listen, the "call of conscience" will act as a spur toward authenticity.

In the second place, *Being* lures us. *Being* is "that-which-regions" in us, provided we wait in the right way for that

10. *Adventures of Ideas* (New York: The Macmillan Co., 1933), p. 357.
11. *Ibid.*, p. 341.

regioning, *i.e.,* creatively absorb ourselves in beings. Whereas in Whitehead possibilities are grounded in the primordial nature of God, in the later Heidegger the possibilities that give us a "world" and its "horizon" or limit are grounded in *Being*. In the early Heidegger we project the possibilities that form our world, but in the later Heidegger the emphasis is upon *Being* as the power that makes our projection of possibilities possible. Moreover, these possibilities are a primordial lure for us, for only by becoming explicitly aware of them as grounded in *Being* can we achieve our destinies— to be fully actualized *Dasein,* to be the kind of being that thinks *Being.*[12] *Being* cooperates by luring us, by initiating our reception of *Being.* Thus for Heidegger also, although he never would state it this way, "the teleology of the Universe is directed to the production of Beauty."

There is, finally, one further aspect of Whitehead's theory of perception that clarifies the participative experience. For Whitehead the depth dimension of anything, its enduring value, is felt by means of its breadth of context. "Importance, limited to a finite individual occasion, ceases to be important. In some sense or other, importance is derived from the immanence of infinitude in the finite."[13] "The zest of human adventure presupposes for its material a scheme of things with a worth beyond any single occasion."[14] Every physically given thing as we prehend it stands within a vague infinity of background. The envisagement of this background, the

---

12. In *Being and Time,* Heidegger uses *Dasein* as a descriptive rather than a normative term. In the later Heidegger the term *Dasein* is used much less frequently, but when used the normative implications become progressively apparent.
13. *Modes of Thought* (New York: The Macmillan Co., 1938), p. 28. Also pp. 107f.:

> In the discussion of our deeper experiences, religious and mystic, an unbalanced emphasis has been placed upon the mere sense of infinitude. . . . The full solemnity of the world arises from the sense of positive achievement within the finite, combined with the sense of modes of infinitude stretching beyond each finite fact. This infinitude is required by each fact to express its necessary relevance beyond its own limitations. It expresses a perspective of the universe.

14. *Adventures of Ideas,* p. 372.

conceptual prehension of its relevant possibilities, is *breadth*.
If this breadth is brought into contrast with the physically
given thing, this thing takes on *depth* because of the breadth.
In Heidegger also—or at least a plausible case can be made—
the awareness of a being's context helps give us an awareness
of its *Being* or depth dimension. In Whitehead it is explicitly
stated   and   systematically   developed   that   possibilities
grounded in God compose the depth dimension of anything. In the later Heidegger it is implicitly suggested and
metaphorically developed that possibilities grounded in
Being help compose the depth dimension of anything. Since
Heidegger is exceptionally vague on this point, Heidegger-
ians might disagree with this interpretation. In any case, my
interpretation will be of crucial importance in the analyses
that follow.

According to the early Heidegger of *Being and Time,* man
is *Dasein, i.e.,* open to the "there" of *Being* because he
"exists" or "ek-sists." Because *Dasein* stands (*-sistit*) outside
of (*ek-*) itself, *Dasein* transcends both itself as a being and
other beings and thus allows both to be revealed as beings.
Without this "standing out," *Dasein* would have no perspective from which beings could be unconcealed. Moreover, this
standing out makes it possible for *Dasein* to be open to the
Being of beings. *Dasein,* unlike other beings, is a "being-in-
the-world," for *Dasein's* ecstatic structure projects possibilities and thus a world. This world with its horizon provides
the context within which beings are revealed. If, furthermore, *Dasein* makes explicit the lighting process, *i.e., Being,*
that illuminates beings in this world, then *Dasein* realizes
its destiny of thinking *Being.* Authentic *Dasein* passes
(*-scendit*) beyond (*trans-*) beings, including itself, to the
Being of beings. Thus the fundamental ontological structure
or *Being* of *Dasein* is process, ecstatic temporality—*Zeitlich-
keit* in *Being and Time*—rather than substance. Ecstatic
temporality is the *a priori* condition that makes possible all
meaningfulness, the condition that makes it possible for
Dasein to be in the truth, the unconcealment of beings and

Being. Ecstatic temporality is the *Being* of *Dasein,* for this temporality makes possible *Dasein's* being-in-the-world. Through its ecstatic existence *Dasein* finds a matrix of meaningful relationships among beings governed by a finite limit of possibilities which *Dasein* projects. This limit is the horizon of *Dasein's* world. What is an instrument, for example, for *Dasein* is revealed within a region of relationships unified by *Dasein's* projection of possibilities. A hammer is a ready-to-hand equipment for me only if I project the possibility of an end to which the hammer is useful as a means. My world is not the sum of beings, the cosmos; my world is the complex of my concerns.

In the later Heidegger, it is not only the *Being* of *Dasein, Being-as-immanent,* but also *Being-as-transcendental* (inclusive of the *Being* of *Dasein*) that is central in his thinking. *Being-as-transcendental* comes to *Dasein. Being-as-transcendental* has the initiative now, whereas in *Being and Time* it was the *Being* of *Dasein* that initiated *Dasein's* projection of its world. This coming of *Being-as-transcendental* is *Dasein's* future. But this coming is to a *Dasein* that is "thrown," that already is. This already-having-been is the past of *Dasein.* Because of the coming of *Being-as-transcendental* to *Dasein,* all beings present to *Dasein* are rendered meaningful. This presence of beings as meaningful is *Dasein's* present. Future-past-present are the components of *Dasein's* ecstatic temporality. *Dasein* is ecstatic, on the one hand, because in projecting its world *Dasein* stands out from its ontical self. Because of *Being-as-transcendental, Dasein's Being* thrusts *Dasein's* ontical self out of what otherwise would be meaninglessness and *Dasein* creates its world. *Dasein* is temporal, on the other hand, because the future-past-present of *Dasein's Being* are inseparable components of a unified process.

Whitehead also asserts than man is ecstatically temporal. In a concrescence the subject withdraws from time. A concrescence is private, a duration that unifies past-present-future in such a way that during the duration they are neither separable nor measurable. It is only after the concrescence has been concluded, after the subject of the concrescence has perished and become an object, that by analysis the distinction between and the measurement of past and present and future become possible. Temporality is private; time is public. What is especially pertinent for my purposes is Whitehead's explanation of the unification of temporality, a clarification that is consistent with what Heidegger claims but fails fully to explain.

The feeling of the future, according to Whitehead, always accompanies propositional feelings. A propositional feeling, as previously described, relates a possibility to something physically given. Therefore the possibility is felt not simply as abstract but as a tale that might be told about particular actualities. But this feeling of the future is fused, except for analysis, with the feeling of the past. For the physically given comes to us through causal efficacy, and thus the feeling of that given inevitably carries with it that given's origin from the past, heavy with the contact of things gone by. Finally, the integration in a concrescence of past and future is felt by the subject as occurring in the vivid, vital present.

What is given in the present duration is given necessarily in a context stretching from past to future. Without that context there would be no present. This context is what Whitehead usually calls "background," and Heidegger usually calls "world." Now when a being is experienced in the present, its world, although necessarily there, will be more or less out of focus if we control and manage that being for strictly ontical purposes. Then the being is abstracted, torn out from the full dimensionality of its world. But in the participative experience, the being reasserts itself, and through its ragged edges we begin to see its world with widening horizons. Possibilities relevant to that being enrich the density of that being. In that breadth of relationships the being begins to take on depth and enduring value. The being now begins to be explicitly experienced as a being-*Being*. The wounds, both in the being and in us, caused by our attempt to dominate that being begin to heal.

"The thing thinks in me" whenever a significant breadth

of possibilities is suggested by the thing and yet the thing
stays in the focal center. The thing points to possibilities and
draws them back like a powerful magnet drawing back fil-
ings. Then we participate with the thing. Then we are aware
of its *Being* or depth dimension. Then we sense the enduring
value of the thing. If, furthermore, the pressure of *Being-as-
immanent* is strongly coercive, we will also have explicit
awareness of *Being-as-transcendental,* of *Being* as a unity
that somehow is more than its embodiment in beings, of a
further reality. Then we comprehend the empirical grounds
that are the foundation of the religious experience. Only
then can the belief in *Being* as supremely important, and
feelings such as ultimate concern, reverence, and peace, and
the various theoretical, practical, and sociological forms of
religious expression be authentic.

Art is the gift that lures us, more than any other thing,
to the participative experience, for in art there is a presentation of reality in a form least reducible to the categories and
functions of the ontical. Art traces openings to *Being* on its
ontical surfaces. Through those openings new worlds are
revealed. Yet those openings are translucent, not transparent,
for the widening horizons can be seen only through the lens
of the specific surfaces of art. Each art lures us to *Being* in
its distinctive way. There are four basic ways: the bringing
to the fore of process, or presentational immediacy, or immanent recall, or sublimity. In the following chapters these
four ways will be examined in those arts respectively in
which they dominate—process in music, presentational immediacy in painting, immanent recall in literature, and sublimity in architecture. Thus the analyses of these four arts
may be taken as paradigms for the arts not discussed. However, in all the arts a unique combination of the four ways
is achieved. The four ways and their combinations are extraordinary ways, the ways most unlike the ways of ordinary
experience in which we try to master rather than let things
be. There is a magic in art, for our perception of art objects
as they claim us, in one way or another, always puts time out
of gear.

3

Music and Process

"And when the minstrel played, the power of the Lord came upon him" (2 Kings 3:15). And Goethe told Eckermann that music "stands so high that no understanding can reach it, and an influence flows from it which masters all, and for which none can account. Hence, religious worship cannot dispense with it; it is one of the chief means of working upon men miraculously."[1] In his last sermon Paul Tillich asked: "What would religious life be without hymns and organs. . . ?"[2] Gerardus van der Leeuw in his monumental study of the beautiful and the holy concluded that "with the possible exception of architecture, music, of all the arts, stands the closest to religion. . . . With few exceptions, Christian and general worship is not possible without music."[3] Schopenhauer explained music's intimate relation to the religious experience by identifying the Will and God, and then claiming that music, unlike the other arts, is an image

---

1. *Conversations of Goethe with Eckermann,* trans. John Oxenford (London: J. M. Dent and Sons, 1930), p. 394.
2. *The University of Chicago Magazine* (November 1965), p. 19.
3. *Sacred and Profane Beauty: The Holy in Art,* trans. David E. Green (New York: Holt, Rinehart and Winston, 1963), p. 225.

not of Ideas derived from the Will but rather the image of
the Will itself.[4] According to the Nietzsche of *The Joyful
Wisdom* and *The Genealogy of Morals,* Schopenhauer made
the composer into a "ventriloquist of God," a "telephone of
the Beyond."

Most aestheticians closest to music tend to be either Formalists or Absolute Expressionists, and both groups relish
Nietzsche's scorn. (The term *music* will be used to mean
pure or nonprogrammatic music.) Their grasp of the tonal
relationships is an experience so intrinsically valuable that
any attempt to relate music to anything, such as the religious
experience, is, for them, spurious. The tonal structures have
meanings, claim the Formalists, for example Eduard Hanslick and Edmund Gurney, but these meanings are strictly
musical. The aesthetic perception and understanding of these
meanings involve intellectual processes full of pleasure but
empty of emotion.[5] On the other hand, the Absolute Expressionists, for example Leonard B. Meyer, affirm the legiti-
mate evocation of emotion by the musical meanings, but this
emotion is strictly musical. Both the Formalists and the Absolute Expressionists are nonreferentialists. They agree that
musical meanings are intramusical. For both, music is essentially "significant form," to use the phrase Bell and Fry made
famous with reference to painting. Musical meanings do not
properly, *i.e.*, aesthetically, function as either signs or symbols that designate or refer to anything in the extramusical

---

4. *The World as Will and Idea*, trans. R. B. Haldane and J. Kemp (London:
Routledge and Kegan Paul, 1957), 1: 331–44 and 3: 231–44.
5. The following argument by Carroll C. Pratt is typical:

> In the fugue from the funeral march in Beethoven's *Eroica* the fortis-
> simo clashing of the dissonances and the pounding of the double
> against the triple rhythms build up for some twelve or fifteen restless
> measures the inescapable impression of bitter strife and acute anguish.
> Now bitter strife and anguish, if felt as one's own emotions, are in-
> tensely unpleasant. But is the listening to the second movement of
> Beethoven's *Third Symphony* an intensely unpleasant experience?

The Meaning of Music (New York: McGraw-Hill, 1931), p. 200. For a
rebuttal to this kind of argument, see my "On the Supposed Incompatibility of Expressionism and Formalism," *The Journal of Aesthetics
and Art Criticism* 15 (Sept. 1956): 96–99.

world. "Music is by its very nature," Stravinsky insists, "essentially powerless to *express* anything at all. . . ."[6] Musical meanings are *in* the music, entirely internal.

The Referential Expressionists, conversely, claim that musical meanings do legitimately refer to the extramusical world,[7] ontical or ontological as the case may be. The theory of the Referential Expressionists, unfortunately, is in bad repute, because as usually formulated it seems to suggest that we should concentrate upon what the music designates rather than listening to the music. But this need not be the case and, as reformulated, this theory is the only one that can adequately account for such comments as those of Goethe, Tillich, and Van der Leeuw. These comments are so typical —granting a few dissenting voices such as Plato's and St. Augustine's—and music is so universally utilized in religious worship, even by the Puritans, that it seems highly unlikely that the intimate relation of music to the religious experience is accidental. Thus an explanation should be possible. And if it can be explained how music may not only open us to *Being* but also interpret *Being,* then some of the puzzles about the role of the other arts in the religious experience may also be solved.

I

No other art, assuming equal capacities for the arts by the recipient, is so likely as music to directly engage us in a participative experience or to move us from the spectator to the participative experience. For music more than any other art forces us to feel causal efficacy, the compulsion of process, the dominating control of the physically given over possibilities

---

6. *Stravinsky: An Autobiography* (New York: Simon and Schuster, 1936), p. 83.

7. The differences among the positions of the Formalists, Absolute Expressionists, and Referential Expressionists have been carefully worked out by Leonard B. Meyer. *Emotion and Meaning in Music* (Chicago: The University of Chicago Press, 1956), pp. 2ff.

throughout the concrescence of an experience. The form of music binds the past and future and present so tightly that as we listen we are thrust out of the ordinary modes of experience, in which time rather than temporality dominates. Ecstatic temporality, the rhythmic unity of past-present-future, is the most essential manifestation of the *Being* of human beings, the power that makes it possible for us to project a world, but in ordinary experience our consciousness is so measured by time that the temporality from which time abstracts is forgotten. Music, however, returns us to our foundations by bringing temporality to the forefront of our awareness and making us forget time. We cannot listen to music participatively and also be conscious of time. Listening to music is ecstatic because it thrusts us out of time into temporality. As Nietzsche knew, music is the most Dionysian of the arts. Music possesses this exceptional power to make us feel process directly because 1) the meanings of music's percepta or tones are basically embodied or internal, any designative or external meanings of the percepta being completely dependent upon the iconic structuring of the embodied meanings; and 2) the tones are presented successively. Although the percepta of the other major arts may be qualified by one or the other of these characteristics, none are qualified by both.[8]

Anything acquires meaning if it indicates something beyond itself, its full nature being revealed by that connection. Meaning is the product of the relationship between something as a stimulus and the something it signifies, this connection requiring, of course, the cognizance of an observer. Meaning arises out of what Morris Cohen calls the "triadic"

---

8. There are apparent exceptions, especially in the plastic arts, for example, Thomas Wilfred's *Aspiration, Op. 145* in The Museum of Modern Art, with a 42-hour, 14-minute, 11-second cycle of lights playing through abstract color formations. This kind of work, however, is still mainly experimental. It may be that similar works, mobiles, and other forms will be developed that will present basically embodied relations as dynamically as music. See George Rickey, "The Morphology of Movement: A Study of Kinetic Art," in *The Nature and Art of Motion*, ed. Gyorgy Kepes (New York: G. Braziller, 1965).

relationship between 1) a stimulus or antecedent; 2) that to which the stimulus points—its referent or consequent; and 3) the conscious observer.[9] Following the distinctions of Leonard Meyer, *designative meaning* occurs when the stimulus and the referent are different in kind, are composed of different media, as when a word refers to a nonverbal object or event. *Embodied meaning* occurs when the stimulus and the referent are the same in kind, as when "one musical event (be it a tone, a phrase, or a whole section) has meaning because it points to and makes us expect another musical event."[10] Similarly, in a painting, whether representational or abstract, there are the embodied references of color to color, light to light, line to line, texture to texture, and so on, usually in very complicated combinations and all related, more or less, to the form as a totality. Thus in Helen Frankenthaler's *Saturn* (Plate III), the yellow areas (colors, lights, lines, and textures in all their variations), require the blue areas, the yellow areas acting as stimuli to activate tensions anticipating or requiring the blue areas as their resolutions or referents. Embodied meanings are the medial or internal interrelationships of a work of art, and they must be present in every work of art because without them the artistic elements or media would not be interrelated, *i.e.*, formed or organized. And without form a work cannot inform. Such a work lacks meaning or content, and thus is without artistic significance.[11] It is not so evident, however, that designative meanings must be present in a work of art. Obviously they are present in program music: the title *The Fountains of Rome* by Respighi designates nonverbal objects. In a representational painting such as Cézanne's *Mte. Ste. Victoire* (Plate 15), the two-dimensional image of a mountain designates a very three-dimensional object. And in the aesthetic experience of such works, unless they are

9. *A Preface to Logic* (New York: H. Holt and Company, 1944), p. 29.
10. *Emotion and Meaning in Music*, p. 35.
11. Most works have form without informing. When such works please, they are works of decoration. They have an important role in making life agreeable, but they should not be confused with art.

artificially restricted by ignoring the designations, the associations and feelings we may have for the actual fountains of Rome and actual mountains, respectively, are fused with the embodied meanings of such works.[12] But in the case of pure music and abstract painting, on the other hand, it seems to be the very lack of designative meaning that distinguishes them respectively from program music and representational painting.

I shall use the term *sign* for any stimulus that designates anything ontical, and the term *symbol* for any stimulus that designates anything ontological. Signs and symbols are the stimuli in works of art that make designative meaning possible. Since musical meaning is entirely embodied, according to Meyer, signs and symbols are absent from music. Musical meaning is created by expectation, the felt probability by the listener being a product of the frequency with which a particular musical relationship has been experienced. The value of music, furthermore, is in the unique emotional accompaniment evoked by the musical meanings.

Meyer's theory of emotion is based on the work of psychologists, such as J. T. MacCurdy, who maintain that "emotion or affect is aroused when a tendency to respond is arrested or inhibited."[13] Musical stimuli activate tendencies that are frustrated by means of deviations from the expected, and then these frustrated tendencies are followed by meaningful resolutions. Tonal patterns, actualized or suggested by the composer's stylistic traditions, provide him with the means for building powerful tensions which then can be resolved by embodied referents. The stronger and more

---

12. For how embodied and designative meanings are fused in the aesthetic experience, see my "On the Supposed Incompatibility of Expressionism and Formalism"; Louis Arnaud Reid, *A Study in Aesthetics* (London: George Allen and Unwin, 1931), chaps. 2–4; and Eliseo Vivas, "A Definition of the Aesthetic Experience," *The Journal of Philosophy* 34 (Nov. 1937): 628–34. For the opposing position, see Richard Rudner, "On Semiotic Aesthetics," *Aesthetic Inquiry: Essays on Art Criticism and the Philosophy of Art*, ed. Monroe C. Beardsley and Herbert M. Schueller (Belmont, California: Dickenson Publishing Company, 1967), pp. 93–102.
13. *Emotion and Meaning in Music*, p. 14.

cumulative the tensions and the more unexpected the resolutions, the more valuable the music.[14] Since, furthermore, pure music lacks signs and symbols, "the affective experience made in response to music is specific and differentiated, but it is so in terms of the musical stimulus situation rather than in terms of extramusical stimuli."[15] The emotions of musical experiences therefore differ from the emotions of nonmusical experiences. And yet

> musical experiences of suspense are very similar to those experienced in real life. Both in life and in music the emotions thus arising have essentially the same stimulus situation: the situation of ignorance, the awareness of the individual's impotence and inability to act where the future course of events is unknown. Because these musical experiences are so very similar to those existing in the drama and in life itself, they are often felt to be particularly powerful.[16]

Moreover, images, connotations, moods, and nonmusical emotions may be associated with the emotions controlled solely by the musical stimuli, reinforcing the intensity of the musical emotions unless such associations turn the listener's attention away from the music itself. Such associations, however, are accidental, *i.e.*, uncontrolled by the music through any kind of designative meaning. Meyer's theory of the meaning of music is convincing as far as it goes, providing a wider base for exploration into how music opens us to *Being*. And for the sake of clarity, the analysis in this section will proceed as if music possesses, as in Meyer's theory, only embodied meanings. This assumption will be qualified in section two.

A participative experience of a work of art necessarily involves the mixed mode of reference. The mode of causal

---

14. The relative degrees of value of musical meanings are further explored by Meyer in "Some Remarks on Value and Greatness in Music," *The Journal of Aesthetics and Art Criticism* 17 (June 1959): 486–500. See also my "Unrealized Possibility in the Aesthetic Experience," *The Journal of Philosophy* 52 (July 1955): 393–400.
15. *Emotion and Meaning in Music,* p. 20.
16. *Ibid.,* p. 28.

efficacy alone is precognitive, barely conscious at best, and lacking in the rapt attention that is a necessary condition of the participative experience. The mode of presentational immediacy alone, while satisfying the condition of rapt attention, cuts off consciousness from the embodied and designative meanings in the work of art. In the case of embodied meaning, for example, for those of us conditioned to diatonic music, the tone G in a composition in the key of C is likely to lead to an anticipation for the tone C. G is physically felt as a stimulus whose referent or meaning is conceptually felt, through reversion, as C. If the G were felt without this reference to C or some other pitch, the G would be experienced in the pure mode of presentational immediacy. But if the C is felt as a relevant and contrasted possibility, then a propositional feeling has entered consciousness. In turn, a conscious feeling of causal efficacy occurs because of this reference to the future. For those incapable of feeling that kind of reference, Mozart's music will have little aesthetic value. Similarly, the yellow areas in *Saturn* (Plate III) may be felt as stimuli that refer to the purple areas, and for those incapable of feeling those references, Frankenthaler's painting will have little aesthetic value. Only by feeling such embodied meanings can one experience the forms of works of art, representational as well as nonrepresentational. The form of a work of art is the relationship of part to part and part to whole. A part being sensed in the present is perceived in the mode of presentational immediacy, but since any part is related to other parts and to the whole, the perception of these relationships brings in feelings of past and future. Thus perception in the mode of presentational immediacy involves perception in the mode of causal efficacy by means of the mixed mode of reference.

Yet in the mixed mode of reference in the aesthetic experience of the various arts, the feeling of causal efficacy may be more or less compelling. Since the percepta of music are experienced more dynamically than the percepta of the other arts, causal efficacy is felt more forcefully and insistently. Thus the subjection of our experience to the percepta or physically given, the *sine qua non* of the participative experience, is more likely to occur. Our attention is more likely to be completely controlled. Nevertheless, for sensitive listeners this is likely to happen only if the embodied meanings of the music activate and resolve powerful tensions.

Tones (or phrases or whole sections) have meaning because they anticipate following tones in the case of the first tone of a piece, or satisfy anticipations in the case of the last tone, or generally in the case of all other tones both set up and satisfy anticipations. Hence the perception in the mode of presentational immediacy of the present sounding tone is not allowed to remain static. The reference of this tone directs and lures us to expect a future tone or to recall a past tone or both. We experience in the present an inescapable bondage to the future and the past, an alliance of the silence of what is to come and of what is no more with what is. The future and the past, then, are included in the present, their reciprocity in the present constituting the ecstatic unity of temporality. Furthermore, the successive presentation of the tones makes it impossible to arrest our attention in the pure mode of presentational immediacy, for in just a moment the presently sounding tone no longer will be sounding. Even the same tone played through an extended period without physical variation will be felt, nevertheless, as varied from moment to moment as we sense the strict but cumulative repetition throughout its sounding.[17]

Literature, the film, and the dance are the other major arts whose percepta are presented successively. We cannot experience their forms as a totality, with an "all-at-onceness," in the way that is possible, for example, with most paintings. Yet we set our own pace as we read a poem or a novel,

---

17. It might seem, other things being equal, that music played more rapidly would increase our sense of causal efficacy. But other things in art are not equal. A Stokowski stepping up the momentum of Beethoven's Fifth Symphony does not guarantee a presentation more powerful than a slower presentation by Bruno Walter. The power of music comes from causes much more subtle than a count of notes per second can indicate.

"slowing down" on a sentence and its designative meaning, but if we "slow down" in listening to music the music passes us by. Thus Roquentin in Sartre's *Nausea* described the compulsive presentation of music as

> a myriad of tiny jolts. They know no rest, an inflexible order gives birth to them and destroys them without even giving them time to recuperate and exist for themselves. They race, they press forward, they strike me a sharp blow in passing and are obliterated. I would like to hold them back, but I know if I succeeded in stopping one it would remain between my fingers only as a raffish languishing wound. I must accept their death . . . I know few impressions stronger or more harsh.[18]

The film, the dance, and literature that is read to us are presented in this respect like music. However, in these arts, unlike music, there almost invariably are designative references to specific objects and events.

Designative meanings in the film, the dance, and literature that is being read to us do not, of course, permit us to "slow down" on an image on the screen or on a movement of the dance or on a sentence of a poem. Nevertheless, they have the effect of weakening our sense of the compulsion of process. In the case of embodied meaning the stimulus refers to at least the immediate past or future; and the stimulus may also refer to the mediate past or future, as when a phrase of a melody is introduced and then its completion delayed, a practice delighted in by Stravinsky and characteristic of jazz. Hence in the present the past and the future are felt as immanently related. Process is felt as given, as in such non-aesthetic experiences of causal efficacy as awakening from a deep sleep. In listening to music there is a direct feeling of derivation from an immediate past and of passage to an immediate future. As Étienne Souriau puts it, "the time spent by the auditor . . . is practically predetermined. His psychological experience must pass through a mill, as it were, where the work is measured out to him moment by

---

18. Trans. Lloyd Alexander (Norfolk, Conn.: New Directions, 1949), p. 33.

moment according to the creator's will."[19] "Music," says Monroe Beardsley, "is no symbol of time or process, mental or physical, Newtonian or Bergsonian; it *is* process."[20] However, in the case of designative meaning, the referent, being different in kind from the stimulus (sign or symbol), is detached from the compulsion of the directly given immanence of the past and future in the present. An image on the screen, for example, refers to Rome; but whether to ancient Rome, or Rome today, or Rome tomorrow, there is always for the sensitive recipient an awareness of the distinction between the signs or symbols on the screen and what they refer to off the screen. Thus the temporal succession of the referents— the Christians just about to be eaten by the lions—is felt as imaginary, as not happening "here-now," but "once upon a time" in some other place than in the theater. And the same is true of a film about modern Rome, such as *La Dolce Vita,* except for the recipient who fails to distinguish between art and actuality. Only the succession of screen images with reference to their medial relationships, the embodied meanings, is happening here and now, the images as related with respect to color, light, line, texture, focus, and sound. Only this dimension of the film gives us the direct feeling of causal efficacy. But in the overwhelming majority of films our primary attention is commanded by the designative meanings. And these meanings involve a sense of time and place. For the difference in kind between sign or symbol and referent weakens our captive feeling of causal efficacy and inevitably we reflect about process. Time—the measurement of process—becomes a factor in our experience. And so does place—the location of process—for time and place are coexistent. We can measure time only by place and place only by time. Thus we cannot be prisoners of process, pre-reflectively conscious of causal efficacy, and at the same time be

---

19. "Time in the Plastic Arts," in *Reflections on Art,* ed. Susanne K. Langer (New York: Oxford University Press, 1961), pp. 140f.
20. *Aesthetics: Problems in the Philosophy of Criticism* (New York: Harcourt Brace, 1958), p. 338.

reflectively conscious of spatial objects. Unless we arbitrarily ignore the designative meanings, we are forced to become conscious of being conscious of process, and in that reflection we abstract time and place from that process. We both date the process and get events, and place the process and get objects. The moment we are aware of "once upon a time," causal efficacy is felt as indirect rather than direct, imaginary to some extent rather than just given. We disengage ourselves to some degree from process. As the specificity of these designative references to objects and events increases—as program music, for example, becomes more programmatic—our disengagement from process increases. Our experience, other things being equal, becomes less ecstatic because we are more in control.

Pure music—because it presents embodied meanings successively without designative meanings to specific objects and events—imprisons us in causal efficacy in a willing bondage.[21] Music is the only major art that gives us process

---

21. George Rochberg claims that the "new music" is presented as a *being* rather than a *becoming.*

> It seems as though 20th century man has grown weary of time and history . . . [and] according to Eliade "contemporary man is in terror of history and its increasingly relentless pressure." He would appear to be rejecting three centuries of a doctrine with which he can no longer live because it does not provide him with the means by which he can successfully cope with the reality of his present existence. In the new music, time as duration becomes a dimension of musical space. The new spatial image of music seeks to project the permanence of the world as cosmos, the cosmos of the eternal present. It is an image of music which aspires to being, not becoming.

"The New Image of Music," *Perspectives of New Music* 2 (1963) : 9f. Such a claim, it seems to me, misinterprets most of what is going on in contemporary music, including, for example, the work of John Cage. But if Rochberg is correct, so much the worse for this new music, for as Ruth Wylie points out:

> even if the concept of the "cosmos as eternal present" were a comforting one which could deliver man from the "terror of his own history," its application to music would be a somewhat coy intellectual exercise in false rationalization bordering on the ridiculous. For the only image of music which can *be* without *becoming* is certainly the glacial stillness of silence.

"Musimatics: A View from the Mainland," *The Journal of Aesthetics and Art Criticism* 24 (Winter 1965) : 292.

undiluted by specific times or places. Music, as Sartre so succinctly observes, neither dates nor locates.

I am listening to the Seventh Symphony. For me that "Seventh Symphony" does not exist in time, I do not grasp it as a dated event, as an artistic manifestation which is unrolling itself in Châtelet auditorium on the 17th of November, 1938. If I hear Furtwaengler tomorrow or eight days later conduct another orchestra performing the same symphony, I am in the presence of the same symphony once more. Only it is being played either better or worse. Let us now see *how* I hear the symphony: some persons shut their eyes. In this case they detach themselves from the *visual* and dated event of this particular interpretation: they give themselves up to the pure sounds. Others watch the orchestra or the back of the conductor. But they do not see what they are looking at. . . . The auditorium, the conductor and even the orchestra have disappeared. I am therefore confronted by the Seventh Symphony, but on the express condition of understanding *nothing about it,* that I do not think of the event as an actuality and dated, and on condition that I listen to the succession of themes as an absolute succession and not as a real succession which is unfolding itself, for instance, on the occasion when Peter paid a visit to this or that friend. In the degree to which I hear the symphony it is *not here,* between these walls, at the tip of the violin bows. Nor is it "in the past" as if I thought: this is the work that matured in the mind of Beethoven on such a date. . . . It has its own time, that is, it possesses an inner time [process], which runs from the first tone of the allegro to the last tone of the finale, but this time is not a succession of a preceding time which it continues and which happened "before" the beginning of the allegro; nor is it followed by a time which will come "after" the finale. The Seventh Symphony is in no way *in time.*[22]

22. *The Psychology of Imagination* (New York: Philosophical Library, Inc., 1948), pp. 279f. Or as Susanne Langer puts it, "musical time is not at all like clock-time. It has a sort of voluminousness and complexity and variability that make it utterly unlike metrical time. That is because our direct experience of time is the passage of vital functions and lived events, felt inwardly as tensions—somatic, emotional, and mental tensions, which have a characteristic pattern." *Problems of Art* (New York: Charles Scribner's Sons, 1957), p. 37.

The moment designative references to specific objects and events are involved, as in opera and program music, the feelings of date and place are relevant. All operas refer to more or less certain times in more or less definite settings. Program music that approaches pure music is less specific. Yet Debussy's *La Mer* suggests a place, however generalized, and even Hindemith's *Four Temperaments* vaguely suggests times in life appropriate for certain propensities—although without the titles these works probably would be experienced by most recipients as pure music.[23] The more programmatic the music, the more process is brought under our control, for the program makes us reflect about process rather than directly encountering it. And, in turn, we are freed to just that extent from the enchainment of process, the power of causality over consciousness. Our experience becomes less ecstatic, and, other things being equal, less intense.

Pure or nonrepresentational dance, next to the abstract plastic arts, comes closest to music in avoiding designative meaning to specific objects and events. But whereas tones are the basic medium of music, completely or almost completely lacking designative reference, the basic medium of the dance is the human body. Thus no matter how tightly the dancer's body is woven into the embodied meanings of the dance's patterns, the inevitable recognition of the body results in designative references to human bodies and movements outside the dance, granting that these references become vague and ambiguous to the degree that the dance is abstract. "Yet," as Selma Jeanne Cohen points out, "even in the so-called 'abstract' dance we have a feeling for the presence or absence of consistency of movement quality that suggests quality of human behavior."[24] Even the purest of dances, like program music of the vaguest kind such as Hindemith's *Four Temperaments*, still contains some specific

23. See my "Naming Paintings," *The Art Journal* 25 (Spring 1966) : 252–56.
24. "A Prolegomenon to an Aesthetics of Dance," *Aesthetic Inquiry*, p. 279.

designative references. There is some backing away from the direct encounter with process. Although designative references to specific objects and events can be eliminated in the plastic arts, the compulsion of the successive presentation of the percepta is lacking, even in the mechanically driven "strabiles" and the wind-propelled mobiles produced so far. Pure music is the only major art that both presents its percepta successively and refuses specific designative references.

If music grips our attention we are immediately forced to submit to the physically given in such a way that we are "at one" with the music. The embodied meanings of the music strike us, as it were, against our will and in spite of ourselves. We are thrust out of the ordinary modes of experience. Consciousness of the "music there" and "I here" recedes from the foreground of attention. The ontical categories of time and place and the functions and habits of practical life are suspended.

> . . . not to get caught,
> not to be left behind, not, please! to resemble
> the beasts who repeat themselves, or a thing like water
> or stone whose conduct can be predicted, these
> Are our Common Prayer, whose greatest comfort is music
> which can be made anywhere, is invisible
> And does not smell.
>
> W. H. Auden, "In Praise of Limestone"

Care ceases and the realities of everyday experience fade away like the transient and distorted images of a dream. Music makes us "ek-sist," stand out from self-consciousness. We relinquish ourselves to the music. Our experience is ecstatic. We are open to *Being*. And the music that is art, furthermore, interprets *Being*, reveals something of its mystery in our participative experience.

II

In listening to music, we feel the possibilities of which the given tones are instances. If, moreover, we are seized by the embodied meanings of the music, we also must feel by reversion those possibilities that the tones anticipate and which are later satisfied by the tones which succeed. Thus a chord based on the dominant is felt propositionally as setting up the possibility for a chord based on the tonic, as any church-going Protestant well knows. If the tonic chord does in fact follow, we have what may be called a "satisfied proposition" or "realized possibility," and any doubt as to whether the possibility was really immanent in the physically given is resolved.

Now what about those reversions which reveal possibilities that are not actualized by the succeeding tones, the "hushed reverberations"? They are immanent in the physically given insofar as through contrast they intensify our feeling of the physically given. Whether these possibilities happen to be physically realized or not by succeeding notes does not change their relevancy. Thus the consciousness of "unrealized possibilities" does not disrupt the participative experience but is rather a condition for maintaining it, provided always, as Whitehead emphasizes, that the possibilities "must be graded in relevance so as to preserve some identity of character with the ground [the physically given]."[25] "For if the subjective form of reception be not conformal to the objective sensa, then the values of the percept would be at the mercy of the chance make-up of the other components in that experience."[26]

---

25. *Process and Reality* (New York: The Macmillan Co., 1929) , p. 427.
26. *Adventures of Ideas* (New York: The Macmillan Co., 1933) , pp. 321f. Cf. Charles Hartshorne, *The Philosophy and Psychology of Sensation* (Chicago: The University of Chicago Press, 1934) , p. 189: "The art of aesthetic appreciation [or participative experience] is to 'associate' with the object solely the images and reactions whose affective content will permit the sensory content to remain in the focal center rather than such as will displace it therefrom."

When a theme beginning in a particular key shifts before its completion to a different key—such as the second theme of the second movement of Beethoven's Fifth Symphony— we are surprised and delighted by the contrast between the expected continuance of the beginning tonality and the actual change in tonality. This theme, in measures 23–32, begins in the key of A flat; but in the fifth measure, where the G flat first appears, the theme begins to be uncertain as to tonality because of its equivocal diminished seventh harmony. The G flat changes enharmonically to F sharp, which is the same pitch, but the accompanying harmony (an augmented six-five chord) demands resolution in C major and the melody suddenly veers off to a close in the distant key of C major, producing a most pleasurable surprise. This delight would be impossible if we were aware only of the physically given and the realized possibilities. Indeed the unexpected, so important in all art, depends upon the contrast yet closeness between the physically given and unrealized possibilities. In the nonparticipative experience of music, reversions have little or no contrasting similarity with the tonal patterns, as in the conception of running feet associated with a rapid passage of Mozart's violins. Such images turn our attention away from the music. In the participative experience of music, on the other hand, the reversions are tonal conceptions rather than visual images and thus enhance rather than slacken our feeling of the physically given. Thus I hear the tone F and, because of the key and previous resolutions, I anticipate an A or G to follow. A is sounded. Nevertheless, the G rings in my inner ear as an unrealized possibility, enriching my hearing of the A, the realized possibility. In the participative experience, furthermore, consciousness of unrealized possibilities is subordinated to the realized possibilities; for not only is the contrast based on the physically given, but physical feelings always have a greater richness and definiteness than the feelings of possibilities. "The essence of depth of actuality—

that is of vivid experience—is definiteness."[27] Thus the reading of a score, other factors being equal, lacks the vividness of listening to an actual performance. In inward hearing the quality and volume of tones and their duration lack the specific determination of outward hearing.

Unrealized possibility is rarely explicitly acknowledged by sensitive listeners, unless there is prodding, because that acknowledgment seems to compromise their love of music. They consider the structure of significant music so intrinsically valuable that any experience of music in which the listener does not concentrate all his attention upon the structure or the physically given is not a musical experience. As we have seen, however, Whitehead's theory of perception, as here interpreted, allows for an awareness of unrealized possibilities in the musical experience without lessening the control of the physically given. Furthermore, in questioning sensitive listeners about unrealized possibility, I have found general agreement that it is a powerful factor in their experiences. Such statements as the following by Maritain and Lucien Price, respectively, are corroborating: "Unexpressed significance, unexpressed meanings, more or less unconsciously putting pressure on the mind, play an important part in aesthetic feeling and the perception of beauty."[28] "I don't pretend that I understand them [Beethoven's last Quartets] except in parts, but they, too, like the beauty of a star, gain from the grandeur of their surrounding immensities of thought." [29] Whitehead's theory clarifies

27. Whitehead, *Religion in the Making* (New York: The Macmillan Co., 1926), p. 113.
28. Jacques Maritain, *Creative Intuition in Art and Poetry* (New York: Pantheon Books, 1953), p. 9.
29. Lucien Price, *Dialogues of Alfred North Whitehead* (Boston: Little, Brown and Co., 1954), p. 231. Compare also Price's statement that "sometimes, during a good performance of the very greatest music, one has the sense that he is in the presence of infinitude somewhat similar to what the composer must have felt when he was having to choose between one concept and another in hope of expressing it. The definite concepts are there, in tones or phrases, but all around them hover the infinitudes of possibility—the *other* ways in which this vastness might have

and helps explain these significant and yet elusive statements about unrealized possibility.

There are three stages or levels of listening to music in the participative experience. In the first stage, the stage of partial prehensions, the listener is summoned to the various parts as parts. In the second stage, the listener succeeds, more or less, in relating the partial prehensions to one another and to the work as a whole. In these first two stages the awareness of unrealized possibilities is mainly a vague premonition. Finally in the third stage, since less effort is now called for in prehending the realized possibilities, awareness of unrealized possibilities tends to develop more distinctly than in the previous stages. Judging from my experiences of music, I find that unrealized possibilities in the first two stages tend to be a vague massive background which serves as a lure for feeling and becomes relatively clear only after the second stage has been achieved. "Consciousness flickers; and even at its brightest, there is a small focal region of clear illumination, and a large penumbral region of experience which tells of intense experience in dim apprehension."[30] It is the penumbral region of unrealized possibilities which gradually becomes less dim as we comprehend more and more of a work of art.

It should be noted that the alternatives rejected by the artist, all those destroyed notations of Beethoven and sketches of Cézanne, are not quite so literally lost as at first might be supposed—provided that they are relevant to what was finally selected. Physically, of course, they are lost, but conceptually they may be felt as part of the penumbral region of unrealized possibilities that surrounds what was not negated. "The negative prehensions have their own subjective forms which they contribute to the process. A feeling bears on itself the scars of its birth; it recollects as a sub-

---

been expressed" (*ibid.*, p. 164). Music was not Whitehead's favorite art, and I know of no statements by him that specifically refer to the role of unrealized possibility in music.

30. *Process and Reality*, p. 408.

jective emotion its struggle of existence; it retains the impress of what it might have been, but is not. . . . The actual cannot be reduced to mere matter of fact in divorce from the potential."[31]

With music that is great art, unrealized possibilities are seemingly inexhaustible. This inexhaustibility accounts for our ability to come back to such music time after time, even after we have achieved complete comprehension of the physically given whole, and discover something fresh. It must be remembered, however, that the felt possibilities must intensify our perception of the music, and they can do so only if they have a close contrasting resemblance to the physically given. Otherwise our attention will no longer be controlled by the presented music and our participative experience will be dissipated. When Mozart attended the operas of other composers, the music usually served as a springboard for his own composing. Posterity was indeed fortunate, but Mozart was not participating with the presented opera.

Music makes us feel the inexhaustibility of unrealized possibilities immanent in the music itself. The stronger and more cumulative the tensions and resolutions of the embodied meanings, the stronger the sense of inexhaustibility. Perhaps the most fundamental standard used to distinguish major works from minor ones, although so difficult to apply that only a consensus of experts over a considerable period of time justifies its usage, is the degree of inexhaustibility possessed by a work of art, its resistance to monotony. Only the inexhaustible can be continually interesting. All works of art are apparently inexhaustible, but only masterpieces seem to be obviously inexhaustible after repeated participations. Inexhaustibility is part of the mystery that is part of the *Being* of anything, whether a blade of grass or music that is not art. But in a work of art something of this mystery is unveiled and articulated. This is one of the essential

---

31. *Ibid.,* p. 346.

demands that the artist must satisfy. He must construct a work that easily resists monotony despite our cumulative understanding of that work. He does this by creating a work that excites reversions that seem to have no end, an infinite wealth streaming forth from it, thus creating a fascinating uncertainty by making present the silent but mighty force of the possible. He may do more than this in the way of interpreting *Being*, but unless he does at least this, he is not an artist. In turn, and seemingly paradoxically, the more aware we become of the physically given work, the more reversions also come into our awareness and the more the mystery of *Being* is understood. As the music as physically given begins to be mastered, more and more unrealized possibilities begin to escape our grasp. The closer we come to the music, the more alarmingly aloof the music becomes. Music moves into silence.

When *Being* is unveiled there is always at the same time a concealment, as the later Heidegger has been pointing out in so many different ways. The mystery of *Being* is unveiled in art not as the mystery at the end of every scientific truth, *i.e.,* that the solution of any problem sets us *ad infinitum* new problems to solve. Nor is this mystery in the sense that we recognize the limitations of our comprehension in face of the unknown, as in Kant's concept of the sublime. Rather, the mystery of *Being* is unveiled within the boundaries of the work of art itself. In the case of music, usually, the clarity of beat and stress in the rhythmic evolution and restrospectively the apparent inevitability of the way possibilities are realized may seem to corner the mystery of *Being* entirely. The mystery of *Being* may seem to be measured by the music. But that very cornering carries a concealment. The unrealized possibilities that continually expand beyond our grasp symbolize the mystery of *Being* that cannot be measured. This account helps explain why music is so intimately related to the religious experience, but it does not explain why some music is generally considered to be secular, such as Bach's *The Well Tempered*

Clavier, and other music is generally considered to be religious, such as Bach's *St. Matthew Passion* or, less obviously, *The Art of Fugue.*

The *St. Matthew Passion* is program music for liturgical use, the designative meanings of the words referring to religious events and doctrines, in this case Christian, that express theoretical, practical, and sociological interpretations of *Being.* Furthermore, since this music is such an exceptional example of inexhaustibility and thus the revelation of mystery, the *St Matthew Passion* is universally accepted in the Western World as religious music. Yet music can have a religious program and even be put to liturgical use and still not be religious, except in the sense, as previously indicated, that all works of art are religious insofar as they reveal something of the mystery of *Being* in their seeming inexhaustibility. There must be a more essential or further inner continuity between the music and the religious dimension. For example, Bach took the melody of the cradle song "Schlafe mein Liebster" in his *Christmas Oratorio* from a song about lust tempting the young Hercules. Bach darkened the tone and produced a lovely song of gentle love specifically related by the words to Jesus, but there is, nevertheless, no inner continuity with the religious dimension. Van der Leeuw has given us many examples of this kind,[32] but he is not clear about the "how" of this inner continuity. *The Art of Fugue* and *The Well Tempered Clavier* lack religious programs and they are not designed for liturgical use. How is it possible, then, that *The Art of Fugue* possesses an inner continuity with the religious dimension that *The Well Tempered Clavier* lacks?

The distinction between iconic signs and conventional signs in works of art helps prepare the way for an answer. (The following analysis is also applicable to iconic symbols and conventional symbols, *i.e.,* to stimuli that designate ontological reality.) The meaning of a conventional sign is

---

32. *Sacred and Profane Beauty: The Holy in Art,* pp. 217ff.

arbitrarily attached to it by individual fiat or social convention, as in the case of words other than the onomatopoetic. In order to follow the reference of the sign to the referent, we must know the convention. An iconic sign, on the other hand, incorporates characteristics significantly similar to those of the referent for which it stands. The reference is grounded in a resemblance between sign and referent. "Anything whatever . . . is an Icon of anything, insofar as it is like that thing and used as a sign of it."[33] Thus the sound of the word *buzz* resembles the sound of a bee, and because of this similarity the word connotes the bee as its referent. The similarity or parallelism between an icon and its referent is not necessarily a physical resemblance, however, although this has been the traditional usage. Actually a great many meaning situations cannot be adequately analyzed when iconicity is restricted to physical resemblance. For example, the color white in certain contexts may refer to sacredness. Yet the idea of sacredness has no physical properties, and therefore the reference of whiteness to sacredness cannot depend upon physical resemblance. It can be argued that the reference is simply a matter of convention, but this is not a complete explanation because it fails to explain why white is chosen so often for sacred usage in many disparate cultures. Muddy brown, so I have been informed by anthropologists, has never been used to refer to sacredness, and this fact suggests that underneath the accretions of conventional signs and symbols lies an iconicity dependent upon psychosocial factors not yet fully known. Thus whiteness generally evokes an emotive response resembling the emotive response to the idea of sacredness, and this similarity in responses rather than in the physical aspects of the symbol and referent helps account for the origin of the meaning function. Furthermore, even the iconicity of physical resemblance is a less obvious relationship than might at first appear. In the

---

33. Charles Sanders Peirce, *Collected Papers of Charles Sanders Peirce*, ed. Charles Hartshorne and Paul Weiss (Cambridge, Mass.: Harvard University Press, 1932), 2: 143.

first place, the degree of likeness necessary for an iconic reference is not a function simply of imitative accuracy but involves the characteristic aspects or perspectives. A Mexican sombrero looked directly down upon from a third-floor hotel window looks more like a doughnut than a hat. Second, an icon is always presented in a context or environment that partially controls the reference. If the doughnut shape were inserted into Degas's *Millinery Shop* it probably would signify a lady's hat, whereas in Grünewald's *Crucifixion* (Plate 9) in the Isenheim Altarpiece it would probably suggest a head and halo.

The less intrinsic value that conventional signs possess, the more likely the success of unambiguous reference, an ideal most nearly achieved with the signs of applied mathematics. A sign "which interests us *also* as an object is distracting. It does not convey its meaning without obstruction. . . ."[34] Iconic signs may also have little intrinsic value,

as in the case of this stickman $\stackrel{\circ}{\lambda}$. However, when the iconic character is vividly embodied in the sign, intrinsic interest is aroused, for attention must be centered on the icon if the subtleties and complexities of its references are to be experienced. For example, the figure on the cross in Grünewald's *Crucifixion* refers to a human being, like the stickman, but the references include much more, such as unearthly suffering and the power of the divine in this human body. Such references, if they are to be understood fully, require careful attention to the icon in all its detail. Both the stickman and Grünewald's Christ are icons, but the parts and the interrelationships of the parts of the stickman have little or no intrinsic value. The configuration or *Gestalt* of the icon is immediately recognizable, and in turn its reference is obvious. On the other hand, the *Gestalt* of Grünewald's Christ requires rapt attention to its elements and their interrelationships if the subtleties and complexities of

---

34. Susanne K. Langer, *Philosophy in a New Key* (Cambridge, Mass.: Harvard University Press, 1942) , p. 61.

the references are to be understood. We can skip from this icon to a meaning, but at the cost of missing the most significant meanings. Note, for example, how the tension of Christ's fingers is intensified by their interrelationships—thrust out in a pattern that suggests supernatural energy. The references of Grünewald's Christ accumulate and integrate as the various parts of the icon concresce in our experience into a unified *Gestalt*.

Conventional as well as iconic signs usually contain embodied references. Since every sign has related parts, and these parts usually are the same in kind, these relationships are embodied. But, as in the case of the interrelationships of the segments of the stickman, the embodied references of a conventional sign have little or no intrinsic importance. The value of a conventional sign is extrinsic, its ability to clearly and distinctly point to its referent. The more transparent the sign, *i.e.,* the less we notice the sign for its own sake, the better, just as a "good" window is one through which we see clearly and distinctly because there is nothing about the window that attracts our attention. The parts of a conventional sign are self-effacing, like the plaster of an inlay or the glue of a collage, necessary for the sign but unnecessary for us to notice carefully. The parts of an iconic sign that lack vivid embodiment are also self-effacing. We see straight through the lines of the stickman to the referent, for the lines lack intrinsic interest. They have no tension—one segment anticipates the next as obviously as the words "tit-for" anticipate "tat." Thus they have no power for attracting and holding our attention. The lines of Grünewald's Christ, on the other hand, are charged with tension because their anticipations and resolutions are extraordinary. Our sight is ensnared. And as we carefully attend to these embodied meanings, something of Christ's divinity and suffering are designated. Because of this rapt attention on the icon, moreover, we fuse the designative with the embodied meanings. We see the divinity and suffering *in* the lines. Whereas the stickman is a "transparent icon,"

Grünewald's Christ is a "translucent icon." The referent of a translucent icon, unlike a transparent icon, cannot be understood independently of careful attention to the icon.

Works of art must possess something of this translucent iconicity, literature other than poetry coming the closest to being an exception. For if translucent iconicity were totally lacking, there would be a separation of the embodied and designative meanings, not just analytically but phenomenologically as well. And then our attention would not be grasped by the physically given. Works of art always make their designative references through the control of vividly embodied icons. At first sight works of art may include what may seem to be conventional signs that are completely transparent, for example the name "J. S. Bach" in Braque's *Homage to J. S. Bach,* and they may seem to include transparent icons as well, for example the stick figures in Klee's *Dancing from Fright.* However, in these examples the name and stick figures, respectively, are tightly incorporated into environments of translucent icons. Thus if we see these pictures sensitively, we will be restrained from seeing straight through the name and stick figures as habit would have us. Their context has transformed them, provided them with a translucency that usually they lack. Sometimes, however, instead of transformation there is either subordination or dismissal. For example, in program music the sound and the rhythm of the words may be noniconically organized, as so often in Protestant hymns. Then we hear straight through the words to their designations, subordinating the sound and rhythm of the words to the fringe of our attention. If the verbal designations, furthermore, are incompatible with the designations of the music, the verbal designations will have to be dismissed. Otherwise our attention will be divided rather than rapt because we cannot unify the meanings of the program and the music. The program has to be dismissed or the possibility of a participative experience is lost. When the program is iconically organized and consistent with the meanings of the music, then all the meanings of music and

words, embodied and designative, can be incorporated into
the participative experience. This kind of synthesis is
achieved by Benjamin Britten in his utilization of the poems
of Wilfred Owen in his *War Requiem.* For example in the
"Libera Me," the final section of the *Requiem,* Britten incorporates Owen's "Strange Meeting" in which two dead
soldiers meet in "some profound dull tunnel, long since
scooped / Through granites which titanic wars had groined."
After the tenor solo the baritone concludes his reply (Example 1).

The melody line is very simple, and there is no accompaniment except for chords by muted strings that punctuate the
solo. The iconic structure of the music is extremely stark,
perfectly harmonizing with the embodied and designative
meanings of the words. This emptiness is particularly moving within the context, for what had gone before had been
very thick and colorful. But now all the drama and vitality
have been drained out. There is only gray and cold futility.

The inner continuity of some works of music with the
religious dimension, such as the *War Requiem,* the *St. Matthew Passion,* and *The Art of Fugue,* is a consequence of
the iconicity of the tonal structures—their embodied meanings—with the feelings of ultimate concern, reverence, and
peace, or feelings closely allied, that accompany a coercive
experience of *Being.* In our reaction to such music, as Rudolf
Otto points out, "musical feeling is rather (like numinous
feeling) something 'wholly other,' which, while it affords
analogies and here and there will run parallel to the ordinary
emotions of life, cannot be made to coincide with them by a
detailed point-to-point correspondence."[35] Secular music is
iconic with feelings mainly relevant to ontical reality. Sacred
music is iconic with feelings mainly relevant to ontological
reality experienced coercively. While the content of secular
music necessarily contains iconic symbols—otherwise it
would not reveal anything of *Being*—it is dominated by

35. *The Idea of The Holy,* trans. John W. Harvey (London: Oxford University Press, 1928), p. 50.

Example 1 From Britten's War Requiem

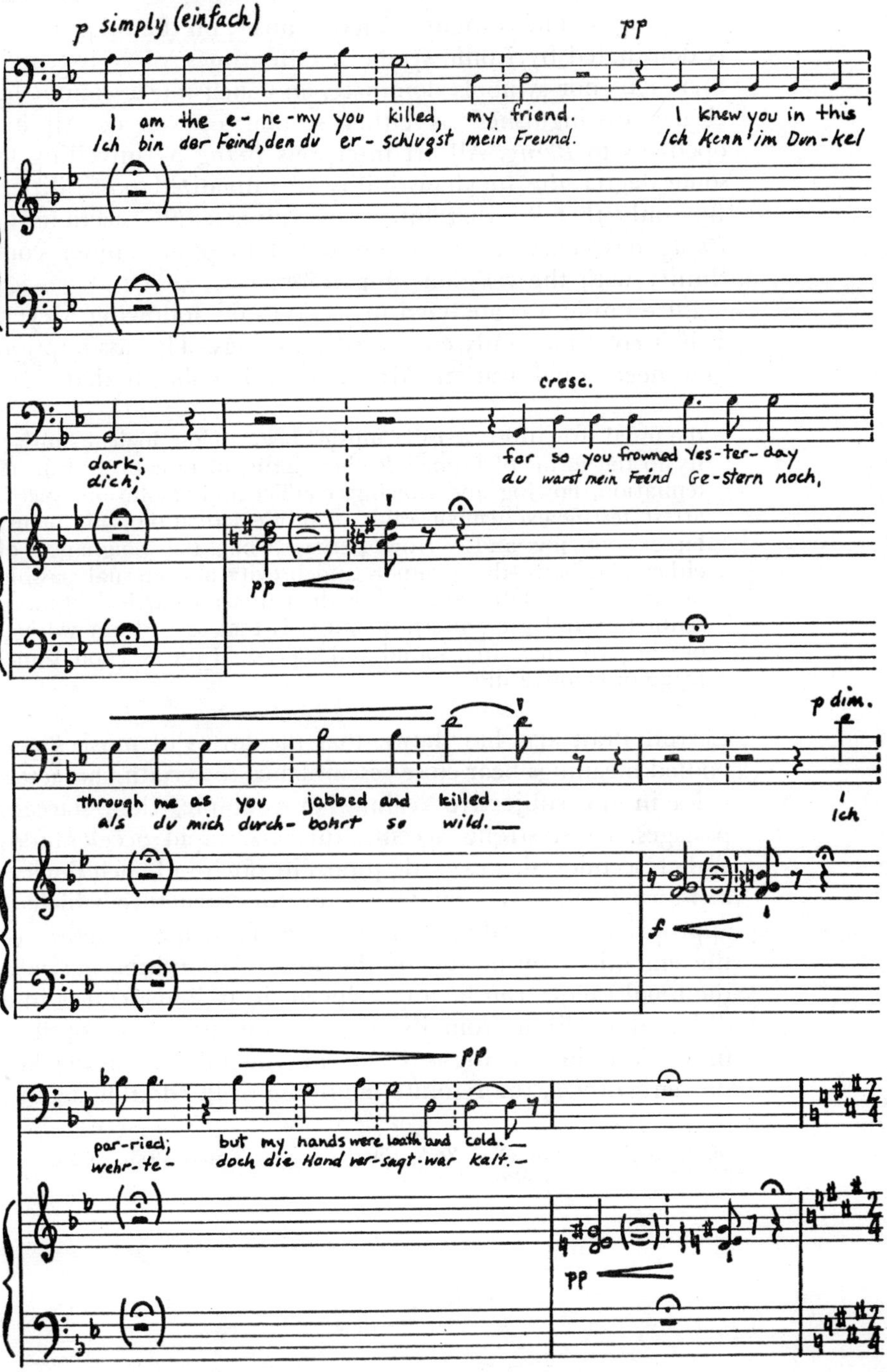

iconic signs. The content of sacred music, on the other hand, is dominated by iconic symbols. Oftentimes, of course, neither signs nor symbols dominate, and such music cannot be clearly distinguished as either secular or sacred. All art opens us to *Being*. All art interprets *Being* by unveiling to some degree the inexhaustibility of unrealized possibilities. But only that art that interprets our awe-full reactions to *Being* has generally been considered to possess inner continuity with the religious dimension.

Pure music was analyzed in section one, following Meyer, as if it contained only embodied meanings. This assumption now needs qualification. Mrs. Langer has shown that

> the tonal structures we call "music" bear a close logical similarity to the forms of human feeling—forms of growth and of attenuation, flowing and stowing, conflict and resolution, speed, arrest, terrific excitement, calm, or subtle activation and dreamy lapses—not joy and sorrow perhaps, but the poignancy of either and both—the greatness and brevity and eternal passing of everything vitally felt. Such is the pattern, or logical form, of sentience; and the pattern of music is that same form worked out in pure, measured sound and silence. Music is a tonal analogue of emotive life.[36]

Carroll Pratt also has shown that the forms of music's embodied meanings bear close resemblance to certain characteristics in the subjective realm. For example, the "staccato passages, trills, strong accents, quavers, rapid accelerandos and crescendos, shakes, wide jumps in pitch—all such devices conduce to the creation of an auditory structure which is appropriately described as restless."[37] Thus the *structure* of the embodied meanings, of the interrelationships between the tonal events, can be a translucent icon. This icon is in a different medium from its referent, the structures of feelings. Thus in the fugue from the funeral march in Beethoven's *Eroica,* the resolute pounding of the double against

36. *Feeling and Form* (New York: Charles Scribner's Sons, 1953), p. 27.
37. *The Meaning of Music,* p. 198.

the triple rhythms, the somber timbre of the tones, and the fortissimo clashing of the dissonances present an auditory structure isomorphic with the structure of the feelings of strife and acute anguish. As we attentively listen we become aware of the iconic reference to the structure of these feelings. The icon, *i.e.*, the structure of the fugue, is translucent because we understand the reference only if we raptly listen to the music. We do not hear the music and then become cognizant of the structures of strife and anguish. We feel these structures *in* the music. The icon, furthermore, is designative; for despite the fusion in our perception of the tonal and feeling structures, they are in different media. Pure music, therefore, has designative meaning, but this designative meaning is completely dependent upon the structuring of the embodied meanings. This structuring makes it possible for music to refer to the external world. The failure to recognize the iconicity and in turn the designative power of music is an error of both the Formalists and the Absolute Expressionists.

Since all music that is art designates, the distinction between program music and pure music must depend on the *kind* of designation. Some of the references of program music, at least, are to definite times or places, whereas the references of pure music are indefinite. For example parts of the last movement of Beethoven's Ninth Symphony are iconic with the feeling structures of joy, as are parts of the last movement of Mozart's *Jupiter* Symphony. The Ninth Symphony is programmatic because Beethoven's use of Schiller's "Ode to Joy" designates specific times and places in relation to the feeling forms of joy. The *Jupiter* Symphony, on the other hand, is nonprogrammatic because there is no suggestion of specific dating or locating. Without a program, it is virtually impossible for music to designate definite times and places. Yet Mozart's music refers to forms of feeling that are just as distinctive as Beethoven's. Mozart's referents are less heroic, more subtle, more mixed, perhaps, with pathos. We cannot avoid awareness of these structures as in time and place, for that is where they occur. But almost any time and place will do. In short, the difference between program music and pure music is one of degree, for the difference between definite and indefinite dating and locating is itself indefinite. That is why the distinction cannot always be easily applied, as in the case of Hindemith's *The Four Temperaments*.

Unlike Mrs. Langer and Pratt, I am claiming that the iconic designations of music are not necessarily restricted to the structure of feelings. All music must, if the previous analysis has been correct, symbolically refer to *Being* by possessing in the structure of its embodied meanings an "icon of inexhaustibility." By stimulating reversions that are seemingly inexhaustibile, the structure is an iconic symbol because it significantly resembles and thus designates an aspect of *Being*. Moreover, all music also possesses an "icon of temporality." The structure of music ties past and present and future into inseparable relationships in our perception, into units or durations which, in turn, rhythmically penetrate into other durations. Music presents in its structure an "objective correlative" of the ecstatic temporality that underlies the projection of our worlds. This icon is not a mirroring of mental *a priori* structures, à la Kant, because in listening to the structure of music we are grasped by a power that is more than our own, that is "other." Music forces us to feel temporality as dominating us, to which we can only be receptive, just as the *Being* of our beings is a power which, although we can forget it, we cannot dominate. Thus music reveals in its process the power that makes it possible for us to "stand out," to "ek-sist"—the power that thrusts *Dasein's* ontical self out of what otherwise would be meaninglessness. "The self," as described by Heidegger, "in its innermost essence is primordially identical with temporality itself."[38] By refusing reference to definite times and places, pure music reveals the *Being* in us that makes possible our projection of

---

38. *Kant und das Problem der Metaphysik* (Bonn: F. Cohen, 1929) , p. 187.

worlds and their horizons within which, in turn, objects and events can be revealed. Pure music is the most introspective of all the arts, but its inward stretch reaches beyond human subjectivity to the *Being* that makes human subjectivity possible. Music reveals the *Being* that is both in us and beyond us. The icon of inexhaustibility unveils something of the mystery of *Being;* the icon of temporality unveils something of the power of *Being* in human beings. Secular as well as sacred music, however, possesses these icons; but secular music, even if it possesses further icons that interpret *Being,* possesses no icons that refer to the structure of religious feelings about *Being.* The primary subject matter of secular music is the structure of ontically oriented feelings. Music that possesses an inner continuity with the religious dimension, on the other hand, may possess other icons that further interpret *Being* and must possess icons that refer to the structure of religious feelings about *Being.*

The *St. Matthew Passion,* for example, is so massive and monumental in structure, and the tensions and resolutions of the embodied meanings are so often overpowering, that a sublimity similar to the sublimity of *Being* is suggested. "There exists a hidden kinship," as Otto emphasizes, "between the numinous [*Being*] and the sublime which is something more than a merely accidental analogy. . . ."[39] And "in the arts nearly everywhere the most effective means of representing the numinous is the 'sublime.'"[40] Given the verbal context of the *Passion* and the liturgical setting, the symbolic reference of this "icon of sublimity" to *Being* is not likely to be missed by anyone carefully listening to the music—provided, of course, that his ontological sensitivities have not been destroyed. This icon of sublimity is a further interpretation of *Being.*

Throughout the *Passion,* furthermore, the structures of the embodied meanings are variously isomorphic with the structures of such feelings as ultimate concern, reverence,

39. *The Idea of The Holy,* p. 65.
40. *Ibid.,* p. 68.

and peace. These icons place the icons of inexhaustibility, temporality, and sublimity in a devotional context. Thus Bach's music not only reveals something of *Being*—all music that is art and all other art does this—but possesses an inner continuity with the religious dimension. The solemnity and humble adoration of the closely associated words, iconically organized for the most part, help decrease any uncertainty about these ontologically oriented references. For example, after the account of Peter's denial of his Master in Part II, Bach introduces the alto aria, "Have mercy, Lord, on me, for the sake of my tears," accompanied by one of the most plaintive violin solos ever written (Example 2).

The reverential references of the iconic structures of the music are made much more definite by the verbal references to Peter and his remorse.

In *The Art of Fugue* the absence of words and a liturgical setting make the existence of icons of religious feelings more dubious. Yet in most of the work—Contrapuncti 1–11, 14, 17–18, and above all 19, the unfinished quadruple fugue— there is in the structure of the embodied meanings an unearthly inevitability about the resolution of the tensions that is iconic with the sense of reverence and peace that accompanies coercive experiences of *Being*. For example, in the opening sixteen measures of Contrapunctus 11 (Example 3), the three-note phrases that form the subject of this four-voiced fugue sound in isolation somewhat baseless and suspended. Despite their majestic pace, there is unfulfilled tension, anxiety in each one. Yet this theme of $4\frac{1}{4}$ measures is centered around the tonic pitch, and when it arrives at the D there is a sense of quiet release, although there is no final release until the last chord of the fugue.

The Well Tempered Clavier, on the other hand, despite its perhaps equally powerful icons of inexhaustibility and temporality,[41] generally lacks icons of religious feeling and

41. A case can be made that both *The Well Tempered Clavier* and *The Art of Fugue* also possess an icon of sublimity. However, the existence of this icon in these works is not so obvious, I believe, as in the *St. Matthew Passion.*

Example 2 From Bach's *St. Matthew Passion*

Example 3   From Bach's The Art of Fugue

thus fails to possess an inner continuity with the religious dimension. In turn, *The Well Tempered Clavier* would be inappropriate in a religious service, whereas Contrapuncti 1–11, 14, and 17–19 of *The Art of Fugue* would be appropriate. Often, no doubt, we will differ about such judgments. Nevertheless, although not verifiable in a scientific sense, such judgments have an objective basis and thus are subject to justifying reasons. Most sensitive listeners, for example, who do not understand the German of the *St. Matthew Passion,* or even that it is German or a Passion, are still likely to be aware of its inner continuity with the religious dimension.

When pure music has such continuity, a religious program is appropriate. The conventional symbolism of language pins down the iconic symbolism of the music to some extent, clarifies some of its vagueness. Without this clarification through convention, the iconic symbolism would generally be considered too subtle for religious institutional purposes. Thus, following ordinary language usage, music must have a religious program if it is to be appropriately described as religious art. Hence *The Art of Fugue* is no more than implicitly religious. Music that possesses both an inner continuity with the religious dimension and a religious program compatible with that inner continuity, such as the *St. Matthew Passion,* is explicitly religious.[42]

The inner continuity of pure music with the religious dimension is made possible by stimuli whose referring power is iconic rather than conventional. Inevitably, nevertheless, even if the designative meanings of a program are lacking, some weakening of our feeling of causal efficacy results. The difference in kind between icon and referent disrupts our direct encounter with process and, consequently, we abstract time and place. This disruption causes only a very slight weakening of our awareness of process, however, and does

---

42. How religious art can be distinguished from nonreligious art is a matter of great importance but of baffling complexity. In the concluding pages of the next chapter, this problem will be discussed in some detail.

not begin to go nearly as far as most program music. In the first place, the iconicity between symbol and referent diminishes our awareness of their differences. The translucency of the iconic symbol fuses the symbol and referent in our experience more tightly than in the case of conventional symbols. Thus the icons of inexhaustibility and temporality in *The Art of Fugue* seem to incarnate the mystery and process of *Being*. Second, since the symbols refer to *Being*, the references are ontologically rather than ontically oriented. Thus there is no reference to specific times and places. Nevertheless, there remains some loss in the sense of the compulsion of process, and, it would seem, some loss in intensity of experience compared to the experience of pure music that is completely lacking in designative meaning, *i.e.*, music that is decoration rather than art. Music that is decoration has form, the organization of tones to attract our attention and arouse our emotions and give us pleasure, but the form does not inform. There is no revelation of a subject matter, no content. There is no insight into anything beyond the music. Thus "rock" music (nonprogrammatic for the purpose of illustration) can be experienced with great intensity. But this kind of intensity is primarily a physical or Dionysiac seizure, as is indicated among other things, by the need for blaring sonorities amplified by electronic devices *ad infinitum* and *ad nauseam*. This kind of intensity fails to thrust us into an awareness of ecstatic temporality because the tensions and resolutions of the embodied meanings are trivial and monotonous. The presently sounding tone anticipates, more or less, the succeeding tone and maybe a few after that, but there is no "stretch," no far-reaching references. Thus in *All My Loving* (Example 4), one of the earliest and weakest works by the Beatles, the embodied meanings of the music are as restricted and obvious as the insipid designations of the words. The embodied meanings are trite because they make no significant demand upon our imaginations. To feel reversions, except of the most obvious kind, is to listen away from the music. This kind of music

Example 4 From Lennon's and McCartney's "All My Loving"

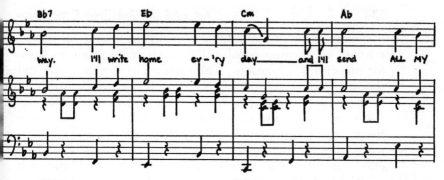

way. I'll write home ev-'ry day___ and I'll send ALL MY

LOV-ING to you.___ I'll pre-___ ALL MY

LOV-ING, I will send to you.___ ALL MY

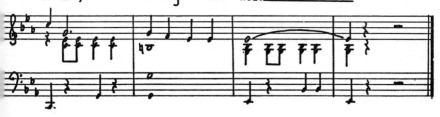

LOV-ING, Dar-ling I'll be true.___

is quickly exhaustible because it lacks the power to suggest relevant contrasting possibilities. There is no room, in turn, for surprising resolutions. The mixture of the expected and the unexpected, part of the power of music that is art, is almost totally lacking. The forms of these embodied meanings along with the noise may evoke emotion; but because these forms lack translucent iconicity, they fail to inform about these emotions or anything else. Thus the intensity of their effects, no matter how strong, is a passing thing. Music such as Bach's both evokes emotions and reveals their structures.[43] Music such as *All My Loving* at best evokes only emotions, turns us into squealing masses of emotion, for, lacking content, such music has no meaning. Its message is a massage.

The designations of program music weaken our feeling of ecstatic temporality. In this respect program music is less likely than pure music to thrust us out of time, to open us to *Being*. Even when the conventional signs or symbols of the program are iconically organized, and even when the designations are ontologically oriented, they usually refer, as in the *St. Matthew Passion,* to definite times and places. There is, unless the meanings of the words are ignored, a pulling back of the listener from the power of process. This weakening of our direct encounter with causal efficacy is especially noticeable when the program is not iconically organized, as in the first verse of Hymn 309 in the *Pilgrim Hymnal:*

> Jerusalem the golden, With milk and honey blest,
> Beneath thy contemplation, Sink heart and voice
>   oppressed.
> I know not, O I know not, What joys await us there,
> What radiancy of Glory, What bliss beyond
>   compare!

---

43. See my "On the Supposed Incompatibility of Expressionism and Formalism."

When the program is more iconically organized, the sense of
difference between the signs or symbols and their referents
is not so obvious, as in the "Sanctus" of Bach's *Mass in B
Minor:*

> Sanctus, Sanctus, Sanctus
> Domine Deus Sabaoth
> Pleni sunt coeli et terra gloria ejus.[44]

The loss in the feeling of ecstatic temporality in listening
to program music may be compensated, depending on the
interests of the listener, by the greater breadth and specificity
of designative meaning provided by the program. Listeners
who are not Christian or who have little interest in theoretical, practical, and sociological expressions about *Being* are
likely to prefer listening to the *St. Matthew Passion* without
paying attention to the meanings of the words. The program
is likely to distract them from the power of music. They are
likely to find *The Art of Fugue* as religious as the *St. Matthew Passion.* On the other hand, for the Christian or someone who takes seriously theoretical, practical, and sociological expressions about *Being,* the program of the *St. Matthew
Passion* is much more easily fused with the symbols of the
music. The loss of intensity due to the weakening of the
direct encounter with causal efficacy is compensated by the
breadth and specificity of references. Such listeners are likely
to be skeptical of a judgment that affirms the religious character of *The Art of Fugue.*

The compulsion of process in music opens us to *Being.*
The iconicity of the structures of music interprets *Being.*
Music that is implicitly religious gives these interpretations
an awe-full context. Music that is explicitly religious adds

---

44. Furthermore, the ancient character of Latin and its association with
Christianity probably have for many Western people, especially Catholics,
an external connection with *Being.* Latin for non-Catholics is so different
from anything in the everyday world that it also may suggest the ontological. This raises the interesting question whether the Second Vatican
Council was wise in permitting the use of the vernacular in the mass.

a program of conventional symbols. By referring to definite times and places, a religious program clarifies the references of music's interpretations of *Being* and our feelings about *Being* at the peril of blocking our opening to *Being*. When the program is successfully harmonized with the iconic symbols of the music, as in Britten's *War Requiem,* this peril is minimized. But, in the final analysis, all such programs depend upon the magic of music's process to impel us into an explicit awareness of the ecstatic temporality that is the *Being* of our beings, the pulse of *Being* in us.

4

Painting and Presentational Immediacy

Painting charms us from the frenzy of functions. Painting is to music as woman is to man. The driving power of music thrusts us from time into temporality. But the framed "all-at-onceness" of painting, by accenting presentational immediacy, frees our perception from both time and temporality. And so the path of painting to *Being* is very different from the path of music.

The persistent presence of a painting provides a context that allows the visually perceptible to be enjoyed for its own sake, rather than being managed or mastered by some form of quantification. In all meaningful experiences except the participative, sense data are extracted from sensa, blinding us to some of the sensa's qualities and tarnishing the splendor of the rest. Since these extractions are made habitually—by everyman as well as the theoretician and technician—they are for the most part made unconsciously. Even such a simple act as walking safely on a sidewalk requires an automatic thinning out of sensa into data. Usually we have to see data. Otherwise we could not survive in the world of things. Yet, fortunately, there are times when it is possible fully to en-joy rather than reduce sensa. When we are driving a car this enjoyment is impossible. But if someone else takes the wheel, and if we are creatively receptive, then the visually perceptible in its qualitative fullness has a chance to unfold itself. Sensa and the things in which they adhere are primordial. Sense data are always derivative from sensa but—unless we are painters or sensitive to paintings—this is likely to be forgotten.

> For, don't you mark, we're made so that we love
> First when we see them painted, things we have passed
> Perhaps a hundred times not cared to see.
> Robert Browning, "Fra Lippo Lippi"

Although sensa appear everywhere, in paintings sensa shine forth. In nature the light usually appears as external to the colors and textures of sensa. The light plays *on* the colors and textures. In paintings the light usually appears immanent *in* the colors and textures, seems to come, in part at least, through them, even in the flat polished colors of Mondrian or Malevitch. When a light source is represented —the candles in the paintings of La Tour, for example, or the windows in the paintings of Rembrandt or Vermeer— the light seems to be absorbed into the colors and textures. There is a depth of luminosity about the sensa of paintings that even nature at its glorious best seldom surpasses. Generally the colors of nature are more brilliant than the colors of art; but usually in nature sensa are either so glittering that our squints miss their inner luminosity, or the sensa are so changing that we lack the time to participate and penetrate. The swift currents of sensa tend to stupefy our sensitiveness. In paintings, except in some Op Art, glittering change is absent. There is a fixation of the flux. Thus the depth of sensa is unveiled primarily by simply allowing the sensa "to be." This is the piety to sensa that all painters possess. To ignore the allure of the sensa of a painting by reducing them to data, as my historian friend did in measuring haloes, requires special training and has its purposes. Unfortunately such contractions can become a kind of sadism. It is especially the abstract painter—the Shepherd of sensa—who is most likely to call us back to our senses.

The sensa of painting—color, line, light, and texture—entice us leisurely, for unlike the tones of music they are omnipresent as an entirety. The sensa are all there and they stay put. Even our memories are rested. By simply a turn of our eye the forgotten can be taken in again. Thus our sight is seduced, so charmed by sensa in the "here-now" that the time and temporality flowing over a painting are screened off. The brightness of the present not only conceals the clock but casts haze over the future and past, the indispensable components of temporality that make consciousness of the present possible. The radiancy of sensa glows in all paintings, not only in Renoirs and Matisses but even in gloomy abstractions, such as the "black paintings" of Ad Reinhardt, or gruesome representational paintings, such as Grünewald's *Crucifixion* (Plate 9). The bracketing of sensa in the present as ends or intrinsic values, rather than shrinking them into means or instrumental values, lights up even the most somber elements of the sensuous. In that glow, the silence is extraordinary. In that moment, if we allow that silence to ring, *Being* comes to presence.

Abstract is to representational painting as pure is to program music. Abstractions contain designative as well as embodied meanings, for every work of art through its informing form interprets some subject matter. But abstract painting, like pure music, excludes specific places and times, objects and events, from its content. Representational painting like program music includes such references. However, the distinction between abstract and representational painting, as between pure and program music, is not always easily applied. Is Arshile Gorky's *Waterfall* (Plate I), for example, abstract or representational? Without notice of the title, we probably would not see a waterfall. Or what about Gorky's *Agony* or Mondrian's *Broadway Boogie-Woogie* or Robert

Motherwell's *Elegy to the Spanish Republic, 54?* They all seem, if the titles have been missed, to have as their content nothing more than the "schema of the sensuous"—the revelation of sensa abstracted from definite objects and events. But if the titles have not been missed, we locate the schemas specifically in the spatiotemporal continuum. Attention to these titles does not trap us in the intentional fallacy because these paintings not only support the designative references of the titles but, much more importantly, these references illuminate our perception of what is *in* the paintings. This is the *use*, as Wittgenstein would put it, of appropriate or aesthetically relevant titles.[1] Then we see the twist of lines in Gorky's *Agony* as more tortured; the rhythm of Mondrian's colors as more bouncy; and the slashing black planes over the harsh background in Motherwell's painting as more keenly terrorizing. Thus these works are representational or, if greater precision is useful, quasi-representational.

Arp's *Mountain, Table, Anchor, Navel* (Plate 17), on the other hand, is an abstract painting. The references of the title are supported by the painting, it is true, for we can see a mountain, and so on, in the painting once we have noted the title. But this title is misleading, if taken as anything more than an identification tag, because the recognition of the objects designated is of no importance in our perception. *Colors, Structures, and Positions*—for they are what Arp's painting is about—would be a much more appropriate title.

Sometimes, as many of the works of Klee and Miró attest, it is extremely difficult to distinguish between abstract and representational painting. What is iconic with definite objects and events may differ with the differences in tempera-

---

1. Titles, unless they are obviously jokes or serve only as instruments of identification, focus the eye on certain aspects of an image at the expense of others. Thus the function of titles can be decisively important in the perception of paintings. Contemporary painters especially are often confused about how to name their paintings, with the result that they often mislead their public. See my "Naming Paintings," *The Art Journal* 25 (Spring 1966) : 252–56.

ment and background of the recipients. (A well-known aesthetician once insisted, in public debate with me, that the recognition of the mountain, table, anchor, and navel was indispensable in seeing Arp's painting.) Even if the temperament and background of the recipients are closely similar, the line between the definite and the indefinite—Gorky's *Agony* is a case in point—is not always easily drawn. Nevertheless, the distinction between abstract and representational painting is useful, because it points up this important phenomenological fact: whereas in abstract painting definite objects and events are not designated as part of the content, in representational painting they are. Thus abstractions open us to *Being* and interpret *Being* somewhat differently from the way that representational paintings do. Abstract painting will be the subject of the first section of this chapter, representational painting the subject of the second.

I

According to Jerome Ashmore, "pure music and non-objective painting are alike in richness of purely aesthetic experience, that is, as an experience of sensuousness; and also are alike in ignoring physical objects as models for representation."[2] Abraham Walkowitz claims that abstract painting "dwells in the realm of music with an equivalent emotion. Its melody is attuned to the receptive eye as music to the ear."[3] And abstract painters tend to agree with Pater that "music is the ideal of all art." The following statement by Arthur Dove, one of the earliest and best of the abstract painters, is typical of many if not most abstractionists: "I

2. "Some Differences Between Abstract and Non-Objective Painting," *The Journal of Aesthetics and Art Criticism* 13 (June 1955): 492. Ashmore makes some valuable distinctions between abstract and nonobjective painting. For my purposes, however, these terms will be used as synonyms, since this is the way they are still used by most painters, critics, historians of art, and aestheticians.
3. Sidney Janis, *Abstract and Surrealist Art in America* (New York: Reynal and Hitchcock, 1944), p. 44.

should like to take wind and water and sand as a motif and work with them, but it has to be simplified in most cases to color and force lines and substances just as music has done with sound."[4] Such conceptions of abstract painting as a kind of visual music if taken without qualification are highly misleading. They can blur our view of abstractions, weakening our insight. I shall maintain that the mode of perception in the participative experience of abstract painting is fundamentally dissimilar from the mode of perception in the participative experience of pure music. This difference in modes helps explain why abstract painting and pure music, despite their similarities, not only open us to *Being* but interpret *Being* in very different ways.

Pure music designates solely through the iconicity in the structure of its embodied meanings. Pure music cannot designate through the qualities of its percepta because tones are very different from the sounds of the nonmusical world. Even if it be granted, as John Dewey claims,[5] that tones are abstracted from the sounds of nature, the imprints of music's origins are irrelevant in the musical experience. Tones are established and organized in pitch or scale relationships so artificial that tones have no significant resemblance to sounds. Thus tones lack qualitative iconicity. That is why pure music does not deepen our sensitivity to the sounds of the external world. That does not mean, however, that the timbre of the tones is irrelevant. If Beethoven's funeral march in the *Eroica* were played by an ensemble of piccolos, the designation, if any, would no longer include the structure of grief. The qualities of the percepta of a work of art are never irrelevant. But in pure music the tonal qualities, although helping to form the icons of structure, are not icons. Such devices as the crashing bottles, bangs, and burps in the music of John Cage are no exception despite their qualitative iconicity. For these sounds are not tones—they

---

4. Quoted by Sam Hunter, *Modern American Painting and Sculpture* (New York: Dell Publishing Co., Laurel Edition, 1964), p. 90.
5. *Art as Experience* (New York: Minton Balch and Co., 1934), pp. 236ff.

are not susceptible to pitch organization. They function in music, *i.e.*, if they are accompanied by tonal structures, very much as an onomatopoetic verbal program. This kind of music is a species of program music.

Abstractions, unlike pure music, designate through qualitative rather than structural iconicity. As in all works of art, abstractions necessarily must have structure. But the structure of an abstraction helps make possible "icons of quality," just as, conversely, the qualities of pure music help make possible icons of structure. Thus in Frankenhaler's *Saturn* (Plate III), the structure of the percepta—the interrelationship of colors, lines, light, and textures—helps establish the qualitative iconicity of the yellows and blues. Similarly in Cameron Booth's *April 2, 1960* (Plate II), it is the qualities of the sensa as pointed up by the structure, especially the wet, slick, "springy" greens, that suggest spring's sensuous surface. However, since the references here are tied by the title to a specific event, *April 2, 1960* probably should be classified as representational.[6] In any case, if we participate with paintings, whether abstract or representational, our sensitivity to the sensa of the external world is refined. Then the mists of a Monet, for example, help us see the mists of nature with finer discrimination. The grays and reds in certain works of Léger sharpen our sight of the grays and reds of industry. The colors, textures, and lines in Pollack's *Autumn Rhythm,* in The Museum of Modern Art, bring the sensuous schema of fall into clearer focus.[7] The amber in Marcelle Loubchansky's abstraction, *Grain of Amber,* in the Galerie Kléber in Paris, makes it difficult to ignore any amber again.

The dominance of icons of structure in pure music as con-

---

6. If the title had been *April 1, 1960,* jocular connotations would have been introduced that would have weakened the representational references. Usually the use of a date for a title serves merely as an identification tag, although the suggestion of chronological ordering may have some significance, as in Robert Natkin's *1963–1.*

7. *Autumn Rhythm,* like Booth's *April 2, 1960,* is a borderline example between abstract and representational painting.

trasted with the dominance of icons of quality in abstract painting makes profound differences in what and how these arts designate. Thus the primary subject matter of pure music is the forms of feelings, whereas the primary subject matter of abstract painting is the schema of the sensuous. There are abstractions that also refer to feelings, such as Gorky's *Agony,* Hans Hofmann's *Exuberance,* and Kandinsky's *Élan tranquille.* However, these references are primarily to the qualities rather than to the forms of those feelings—the harshness of color and line in the Gorky resembles the qualitative feel of agony; the bounce of color and line in the Hofmann resembles the qualitative feel of exuberance; the glasslike smoothness of color and light in the Kandinsky resembles the qualitative feel of serene spirit. Since the forms of feelings are inherently temporal, only an art that presents its percepta successively, such as music, can be iconic with these forms. It is true, also, that some abstract painters like to baptize their works with musical names. Thus among Rudolf Bauer's abstractions there are several that are entitled *Andante, Allegro, Allegretto,* and *Presto.* These titles, however, in the context of their use suggest qualities of the sensa rather than forms of feeling. Thus the colors in any *Andante,* for example, are cooler than the colors in any *Presto.*

These similarities between pure music and abstract painting, however tenuous, tend nevertheless to makes us overlook the differences between pure music and abstract painting, especially since both arts lack signs and symbols referring to specific places and times. Yet in just as fundamental a respect, abstract painting is at the opposite pole from music. The sensa of an abstract painting are not presented successively but as a totality. This "all-at-onceness" frees our perception from any sense of compulsion. Normally we can "hold on" any part or region or even sometimes the totality as long as we like, and follow any order of parts or regions at our own pace. Or, as Husserl puts it, "I can always do so again." No part or region of an abstraction strictly presup-

Plate I Arshile Gorky: *Waterfall* (c. 1943). 60½" x 44½".
Private Collection. Courtesy Mrs. Agnes Gorky Phillips.

Plate II Cameron Booth: *April 2, 1960.* Acrylic on linen, 40″ x 50″. Private Collection. Courtesy the artist.

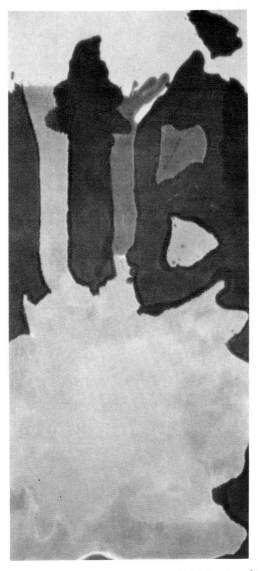

Plate III   Helen Frankenthaler: *Saturn* (1964). Acrylic on canvas, 105″ x 49″. Private Collection. Photo by Edward Meneeley. Courtesy ESM Documentations.

poses another part or region temporally; their sequence is subject to no absolute constraint. Whereas there is only one route in hearing music, there is a freedom of routes in seeing abstractions.

The persistent presence of the whole of an abstraction provides a context that permits the percepta to be experienced mainly for their own sake. In everyday experience such a context usually is lacking, and, as Whitehead points out, abstract painters have to learn to ignore the designative references of sensa.

> We look up and we see a coloured shape in front of us, and we say,—there is a chair. But what we have seen is the mere coloured shape. Perhaps an artist might not have jumped to the notion of a chair. He might have stopped at the mere contemplation of a beautiful colour and a beautiful shape. . . . I am very sceptical as to the high-grade character of the mentality required to get from the coloured shape to the chair. One reason for this scepticism is that my friend the artist, who kept himself to the contemplation of colour, shape and position, was a very highly trained man, and had acquired this facility of ignoring the chair at the cost of great labour.[8]

The artist in such a case perceives primarily in the mode of presentational immediacy: stops at the present and enjoys the sensations provided by the show of the percepta.

When the awareness of sensa is exceptionally vivid, awareness of causal connections—past and future—is inhibited. Thus the striking hue of that green so rivets our attention that we ignore the reference of the green to that field of grass. Such forceful awareness of sensa, unless we are artists, occurs only occasionally—when, for example, we are resting with no pressing worries and time on our hands and the sunset is so striking that our attention fixes on its redness. Even then darkness descends. But in front of an abstraction there is a self-sufficient totality that provides a context that allows the red in the abstraction to "stand still." The red is

8. *Symbolism, Its Meaning and Effect* (New York: The Macmillan Co., 1927), pp. 2f.

peculiarly impervious and reliable, infallibly fixed and settled in its place. It can be surveyed and brought out again
and again; it can be gone over with closed eyes, and checked
with open eyes. Moreover, that red abstains from referring
to definite objects or events—like good weather tomorrow—
for the only definite references of that red are embodied
references, *i.e.*, references to other sensa within the painting.
And there is no hurry, furthermore, about getting to these
referents, for all of the painting is present and under normal
conditions it is not changing in any significant perceptual
sense. Liberated from references to specific objects and events
and the press of successive presentation of percepta, we can,
for once, focus on the qualitative values of the sensa themselves. If the abstract painter has done his job, he will have
painted the sensuous in a context that, assuming our sensitiveness, will hold our attention on the "here-now." Then
instead of our controlling the sensa, transforming them into
data, the sensa control us, transforming us into participators.
The spectator to some extent reduces the sensa to data, for
he keeps his distance and stares at the surface of an abstraction from a standpoint. His sight glides over the sensa as
smooth and impenetrable. The spectator experience is an
affair of the surface. The participator, conversely, releases
himself to the sensa, loses his self-consciousness, and thus
goes beyond intuitions of the surface of the sensa to an awareness of their depth. A series of durations follows, vivid solip-
sisms of present moments—"spots of time" (Wordsworth) —
that are ordered by the embodied references, but are divided
from one another in a different way from the more fluid
progressions felt in listening to music. Whereas when we
listen to music the percepta interpenetrate, when we see an
abstraction the percepta are more juxtaposed. Whereas the
rhythm of perceiving music is continuous, the rhythm of
perceiving abstract painting is discontinuous. Whereas music
is perceived as motion, abstract painting is perceived as mo-
tionless. We are fascinated by the vibrant novelty and the
primeval power of the red of an abstraction for its own sake,

cut off from explicit consciousness of past and future. But then, sooner or later, we notice the embodied reference of the red to the green, and then we are fascinated by the green. Or then, sooner or later, we are fascinated by the interaction or the contrast between the red and the green. Our eye travels over the canvas step by step, free to pause at any step as long as it desires. "Paths are made," as Klee perceived, "for the eye of the beholder which moves along from patch to patch like an animal grazing." The rhythms of hearing music and seeing abstractions are at opposite poles. But both are extraordinary, quite different from the rhythms of ordinary experience somewhere between.

Music, more than any other art, is perceived mainly in the mode of causal efficacy. Abstract painting, more than any other art, is perceived mainly in the mode of presentational immediacy. Thus music appears in part elsewhere, whereas abstractions appear to be all here. In listening to music, we experience presentational immediacy because we hear the presently sounding tones. But there can be no "holding" and we are swept up in the flow of process. In seeing an abstract painting, we experience causal efficacy because we follow the reference of the embodied meanings and this involves a sense of process. But there can be and generally is a "rapt resting" on any part, an unhurried series of one-after-the-other of "nows," each of which may have a temporal spread that for a while ignores any further embodied references. Usually abstractions have a feudal constitution: although certain parts or regions may have hierarchical rights over others, each part or region maintains its personal rights and particularity, its intrinsic value intensity. Each part or region of an abstraction has its own center of gravity and thus is a place of rest—of arrest. Each part or region is a calculated trap for sensuous meditation and consummation. Each part or region fills the mind so completely that there is no desire—at least for a while—to return to a better past or to invoke a more seductive future. Each part or region compresses the dimensions of temporality into the single dimension of a *now*, an intense moment isolated. And thus our sense of the intensified immediate dominates our sense of process.

All the other major arts are perceived in modes somewhere between the extremes of the static dominance in seeing abstractions and the dynamic dominance in listening to music. In general, the feeling of presentational immediacy weakens and causal efficacy strengthens as one proceeds from abstract to representational painting, sculpture, architecture, literature, drama, film, dance, program music, and, finally, pure music. A defense of such a scaling requires an analysis that goes beyond the scope of the present inquiry, but I can illustrate the basic determinants in such a scaling by comparing representational with abstract painting.

The sensa of representational painting, like those of abstract painting, are not presented successively. Yet the cognition of the designative meanings that refer to definite objects or events inevitably involves an indirect feeling of process. In the case of representational paintings that refer primarily to events, such as the *Crucifixion* (Plate 9) by Grünewald, there is an awareness of both time as the dating of the event and a very specific place. But even in a still life where the primary reference is to objects, as in most of the cubistic still-life paintings of Braque and Picasso, the immaculate perception of presentational immediacy is somewhat compromised. Although there may be no definite dating, there is, as in the experience of an "eventful painting," a definite placing, resulting in a referential discursus that directs attention from the sensuous surface of the design to the objects designated, such as fruit and a table. For the sensitive recipient there will be fusion of the stimuli and the referents. He will see the fruit and the table *in* the lines, shapes, colors, and textures of the painting, for the designative references to fruit and table are made possible by translucent icons. Nevertheless, the synthesizing of sensa and objects is a mediated "taking account" that breaks into the sheer immediacy of the perception, and with that meditation comes a feeling of process. Abstractions also refer to objects and events, for designative meaning always requires some location, however indefinite, in the spatiotemporal continuum. But the references of abstractions are so general that, unlike our perception of representational paintings, the mediation is kept at the outskirts of our attention.

Just as a still life is likely to stimulate a sense of presentational immediacy more than a historical painting, so abstractions differ in their ability to stimulate the sense of presentational immediacy. The vast canvas of Pollack's *Autumn Rhythm*, full of the chaos of chance, is so forceful, rhythmic, and seemingly spontaneous in the presentation of its percepta that our eye tends to get caught up in the violent rush in a way that inhibits resting on a part. With work such as this—some of the abstractions of Willem de Kooning and Hans Hofmann, for example, and much of Op Art with its flashing, iridescent colors and shapes—abstract painting comes closest to music in the way it propels perception. Even in our perception of such works, however, there is no more than a sense of the "saddle-back present," as William James called it, of riding the present with a piece of the past and a piece of the future. There is no long stretch into the past and future as in the perception of music. And, furthermore, the persistent presence of the whole of such abstractions inhibits any feeling of process from becoming compulsive. Malevitch's chilly *White Square on a White Background* in the Museum of Modern Art illustrates the opposite extreme. The dimensions are so small, the parts and regions so simply and sharply profiled, and the embodied meanings so economically interrelated that there tends to be simply one rather than a series of timeless moments. The shades of white sit so quietly and subtly side by side that *White Square on a White Background,* like many of the abstractions of Mondrian, is viewed within such a chaste and unified field of vision that it appears to have no parts or regions. And no matter how long we contemplate this painting it seems as if a single glance has sufficed. The vast

majority of abstractions fall between these extremes of restlessness and stillness—for example, those of Robert Motherwell, Mark Rothko, and Clyfford Still—and at the present
time there seems to be no prevailing tendency toward either
extreme.

Abstract painting presents sensa in their primitive but
powerful state of innocence. Thus the persistent presence
of abstract painting arouses our senses from their sleep by
attracting our vision so that it holds clearly and distinctly
on the bits and pieces and structures of sensa that get lost
in theoretical and technical work and get blurred in the
crowded confusion of everyday experience. In turn, this
intensity of vision renews the spontaneity of our perception
in the mode of presentational immediacy and enhances the
tone of our physical existence. We clothe our visual sensations in positive feelings, living in these sensations instead
of using them as means to ends. And such sensuous activity—
sight, for once, minus anxiety and eyestrain—is sheer delight.
Abstract painting offers us a complete rest from practical
concerns and liberates us from the push of embodied references. Abstract painting is, as Matisse in 1908 was beginning
to see, "an art of balance, of purity and serenity devoid of
troubling or depressing subject matter, an art which might
be for every mental worker, be he business-man or writer,
like an appeasing influence, like a mental soother, something
like a good armchair in which to rest from physical fa-
tigue."[10] Or as Hilla Rebay remarks: "The contemplation
of a Non-objective picture offers a complete rest to the mind.
It is particularly beneficial to business men, as it carries them
away from the tiresome rush of earth, and strengthens their
nerves, once they are familiar with this real art. If they lift
their eyes to these pictures in a tired moment, their attention
will be absorbed in a joyful way, thus resting their minds
from earthly troubles and thoughts."[11]

10. *La grande revue* (Dec. 25, 1908).
11. "Value of Non-Objectivity," Third Enlarged Catalogue of the *Solomon R.
    Guggenheim Collection of Non-Objective Paintings* (New York: Solomon
    R. Guggenheim Foundation, 1938), p. 7.

Music opens us to *Being* through the compulsion of causal efficacy, forcing us into an intense awareness of ecstatic temporality, the fundamental characteristic of the *Being* of human beings. Abstract painting, on the other hand, frees us from the grip of causal efficacy by holding us in relatively isolated durations of presentational immediacy. Whereas music opens us to *Being* through the flow of tones, abstract painting opens us to *Being* through the unmoving silence of sensa. The intrinsic values of the sensuous entrance our sight because the "all-at-onceness" of an abstraction and the absence of references to definite objects and events persuade us to be one with the sensa. There is a stillness about that area of blue or green of an abstraction that seems as permanent as anything in this World of Becoming, as Plato might put it, can be. Even the designative references of the blue and green by means of qualitative iconicity are only to the "schema" of the blues and greens of the external world. The designations are not, as in representational painting, to the sensuous as situated in definite objects and events. Thus specific place and time are irrelevant. Furthermore, even the embodied references of the sensa of an abstraction have a static character. The duration of the experience of the blue terminates with the awareness of the blue as a stimulus that refers to the green. The duration of the experience of the green, in turn, may terminate with the awareness of the green as a stimulus that refers to the blue. In this dialectic of durations the next duration may include the blue and green locked together as crossing vectors in a plane which, in turn, may refer to another color or plane, and so on. These reversing and interlocking references of embodied meanings further freeze our sense of temporality. Goethe described architecture as frozen music, but abstract painting is a much better example of that metaphor.

When we view an abstraction we suspend the habits of our ordinary experience. Even the habit of reference, although not abolished, is quieted down. The very framing of an abstraction sets it apart from the tyranny of temporality and time and space, and the fury of functions. "Every man," claims Michel Seuphor,

> awaits the revelation. It takes place today through abstract art in particular, in the clearest and simplest language that was ever found. . . . I believe that religious sentiment, in all religions, resides first of all in an immobilization before life, a prolonged attention, a questioning and expectant attitude that suspends all corporeal activity and that is a prelude to an activity of a quite different nature that we call inner life, spiritual life. Now art—and abstract art above all—is the expression of the attentive life, of the free life of the spirit, of this contemplation.[12]

Abstractions rest our never-resting eyes. Abstractions anchor us from transit-sickness. If anything is likely to calm our nervous souls, it is an abstraction. Then, as we stand in front of Reinhardt's *Abstract Painting* in The Museum of Modern Art, the guardrails disappear. We forget where we are. Instead of staring from a standpoint at a vast black glob of alien meaninglessness that in saying nothing seems to be conspiring against us, the painting comes to us and we begin to see with insight nine very subtly related squares of luminous blacks. We become what we behold. Our awareness becomes black. And in the inner intimacy of that participative experience there is a silence that rings, as in the darkness of the night. "Give her a silence, that the soul may softly turn home into the flooding and the fullness in which she lived" (Rilke). In that resonance, we are opened to *Being*.

How abstract painting can also interpret *Being* is much more difficult to explain. Arp wrote that abstractions "are structures composed of lines, of surfaces, of forms, of colors. They try to reach the eternal, the inexpressible above men." Klee wrote that "art plays an unknowing game with ultimate things, and yet achieves them." And the game of abstract

---

12. *The Spiritual Mission of Art* (New York: Galerie Chalette, 1960), p. 26.

painting is perhaps the most unknowing of all the arts, the best example of Klee's point. In resisting reference to definite places and times, abstractions seem to be able to interpret only the schema of the sensuous. The primary subject matter of abstract painting is surely the sensuous in all its qualitative infinity abstracted from definite objects and events. Colors, lines, textures, lights, shadows, horizontality, verticality, ascent, and descent are a constant concomitant of our everyday experience; but usually we either pay no attention to these incessantly changing patches or see them only as transparent signs, penetrate them like panes of glass to note the things signified. Our survival depends upon it. But sometimes, when the strains of survival slacken, we may again, as when we were children, begin to see the sensuous and its structures as windowless monads. Then the radiant and vivid values of the sensuous are enjoyed for their own sake, satisfying a primal, fundamental need.[13] Abstractions can help fulfill this need if we dare, despite our habits of

---

13. Walter Abell argues that "plastic values are potentially greater in representational art than in abstract art." *Representation and Form* (New York: Charles Scribner's Sons, 1936), p. 164. But is the value of a color *qua* color, for example, lessened because it does not refer to some definite object or event? No one has answered Abell better than Mieczyslaw Wallis:

> Simple and poor arrangements of stimulative factors, for instance, simple geometric figures or juxtapositions of few colored areas, affect us in point of fact more strongly when associated with representative factors. But richer and more complicated combinations of stimulative factors, such as we find in most works of non-objective painting, do not need any aid of representative favors. They are "self-sufficient." Although an association with representative elements would enrich them, it would at the same time impede the spectator in concentrating his whole attention on stimulative elements. Non-objective painting has arisen as the result of the tendency to liberate the stimulative factors from the state of being overwhelmed by the representative factors, as an attempt to bestow upon the stimulative factors the greatest efficiency by separating them from the representative factors. The fact that non-objective painting not only subsists, but flourishes proves that this tendency was reasonable and has achieved its goal.

"The Origin and Foundations of Non-Objective Painting, "*The Journal of Aesthetics and Art Criticism* 19 (Fall 1960): 68.

practice and Puritan heritage,[14] to behold and treasure the images of the sensuous.

Perhaps we should maintain only that abstract painting prepares us for *Being* but goes no further. The pervasive vagueness in the claims of those who do go further reinforces this caution. For example, according to James Johnson Sweeney, abstract painting is a "metaphor of structure"— "essentially an organization of color-relationships, line-relationships, and space-relationships recalling to the conscious, or unconscious mind some basic, organic, relationship in Nature."[15] For Jerome Ashmore "non-objective paintings are attempts," like the old Pythagorean philosophies, "at translations of clues to a mystery—the mystery of what is behind phenomena and what is the key to an adequate interpretation of the universe."[16] For Tillich abstract painting is a mystical style in which "artists have deprived reality of its manifoldness, of the concreteness of things and persons, and have expressed ultimate reality through the medium of elements which ordinarily appear only in unity with concrete objects on the surface of reality."[17] Like Klee these theorists maintain, and I believe correctly, that abstractions reveal "ultimate things" (*Being*), that they are something more than a mental soother or an appeasing influence like Matisse's armchair. Somehow in abstractions the sensuous and its structures, despite their monadic character, possess translucent windows into the depth dimension of reality, but the "how" of this revelation has not been specified.

---

14. "The denial of the sensuous character of the material means of painting has probably been one of the most identifiable marks of American provincialism, and its most damaging weakness, from the journeymen painters of the Eighteenth century to Winslow Homer, from Charles Demuth and Charles Sheeler to Ben Shahn and Andrew Wyeth." Hunter, *Modern American Painting and Sculpture*, p. 103.
15. "New Directions in Painting," *The Journal of Aesthetics and Art Criticism* 18 (Mar. 1960) : 369.
16. "The Old and the New in Non-Objective Painting," *The Journal of Aesthetics and Art Criticism* 9 (June 1951) : 300.
17. "Art and Ultimate Reality," A Lecture at the Museum of Modern Art in *Dimensions* (Feb. 17, 1959), p. 13.

Sensa from a spectator's standpoint are sheer surface, riding in our minds like a sea in continual motion, the wavering waves interfering with each other so much that we see mainly a blur. That is one of the reasons why, in order to anchor ourselves from motion sickness and to manage ourselves in the world of things, we have to reduce sensa to data. Such reduction helps bring order and stability into the swirl, but such reduction removes us from the qualitative fullness of sensa. And sensa as data have little intrinsic value or, unless the data are related to elaborate scientific theories, complexity. Sense data as such are precise but aesthetically impoverished. If, on the other hand, we come close to sensa by means of the participative experience, the sensa become fascinating and mysterious and take on depth. We discover the supposedly finite as complicated when we get down to it as presumably even the infinite would be. When sensa are bracketed without reduction and raptly contemplated, our vision penetrates through the skin of the sensa to their substratum. Then not only are the sensa intuited but the presence of their density comes to awareness. Their radiancy reveals a power—*Being*—that enlightens, that makes the sensa present and gives to our eyes an insight.

In this utter union with sensa we sense the beauty of reality. Sensa are the dress, as it were, of the homeland, and when we participate with sensa we feel the homeland they embody—the further reality which was always there but which we had ignored. For in our sifting of sensa into data we miss the glory of sensa, and, in turn, the charm that can lure us back to *Being*. Participative experiences occur with the sensa of nature, as Thoreau and many others have attested, but with abstractions the participation with sensa, other things being equal, is deeper because it is more concentrated. In seeing an abstraction the sensa "hold still," the lighting usually is unchanging, the mosquitoes do not distract, and other interruptions are less likely. More importantly, the abstract artist has arranged sensa in such a way that irrelevancies—including, especially, the connections of sensa with definite objects and events—are swept aside. "If the world were clear," as Camus insists, "art would not exist." The abstract artist purges from our sight the films of familiarity that confuse sensa, lets them be as they are, just as the pop artist clears away the covers of mundane objects disguised by repetition. Then our sight has a better chance of becoming insight.

Abstract painters with tender care seize sensa, the most transient aspects of reality, and make them stand still in their paintings. In the structure of an abstraction, sensa take on a powerful and pervasive static quality, timeless within time. The transience of the sensuous gives way to a steadily standing "now" that suggests everlastingness. No other art is so unchangeable—the light changes on the cathedral and the sculpture; music and the dance are always performed differently; the designative meanings of representational painting or literature or drama or the film acquire new connotations more rapidly because they are connected with definite objects and events. But an abstraction "is." No other thing in art or nature, unless it be the geological patterns in certain rocks, matches its unchangeability. Thus abstractions symbolize in a unique way the quality of endurance that significantly resembles the eternity of *Being*. Abstractions possess "icons of permanency." From the depths of the sensuous of an abstraction, *Being* comes to presence as everlasting.

Nothing more of *Being*, aside from something of its power, glory, and mystery, is revealed. But no other art interprets so convincingly the eternity that belongs only to *Being*. Every art reveals a new world, opens up some aspect of reality we had missed, but the world that abstractions reveal through the translucency of sensa has only one special specification—it endures. The horizon of this world is more distant and vague than the horizons of the worlds of the other arts. And the world of abstractions is left empty of definite times and places. Hence this world seems more "other," more the world of *Being-as-transcendental* than the world of man. This encompassing emptiness that permanently "is" makes abstractions especially appealing to mystics, and even leads a non-mystic such as Tillich to classify abstract painting as the mystic style *par excellence*. And that is why abstractions, even the frenzied works of some of the abstract expressionists, are calming. Nothing is so likely to save us from the slavery of functions as abstractions. Moreover, the revelation of the eternity of *Being* is reassuring. Despite the otherworldliness of the world that abstractions unveil, the celebration of sensa also unveils that world as benign in its eternal restfulness.

Mark Rothko's *Earth Greens* (Frontispiece) is an exceptional example of the "is-ness" of an abstraction. The underlying blue rectangle, cool and recessive, has a pronounced vertical emphasis (91½″ x 73½″), accented by the way the bands of blue gradually expand upward. However, the green and rusty-red rectangles, smaller but more prominent because they "stretch over" most of the blue, have a horizontal "lying down" emphasis that quiets the upward thrust. The vertical and the horizontal—the simplest, most universal, and potentially the most tightly "relatable" of all axes, but which in everyday experience usually are cut by diagonals and oblique curves or are strewn about chaotically—are brought together in perfect peace. This fulfilling harmony is enhanced by the way most of the lines of these rectangles are soft and slightly irregular, avoiding the stiffness of straight lines that isolate. Only the framing lines of the blue rectangle are strictly straight, serving to separate the three rectangles from the outside world. Within the firm frontal symmetry of this painting's world, the green rectangle is the most secure and weighty. This rectangle comes the closest to the stability of a square, the upper part occupying the actual center of the picture which, along with the lower blue border, provides an anchorage, and the location of the rectangle in the lower section of the painting suggests weight because in our world heavy objects seek and possess low places. But more important, this green, like so many earth colors, is a peculiarly quiet and immobile color. Kandinsky finds green generally an "earthly, self-satisfied repose." It is "the most restful color in existence, moves in no direction, has no corresponding appeal, such as joy, sorrow, or passion, demands nothing." Rothko's green, furthermore, has the texture of earth, thickening its appearance. Although in the green there are slight variations in hue, brightness, and saturation, their movement is congealed in a quiescent pattern. The green rectangle does not look as though it wanted to move to more suitable places. The rusty-red rectangle, on the other hand, is much less secure and weighty. Whereas the blue rectangle recedes and the green rectangle stays put, the rusty-red rectangle moves toward us, locking the green in depth between itself and the blue. Similarly, whereas the blue is cold and the rusty-red warm, the "temperature" of the green mediates between them. Unlike the blue and green rectangles, the rusty-red seems light and floating, irradiating vital energy. Not only is the rusty-red rectangle the smallest, but its winding, swelling shadows and the dynamism of its blurred, more obliquely oriented brush strokes produce an impression of self-contained movement that sustains this lovely shape like a soft cloud above the green below. This effect is enhanced by the blue lit up as if by starlight, thus serving as a kind of firmament for this sensuous world. Yet despite its amorphous inner activity, the rusty-red rectangle keeps its place, also, serenely harmonizing with its neighbors. Delicately, a pervasive violet tinge touches everything. And everything seems locked together forever, an image of eternity.

Abstractions charm and soothe our senses in laying bare the schema of the sensuous. But if we participate, the sensuousness of abstractions lures us on to an awareness of the benign eternity of *Being* in that which is most a becoming. Then our admiration becomes adoration.

II

In the participative experience with representational paintings, the sense of presentational immediacy, so over-whelming in the participative experience with abstractions, is somewhat weakened. Representational paintings possess signs or symbols that situate the sensuous in specific objects and events. These designations—unless we arbitrarily ignore them, as purists such as Clive Bell sometimes propose[18]— make place and time relevant associations. Causal efficacy is not given directly as in music, for a representational paint-ing, just as an abstraction, is "all there" and "holds still." But causal efficacy is felt indirectly because we are seeing portrayals of definite objects and events. Inevitably we become cognizant of place and date, and thus reflect about process. Our experience is a little more ordinary than the extraordinary isolation from specific objects and events that occurs in the perception of abstractions. Representational paintings always bring in some suggestion of "once upon a time." Hence we are not held quite so tightly in presenta-tional immediacy as with abstractions. We are kept a little closer to the kinds of experience of every day, moreover, because images that refer to specific objects and events usually lack something of the strangeness of images that refer only to the schema of the sensuous. Consequently representational paintings, other things being equal, are not quite so seductive as abstractions in charming us beyond our ontical habits.

Representational paintings, nevertheless, entice. Like ab-stractions, representational paintings have a framed "all-at-onceness." An action that in ordinary experience would be-come lost in another action is isolated. Moreover, the sensa of a representation, as of an abstraction, have an inner

---

18. *Art* (London: Chatto and Windus, 1914), p. 208: ". . . to appreciate a work of art we need bring with us nothing from life, no knowledge of its ideas and affairs, no familiarity with its emotions."

luminosity that lures beyond the surface and its meanings. The references to definite places and times are fused with the sensa, "held still" by the form for our leisurely contemplation, allowing us to penetrate into the depth dimension of the sensa and their references. Only abstractions seduce us more securely into durations dominated by presentational immediacy. Thus representational paintings open us to *Being* along the same path as abstractions—the path that soothes our restlessness and allows our vision raptly to focus. Abstractions, however, tend to calm us down more quickly and quietly, primarily because the world that abstractions reveal is an encompassing sensuousness empty of definite objects and events.

Representational painting furnishes the world of abstractions with definite objects and events. The horizon is sketched out more closely and clearly, and the spaces in the schema of the sensuous are filled in at least to some extent. If these furnishings are ontically oriented, *i.e.*, if the interpretation of something ontical is the primary subject matter, then the painting is secular. If these furnishings are ontologically oriented, *i.e.*, if the interpretation of *Being-as-transcendental* is the primary subject matter, then the painting is religious. This distinction, so important in the description of the role of art in the religious experience, needs careful elaboration.

All works of art, if the previous analysis has been correct, reach into the depth dimension of reality and interpret *Being*. All works of art in this sense are religious. This is the presupposition behind Tillich's claim that there is more religion in an apple by Cézanne than in a Jesus by Heinrich Hofmann.[19] Tillich is implying that the sickly sweet paintings of Hofmann are not even works of art, and presumably most of us would agree. However, to describe all works of art as religious not only defies ordinary and most systematic

---

19. "Art and Ultimate Reality," p. 10. There are three canvases by Hofmann in the Riverside Church in New York City. *Christ in Gethsemane,* painted in 1890, was especially irritating to Tillich.

Plate 1 Magdalen Master: *Madonna Enthroned* (c. 1270). Panel painting, 36⅝" x 53¾". Musée des Arts Decoratifs. Courtesy Alinari.

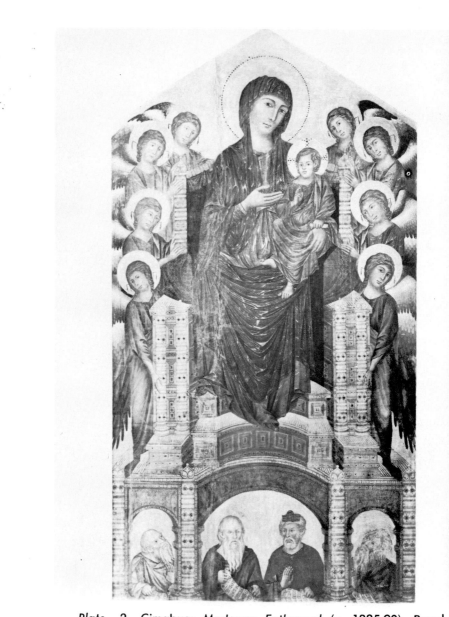

Plate 2 Cimabue: *Madonna Enthroned* (c. 1285-90). Panel painting, 151¾" x 78⅞". Uffizi, Florence. Courtesy Alinari.

Plate 3 Giotto: *Madonna and Child* (c. 1310). Panel painting, 128 3/16″ x 80⅜″. Uffizi, Florence. Courtesy Alinari.

Plate 4 Orcagna: *The Strozzi Altarpiece* (1357). Panel painting. Strozzi Chapel, Santa Maria Novella, Florence.
Courtesy Alinari.

Plate 5 Masaccio: *The Trinity* (c. 1427). Fresco. Santa Maria Novella, Florence. Courtesy Alinari.

Plate 6   Fra Filippo Lippi: *Madonna and Child with Angels*
(c. 1464). Panel painting, 36¼″ x 25″. Uffizi, Florence.
Courtesy Alinari.

Plate 7 Botticelli: *Madonna of the Pomegranate* (c. 1487). Panel painting, Tondo, 56¾" dia. Uffizi, Florence. Courtesy Alinari.

Plate. 8   Raphael: *Sistine Madonna* (c. 1513). 104″ x 77¼″.
Gemaeldegalerie Alte Meister, Dresden. Courtesy
Staatliche Kunstsammlungen, Dresden.

Plate 9 Grünewald: *The Crucifixion,* from the *Isenheim Altar-piece* (c. 1513-15). 105⅞″ x 120⅞″. Courtesy Musée Unterlinden, Colmar, France.

Plate 10 Parmigianino: *Portrait of a Young Prelate* (c. 1529). Panel painting, 20½″ x 16½″. Galleria Borghese, Rome. Courtesy Alinari.

Plate 11 Parmigianino: *Madonna with the Long Neck* (c. 1535). Panel painting, 84⅜″ x 52⅜″. Uffizi, Florence. Courtesy Alinari.

Plate 12 Bronzino: *Christ in Limbo* (1552). Panel painting, 174⅜" by 114½". Museum of Santa Croce, Florence. Courtesy Alinari.

Plate 13   Meindert Hobbema: *A Wooded Landscape* (1663).
37½" x 51⅜". Andrew Mellon Collection. Courtesy
The National Gallery of Art, Washington, D. C.

Plate 14 Photograph of Mte. Ste. Victoire. Courtesy John Rewald.

Plate 15 Cézanne: *Mte. Ste. Victoire* (1886-7). 23½″ x 28½″. Courtesy The Phillips Collection, Washington, D. C.

Plate 16   Van Gogh: *Cypresses* (1889). 36¾″ x 29½″. Courtesy
Metropolitan Museum of Art, New York City.

Plate 17   Jean Arp (originally Hans): *Mountain, Table, Anchors, Navel* (1925). Oil on cardboard with cutouts, 29⅝" x 23½". Collection, The Museum of Modern Art, New York City.

Plate 18   Pablo Picasso: *Guernica* (1937). Mural. Oil on canvas, 11'6" x 25'8". On extended loan to The Museum of Modern Art, New York City, from the artist.

language usage but it also leaves us without sufficient analytic tools to distinguish the differences in the religious roles
between, for example, abstract and representational painting. Within the representational field, moreover, there are
important differences that need to be clarified between works
that contain conventional symbols, such as Cimabue's
Madonna Enthroned (Plate 2), and those that do not, such
as Picasso's *Guernica* (Plate 18). Tillich, for example, has
praised *Guernica* as a great religious painting, but as acute
a critic of painting and philosopher of religion as Paul Weiss
sharply dissents.[20] Furthermore, works such as Parmigianino's
The Madonna with the Long Neck (Plate 11) and Bronzino's *Christ in Limbo* (Plate 12), although containing conventional symbols such as haloes, for example, are surely
religious, if at all, in a very different sense from Cimabue's
Madonna Enthroned. The problem of distinguishing religious painting, as well as religious art in general, has become
increasingly confused in recent writings. The following rule
has been generally used, although more implicitly than explicitly: if the primary subject matter of a work of art, that
which is basically interpreted, is ontological, then and only
then can the work be appropriately described as religious.
But how does one determine whether a work is ontologically
oriented? The answer has usually been: if conventional symbols are present. Much of Tillich's writing on religious art
has been a protest against this answer, and rightly so. But,
unfortunately, Tillich's own answer is not very clear.

All art is religious in the sense that every work of art is a
gift that not only has a special power to open us to *Being*
but interprets *Being*. The ontological is necessarily included,
therefore, in the content of every work of art. But so is the
ontical, of course, for the ontological can be revealed only
in and through the ontical. When, however, the ontological
content is interpreted as supremely important, as *Being-as-
transcendental,* then that work can be appropriately de-

20. *Religion and Art* (Milwaukee, Wis.: Marquette University Press, 1963),
   p. 13.

scribed without qualification as religious. Then and then only will it be readily apparent, although this may require very careful critical inspection, that the ontological is the primary subject matter. *Both* religious feeling and conventional symbols must be portrayed, or it will not be readily apparent that the ontological subject matter dominates the ontical, that *Being-as-transcendental* is the basic content. Iconic symbols may be present in a work of art without any conventional reinforcements, of course—for example, the icon of permanency in abstractions; but iconic symbols when used for religious purposes, for reasons that will be explored in this as well as the next chapter, must draw in conventional symbols. Without the addition of a convention, an iconic symbol cannot function as a "religious symbol." Conversely, all conventional symbols that function religiously must have, I shall maintain, an iconic foundation.

Unless conventional symbols are basic to the content and presented within a context of awe, the ontological dimension will not be revealed as sacred, *i.e., Being-as-transcendental*. A conventional symbol becomes a religious symbol only within an awe-full context. Thus Parmigianino's *The Madonna with the Long Neck* (Plate 11) is a secular work because of the absence of expression of religious feeling, possessing conventional symbols but lacking religious symbols. In this work the reference to *Being* is explicit but not awe-full. On the other hand, the ultimate concern portrayed in *Guernica* (Plate 18) is so deep that its source and redemption imply *Being-as-transcendental*. That is why Tillich describes *Guernica* as a religious painting. Yet this description is strained because of the absence of conventional symbols. If conventional symbols were there, they surely would be religious. In *Guernica* the reference to *Being* is awe-full but implicit. Ordinary language usage tenaciously denies the term *religious* as appropriately descriptive of any work of art that does not include in its content both an awe-full and explicit reference to a further reality. Unless both are present, it will not be readily apparent, even after extended critical analysis, that the ontological has been interpreted as sacred. It is useful, in a matter of such wide popular concern, to respect this usage.

The depth of the religious dimension may be penetrated in a painting or any work of art on three descending levels. On the first level, there is some interpretation of *Being* involving iconic symbolism, as in abstract painting that is a work of art, without any portrayal of religious feeling or conventional symbols. All works of art must include the religious dimension to at least this extent. This is the content that distinguishes works of art from works of decoration, *i.e.,* works that attract our contemplative attention to their surface but go no further, that please but do not inform because their forms lack the force to draw us beyond the surface.

On the second level, there is in addition the portrayal of an awe-full context—including either the suggestion or a rendering of such religious feelings as ultimate concern, reverence, and peace—as somehow derivative from an awareness of the ontological. Thus the concern portrayed in *Guernica* is so deep that its source and its redemption imply *Being-as-transcendental.* That is why the concern is ultimate or ontological rather than ontical. It is inappropriate, nevertheless, to describe *Guernica* as anything more than implicitly religious. There are no conventional symbols, no codifications that stabilize and stand for what *Being* has meant or means to man, nothing that refers to traditional or current theoretical or practical or sociological forms of expression about *Being.* Iconic symbolism, the means of the first level of interpretation, is too vague to make the interpretation of *Being* explicit. If the reference to *Being* is to become explicit, stipulations must be added to clarify the meanings suggested by the iconic symbolism. Thus *Guernica* only implies *Being-as-transcendental,* points to a further reality in its devastating representation of what the ontical "is" when it becomes man's supreme value. *Guernica* calls us back to *Being* by suggesting that "something else" beside secular values ought to be supreme, but that "something else," unlike fascism and Franco as signified by the bull, is given no explicit interpretation. In this sense, as so often in Oriental art, *Being* is left largely a blank. And this is something less than *Being* as sacred, at least in the West.

On the third level, finally, there is the further addition of conventional symbols. When these symbols are used within a governing context in which religious feeling is portrayed—as in Cimabue's *Madonna Enthroned* (Plate 2) and Grünewald's *Crucifixion* (Plate 9) —then the work can be appropriately described as explicitly religious or simply religious. All religious works must include these three levels of the depth dimension. Thus *The Madonna with the Long Neck* fails to be religious because no religious feeling is expressed. In such a context, the conventional symbols appear perfunctory if not profane. Thus *Guernica* fails to be religious because despite the presence of religious feeling there is no explicit reference to *Being* by means of conventional symbols. In both cases, one of the levels of the depth dimension is missing, and so *Being* fails to be interpreted as *Being-astranscendental,* as sacred.

A study of the evolution of Florentine Renaissance painting is especially revealing with respect to this three-level distinction, for in no other period in the West is the conflict between the ontical and the ontological as the primary subject matter of art so sharply engaged. This conflict in art mirrored the conflict in Florentine society.[21] Florence in the eleventh, twelfth, and thirteenth centuries was making great strides in bending nature, for the first time since the Roman Empire, to man's needs. A resurgence in confidence in the powers of man began to clash with the medieval view that

---

21. Art always reflects, directly or indirectly, the fundamental values of the society in which it functions. But no single formula, such as most Marxist theorists provide, can explain this highly complex relationship. See my "The Imperatives of Stylistic Development: Psychological and Formal," *Bucknell Review* 11 (March 1963) : 53–70 and "The Sociological Imperative of Stylistic Development," *Bucknell Review* 11 (Dec. 1963) : 54–80.

man was nothing without God, that nature was valuable only as a stepping stone to heaven, that, as St. Peter Damiani in the first half of the eleventh century asserted, "the world is so filthy with vices that any holy mind is befouled by even thinking of it." The emerging view was not yet "man is the measure of all things," but the honor of being a man began to be taken seriously, an idea that "was to traverse all later Italian art like the muffled, persistent sound of a subterranean river" (Malraux). This is not the place to try to trace the strife between the ideologies of the Middle Ages and the Renaissance—a vast literature going back to Burckhardt exists—but an analysis in some detail of a few typical paintings from the Florentine milieu from the thirteenth through the sixteenth centuries will illustrate how religious or sacred paintings can be distinguished from nonreligious or secular paintings. Sometimes, especially in works of the latter half of the fifteenth century, a clear separation will be impossible. This should not be surprising. Every work of art has a surface and a depth, an ontical and an ontological side, and in a work of art the two dimensions may be given more or less equal emphasis. In art that is clearly religious, however, not only is the ontical subordinated to the ontological but the ontological is interpreted as supremely important, worthy therefore of the portrayal of such feelings as ultimate concern, reverence, and peace. Such portrayal leads to some form of explicit interpretation of *Being-as-transcendental,* and this, in turn, requires conventional symbols. There are other ways by which religious art can be distinguished, of course, but hopefully the following analysis may serve as one useful paradigm not only for painting but for the other arts as well.

In Florence and Tuscany in the thirteenth and fourteenth centuries, paintings were servants of the Church. Thus paintings invariably contained conventional Christian symbols such as haloes, crowns, the blessing gesture of the Child, and the like, as in the central panel of the Magdalen Master's *Madonna Enthroned* (Plate 1), c. 1270. Everything ontical in this panel is subordinated to the portrayal of theoretical, practical, and sociological expressions of the medieval Catholic conception of the sacred. For example, the Child is portrayed as divine (mainly a theoretical expression), as the mediator between us and God (mainly a practical expression), and as a king or prince (mainly a sociological expression). The ontical, furthermore, is interpreted as completely dependent on and almost completely separate from its source of existence—the ontological. The sacred comes very close to being represented as *Being-as-absolute,* for the Madonna and Child are barely incarnated in this world. It is impossible, of course, to interpret *Being-as-absolute* "absolutely," as totally "ab-solved" from all beings, for this would negate the possibility of any portrayal of *Being* whatsoever. But the Magdalen Master's panel is typical of the way the artists of the thirteenth and the immediately preceding centuries came as close as possible to representing *Being-as-absolute* absolutely. Thus the Madonna and Child are bilaterally immobile, symmetrically and compactly enclosed, and their fantastic sizes relative to the bit-like donor at the bottom left of the throne resist any reference to *Being* as incarnate in this world. The Madonna and Child are interpreted more as emblems rather than as living embodiments of the divine. "Love not the world, neither the things that are in the world. . . . For all that is in the world . . . passeth away" (2 John: 15–17). And so the human qualities of the Madonna and Child are barely recognizable. Note, for example, how the fish-shaped, long-tailed eyes of the Madonna cannot blink, and how the popping pupils stare out and slightly up in a Sphinx-like glance that seems fixed forever. Her features are written large and seem added rather than molded with the head. Only in the careful tender way she holds the Child is there any hint of human sorrow and affection. The spirits of this Madonna and Child belong to a supernatural world; and their bodies are hardly bodies at all, but, in the words of St. Thomas Aquinas, "corporeal metaphors of spiritual things." The ontical is mainly appearance, a secondary reality. The ontological is the primary reality.

Nevertheless the ontical, even if it is interpreted as appearance, appears very powerfully indeed, for this panel is a very fine work of art. The sensa shine forth, especially the glimmering gold, the crystal cabochons set in the crowns of the Madonna and Child, and the rhythmic, sharply edged lines. We are lured by the sensa and their designs beyond mere illustrations of doctrine by images. We are caught up in durations of presentational immediacy. But, unlike our experience of abstractions, these durations include, because of the conventional symbols, doctrinal interpretations of the ontological. And if we participate we "understand"— even if we disagree—rather than having mere "knowledge of" these doctrines. The expressions of ultimate concern, reverence, and peace in the Saints and donor provide a context in which the conventional symbols are unlikely to be mistaken for signs by the sensitive recipient, even if he does not know the conventions of the symbols. This painting is the kind of work that can be appropriately described without qualification as religious, *i.e.*, explicitly religious.

Cimabue, active c. 1272–1303, is the ancestral Adam of Florence's very gradual movement in art away from the sacred to the secular. The Cenni di Pepi of the documents, with the apparently opprobrious nickname of Cimabue or Oxhead, is a somewhat legendary character, and, as with Adam, we cannot be certain that he is the beginning. In the first place, the beginning of Florentine Renaissance painting in a sense goes back to the very beginning of Western art, a rather vague Eden. In the second place, other artists in Tuscany during the thirteenth century, such as Bonaventura Berlinghieri, Coppo di Marcovaldo, and Duccio di Buoninsegna, were shyly beginning to enliven the emblematic human and divine figures that had dominated the Western visual arts since the Romans. Moreover, Cimabue's humanization just emerges, but after Cimabue there begins a march toward the secular that ends in the sixteenth century with an exaltation of the secular at the expense of the sacred, an exodus that in retrospect seems as predestined as the story of Adam and his progeny.

To begin Florentine Renaissance painting with Cimabue may seem strange, for he is usually classified, however uncomfortably, as Byzantine, and for good reasons early Renaissance painting usually is begun with Masaccio in the first quarter of the fifteenth century. But periods of art, however necessary for analysis, are conventions, and the currents of artistic styles flow through the nets of sharply drawn analytic divisions. The pre-classic period of the Florentine Renaissance—so far as incarnating the ontological more securely and broadly into the ontical is concerned, and the massive and powerful unrealized possibilities that are suggested and opened up by this development—goes back to work such as Cimabue's *Madonna Enthroned* (Plate 2), c. 1285–90, at least 135 years before Masaccio's Carmine frescoes, c. 1422–27, and over 200 years before the classic or High Renaissance period, c. 1490–1520.

The figures in Ciambue's *Madonna Enthroned* at first sight seem lacking in human liveliness. The fine hands of the Madonna, for example, are extremely stylized. Moreover, the geometricized facial features of the Madonna, very similar to those of the angels, and the stiff, unnaturally regular features of the Child certainly would appear as masks if somehow they were to be inserted into a painting of the classic period such as Raphael's *The Sistine Madonna* (Plate 8), c. 1513. But Cimabue's Madonna and Child begin to grow and glow in liveliness, the ontical begins to seem to have its own intrinsic values, when Cimabue's panel is juxtaposed with contemporary paintings, such as the Magdalen Master's *Madonna Enthroned* (Plate 1). Only in the context of its tradition can a work of art be fully understood and in turn fully appreciated.

Cimabue had assimilated from the Byzantine tradition its conventions, hierography, technical perfection, and richness of detail. He enriched that inheritance, and in turn helped break the ground for the Renaissance, by endowing the old

style with more liveliness and mixing the divine into the
human, as in this panel, by revealing human emotions in the
Madonna. The inert passivity of the Byzantine and the hard
dogmatic grimness of the Tuscan style, both so evident in
the Magdalen Master's work, are revitalized with a spiritual
subtlety and psychic awareness, a warmth and tenderness
that make unforgettable the Madonna's benevolently in-
clined face, to which one returns with unwearying delight.
"Credette Cimabue nella pittura Tener lo campo" (Dante).
With this face begins the scaling down of the divine into this
world. The anthropocentric view is beginning to focus. A
human face has awakened! And it leans forward to come
more closely into spiritual contact with us. Its liveliness fell
like a refreshing shower on a parched and long-neglected
soil, and from that soil a new world began to rise.

Brown-gold tones play softly across the Madonna's features, merging them organically despite the incisive lines,
setting the background for the sweeping eyebrows and
large, deep eye sockets that form a stage on which the
pathetic eyes play their drama of tragic foreknowledge.
These eyes seem to pulsate with the beat of the soul because
they are more flexible than the eyes in contemporary paintings—the irises rest comfortably and dreamily within their
whites, the delicately curved lids, now shortened, detach
themselves gracefully to meet neatly at the inner pockets,
and the doubling line of the lower lid is replaced by fragile
shadows that flow into the cheeks and nose. Although the
Greek or bridgeless nose is still high and marked, furthermore, by a conspicuous triangle, the sensitive modeling of
the nose, its dainty shape, and the tucking in of the pinched
tip help blend it into the general perspective of the face.
Light shadows fall under the shapely chin to the slender
neck and around the cheeks to merge indistinctly with the
surrounding veil, whose heavy shadows add to the contemplative atmosphere. But the full lips, depressed at the
corners and tightly drawn far to the left, add a contrasting
touch of intensity, even grimness, to what otherwise would

be pure poignancy. The immense, exquisitely decorated throne, with the bristling and curiously vehement prophets below, enhances by its contrasting monumentality the feminine gentleness of the Virgin, whose large size, relative to the angels and prophets, is minimized by her robe, one of the loveliest in Western art with its close-meshed lines of gold feathering over the cascading folds. In a skillfully worked counterpoint, the angel heads and the rainbow-colored wings form an angular rhythm that tenses toward, and then quietly pauses at, the Madonna's face. This pause is sustained by the simple dotted edge of the centered halo and by the shape of the pedimental top of the rectangular frame. The facial features of the angels superficially resemble the Virgin's, especially the almond-shaped eyes separated by the stencil-like triangles and the heavy mouths squared at the corners. Nevertheless they lack the refined qualities and liveliness that betray so feelingly the soulful sadness of the Madonna. Now in the City of Florence

> . . . Mercy has a human heart,
> Pity a human face,
> And Love, the human form divine,
> And Peace, the human dress.
> William Blake

But into this peaceful hush that spreads around her sound with anguished apprehension the tragic tones of the Pietà, like the melody of a Requiem continued by our imaginations into the pregnant pause.

In Cimabue's panel, unlike the Magdalen Master's, there is no longer the sure suggestion of *Being-as-absolute*. The ontological and the ontical are only narrowly joined, but the juncture seems much more secure. *Being* is portrayed as clearly immanent at least in some things—the Madonna, Child, and Saints—but the emphasis, of course, is upon the transcendency of *Being*. There is not the slightest hint of the secular taking precedence over the sacred. However, this precedence will come, so much so that by the post-classic or Mannerist period, c. 1520–1600, the sacred is often played with sacrilegiously, as in Bronzino's *Christ in Limbo* (Plate 12), 1552. Cimabue began interpreting in his art, as did St. Francis in his life, the ontological as unmistakably immanent in some areas in the natural world. The Platonic fracture between the World of *Being* and the World of Becoming begins to be healed. And the artists of the first half of the fourteenth century, for the most part, continued the healing process.

Cimabue, according to the legend reported by Ghiberti and embellished by Vasari,

> going one day on some business of his own from Florence to Vespignano, found Giotto, while his sheep were browsing, portraying a sheep from nature on a flat and polished slab, with a stone slightly pointed, without having learnt any method of doing this from others, but only from nature; whence Cimabue, standing fast all in a marvel, asked him if he wished to go live with him. The child answered that, his father consenting, he would go willingly. Cimabue then asking this from Bondone, the latter lovingly granted it to him, and . . . in a short time, assisted by nature and taught by Cimabue, the child not only equalled the manner of his master, but became so good an imitator of nature that he banished completely that rude Greek manner and revived the modern and good art of painting, introducing the portraying well from nature of living people.[22]

Dante confirms: "Ora ha Giotto il grido."

Although Giotto, 1266 (or 1276)–1336, may have received his earliest training from Cimabue, his stylistic links are much closer to the Roman School of fresco painters, particularly Pietro Cavalini and the Isaac Master of Assisi,[23] and the Gothic sculptural tradition as represented in Tuscany by Arnolfo di Cambio and Giovanni Pisano. Giotto's *Madonna and Child* (Plate 3), painted about 1310 for the

---

22. *Lives of the Most Eminent Painters, Sculptors and Architects,* trans. Gaston Duc Devere (London: Macmillan and Co., 1912), 1: 72.
23. Millard Meiss claims that Giotto is the Isaac Master. *Giotto and Assisi* (New York: New York University Press, 1960).

Church of the Ognissanti, now hangs beside Cimabue's *Madonna Enthroned* in the first room of the Uffizi. The contrast is striking. Cimabue's Madonna, who seems to float into our world, is abruptly brought to earth by Giotto; or, as Ruskin puts it, now we have Mama. She sits solidly, bell-shaped, without evasion, in three-dimensional space subject to gravitational forces, and her frank, focused gaze is alerted to her surroundings, whereas Cimabue's Madonna, oblivious of space, is steeped in moodiness. The forms of Giotto's Madonna seem to have been abstracted, however radically, from nature, whereas Cimabue seems to have started from Byzantine forms. In subject matter Giotto seems to have begun from Here, whereas Cimabue seems to have begun from Hereafter.

The eyes of Giotto's Madonna, surrounded by her high forehead and the immense cheeks, have a fascinating asymmetry that gives her face a mark of idiosyncrasy and adds to its liveliness. The fish-shaped left eye with its half-covered pupil is twisted to the left so that it appears to be looking in a different direction from the more realistic right eye. Yet since this is not quite obvious, the resulting tension fixes our attention and heightens our feeling of being caught in her level gaze, which gains further intensity by being the focus of the gazes of the saints and angels. Since the open space below the Madonna provides the observer with a figurative path of access, we are directly engaged with her in a way that Cimabue carefully avoids by, among other devices, putting the throne of his Madonna on a high-arched platform and then placing the little prophets within the arches. The smallness of the sensual mouth of Giotto's Madonna, barely wider than the breadth of her long and snouty nose, accentuates its expressiveness, and for the first time the lips of a Madonna open, however slightly, shyly revealing two teeth, as if she were about to gasp or speak. It does not matter, for the mobility of inner responsiveness is conveyed. Everything else expresses her stoicism, a rock-like kind of endurance—the untooled, centered halo, the steady gaze, the calm, impersonal expression, the cool and silvery skin color with green underpainting that suggests bone structures beneath, the heavy jay and tower-like neck, the long unbroken verticals and broad sweeping curves of the simply colored robe and tunic, the firm hand that no longer points but holds, and, above all, her upright monumental massiveness, as solid as if hewn in granite. The angels and saints are compactly arranged in depth and stand on the same ground as the earthly throne. Although the saints express peace and the angels awe, they are natural beings, not imaginary supporters of a heavenly throne as in Cimabue's picture.

The Child shares with his mother the monumentality of Giotto's style—the square, forthright head, the powerful body, the physical density and solidity that led the Caracci school to describe Giotto's figures as statues. Giotto's Child, compared with Cimabue's, seems almost coarse, especially in the shaping of the hands and feet, and the incorrect indication of his position from a naturalistic standpoint is physically much more uncomfortable, primarily because such a standpoint is almost irrelevant in Cimabue's picture. The hair and ears are not so stylized as in Cimabue's Child, light and shadow sink more organically into the flesh, the eyes and nose are given the most realistic rendition up to that time, and the expression is dynamically alert. Yet the lack of irregularity and flexibility in these less conventional features combined with the effect of maturity in miniature keeps the Child from being Baby. (Shortly thereafter the Baby came in the work of Bernardo Daddi, active c. 1312-1348.) Giotto's painting is clearly religious, but not quite so obviously as the paintings of the Magdalen Master and Cimabue. The portrayal of religious feeling is not quite so strong, and for the first time in Florence there is the suggestion, however muted, of the secular challenging the sacred. If Mama gets much more earthy and independent, then the ontological no longer would be represented as *Being-as-transcendental*.

The Black Death of 1348, class warfare, economic recessions, and severe setbacks in foreign affairs retarded the secu-

lar trend in the second half of the fourteenth century. In reaction to the "bad times," Florence experienced a revival of
the Old Testament, of *Being-as-absolute*. The Franciscan,
humanizing realism set in motion by Cimabue and Giotto and
carried on by Giotteschi such as Daddi and Maso di Banco
was slowed down or even reversed, as in Orcagna's great
Altarpiece (Plate 4), 1357, in the Strozzi Chapel of Santa
Maria Novella, a work of Dominican severity. The medieval
dogma of the chasm between the sacred and the secular,
with the secular in complete subservience, gains ascendency
once again.

In the early fifteenth century, following the impact of the
International Gothic style, the secular revives, especially in
the work of Masaccio, active c. 1418–1428, for example *The
Trinity* (Plate 5), 1427, in Santa Maria Novella. "Giotto
born again, starting where death had cut short his advance,
instantly making his own all that had been gained during
his absence, and profiting from the new conditions, the new
demands—imagine such an avatar, and you will understand
Masaccio."[24] And following Masaccio for the next one hundred years there is a rapid advance toward humanization,
realism and secularism: a result not only of what in retrospect seems to be an inevitable stylistic evolution but also,
very generally speaking, of "good times." There is an unmistakable shift away from even the suggestion of *Being-
as-absolute,* and the interpretation of *Being-as-transcendental*
tends to give way to the interpretation of *Being-as-immanent*.
Moreover, more and more works are not even implicitly
religious. Increasing numbers of paintings have secular subject matters. Portraiture, for example, becomes widely popular for the first time. Man, moreover, is usually interpreted
as supremely self-confident, as in the work of Castagno and
Piero della Francesca. Even in as religious a painter as Fra
Angelico, man is given a beauty and dignity that places his
work firmly in the Renaissance.

---

24. Bernard Berenson, *The Florentine Painters of the Renaissance* (New
York: G. P. Putnam's Sons, 1909), p. 27.

Most of Angelico's contemporaries, even when they used conventional symbols, usually failed, unlike Angelico, to place them in a context that clearly expressed religious feeling. In place of the harmonious synthesis of secular values with the ontological as interpreted by conventional symbols, as in the work of Giotto, Masaccio, and Angelico, a pulling apart of the secular and the sacred is often apparent. For example, Fra Filippo Lippi, c. 1409–1469, after an early Masaccesque period, usually painted Madonnas with Angelico's chaste regularity of feature. The delicacy of the Madonna's face in the *Madonna and Child with Angels* (Plate 6), c. 1464, is further emphasized by its contrast with the large, heavy features of the Child and the roguish angels, typed from the street urchins of Florence. On the one hand, there is an appealing and pathetic melancholy in this girlish, transparently pale face, suggesting an untouched purity. There is an ethereal, dreamlike quality about her, pointed up by the magic mountain, the wraithlike veil and halo, and her strange placement in relation to the frame. On the other hand, there is also fashion in this face—the plucked eyebrows, the elaborate headdress with its dainty ornaments, and the vaulty forehead, artificially produced at that time by plucking the hair. Charles de Tolnay even suggests that this Madonna is modeled after Lippi's famous mistress, Lucrezia Buti, and the Child is Lippi himself in a dream scene of love.[25] There is, in any case, an unresolved tension here between Eros and Agapé.

Many of Botticelli's works reveal a deeper kind of ambivalence. For example, *The Madonna of the Pomegranate* (Plate 7), c. 1487, illustrates Botticelli's genius for opening up the inner mansions of the soul. Although Lippi's demure Madonna is vaguely sad, we sense that it is only a feeling of the moment, whereas the utterly woebegone forlornness of Botticelli's Madonna is plainly beyond transitory changes, her emotions wound so tightly around the central spool of

25. "The Autobiographic Aspect of Fra Filippo Lippi's Virgins," *Gazette des Beaux-Arts* 39 (1952).

her self that no unwinding seems possible. The portrayal of despair in this Madonna seems almost profane, for there seems to be no saving grace. The fact that she is the Madonna and the presence of the other conventional symbols make this despair, unlike that expressed in *Guernica* (Plate 18), absolute. In *Guernica* there is the suggestion, however vague, that somehow redemption is possible if we can find "the way." In Botticelli's painting, however, "the way" is explicitly interpreted, and yet apparently it is of no help whatever. The Madonna's gloom permeates through the somber heavenly light of what appears to be a slowly revolving sphere, affecting the circling angels and the pathetic Child, who is so depressed he can barely raise his hand in blessing, while his other hand lies on the pomegranate, sign of the Fall. Not only does the Virgin seem to be absorbed in the tragedy of her Child's future, but there is something of a sensual reference as well—note the exquisite hands, as if she regrets the renunciation of the natural pleasures of life that conflict with her divine motherhood. Alien and outcast, she seems completely alone. Reverence and peace are lacking here; and so in a way is ultimate concern, for the concern seems as much centered on the secular as the sacred. This work is neither quite religious nor nonreligious.

Most paintings from 1450 to 1490 are more clearly secular, lacking the portrayal of religious feeling or conventional symbols or both. Even when conventional symbols are used, the portrayal of religious feeling is often so weak that the use of the symbols appears perfunctory, apparently a matter oftentimes of fulfilling the terms of the commission. There are many exceptions, for example Botticelli's *St. Augustine in his Study,* 1480, in the Church of the Ognissanti, but the trend toward the secular is unmistakable.

In the classic or High Renaissance period, c. 1490–1520, the depth dimension, when portrayed on the third level, *i.e.,* with conventional symbols, is usually not treated sacrilegiously; but generally the depth dimension seems to be not much more than a backdrop for displaying the secular.

For example, Raphael's *Sistine Madonna* (Plate 8), c. 1513, replete with the ease of execution, economy, and monumentality of the High Renaissance style, has a theatrical-tableau quality even without the drawn curtains. The Madonna is almost just a very beautiful woman, the Child almost just a handsome baby, and both are carefully posed. St. Sixtus and St. Barbara wear their reverence like performers, and the puckish putti are just kids with attached wings. The effect is stunning, but the second level of the depth dimension, the portrayal of religious feeling, is so superficial for critics such as Tillich that the content of the work for them is more secular than sacred. On the other hand, for critics such as John W. Dixon, Jr., "the harmonious humanity of his (Raphael's) figures is handled with such grace and dignity that they communicate the sweetness of an earth newly seen."[26] For Tillich this kind of sweetness is sentimentality; for Dixon it is a celebration of the transfiguration of nature by the divine. In any case, readily apparent religious works, such as Michelangelo's ceiling frescoes in the Sistine Chapel, 1508–1512, which are recognized as religious by almost all contemporary critics of whatever persuasion, are the exception rather than the rule.

In the post-classic Renaissance or Mannerist period, c. 1520–1600, conventional symbols often should be simply ignored, as in Francesco Parmigianino's *The Madonna with the Long Neck* (Plate 11), c. 1535. Parmigianino, 1503–1540, was a North Italian who never worked in Florence and may never have been there. He was raised in Parma on the styles of Francia and Correggio, imbibing Francia's version of the classic canons, not quite so strict as Florence's, and skill and grace from Correggio. In 1523 Parmigianino moved to Rome, where he encountered the Florentine style more directly, mainly through the work of Raphael and Il Rosso. Vasari reports a transmigration of Raphael's spirit into Parmigianino. However that may be, the soft painterly grace

26. *Nature and Grace in Art* (Chapel Hill, N. C.: University of North Carolina Press, 1964), p. 133.

that already was established in the young Francesco's style
under Correggio's influence was polished in Rome, no doubt
accelerated by contact with Raphael's style, into the svelte
sheen and cadential contours that produced the most exquisite style of the Italian Renaissance.

The Madonna with the Long Neck was never quite finished, and so far as we know Parmigianino did not provide
a title. There is no reason to believe, however, that he would
have objected to Vasari's naming the panel *The Virgin and
Sleeping Child.* Most of the earliest references use the title
Madonna, Child, and Angels, and the first mention of *The
Madonna with the Long Neck,* so far as I have been able to
discover, occurs in D'Argeuville's *Abgégé de la vie des plus
fameux peintres* (Paris, 1745), 1:224. Who provided this
unflattering title is unknown, but probably it was so called
after the acquisition of the painting by the Medici and its
removal from the Chiesa dei Servi in Parma to Florence in
1698. Badly hung and preserved in the Palazzo Pitti until
in recent years it was moved to the Uffizi, it generally has
been an object of derision. Burckhardt in the *Cicerone* of
1855 complains of its "unsupportable affectation," and, somewhat more tolerantly, of "the bringing of the manners of the
great world divertingly into the holy scenes." Yet, if there ever
has been a picture in which conventional symbols are an
external formula for the interpretation of the secular, it
surely is *The Madonna with the Long Neck.*

Although natural structures are suggested, they are not
interpreted as natural. The light is neither quite indoors nor
outdoors, the perspectives are inconsistent, gravity is defied,
the bodies are artificially proportioned and drained of mass
and physical power, the protagonists are psychologically detached from one another, and above all the poreless porcelain
facial features allow no hint of liveliness. Thus the head of
the Madonna is shaped like a well-wrought urn, while the
ears, set out abnormally in order to emphasize their serpen-
tine calligraphy, look like its handles. The nerveless skin is
unnaturally cold and pale, glazed like ceramics, and beneath

that polished surface the urn seems hollow. Hence the pure geometrical design of the fastidious lines of the eyebrows, eyes, nose, and mouth is assembled on a surface without organic foundation—no pulsating blood coursing through arteries and veins integrates these features, and no muscular structure can move them. And so the gaze down upon the Child—the most lifeless Child of the Renaissance—is too stylized and superficial to be expressive of any psychic meaning, let alone sacramental intensity. Like an Attic amphora the head of the Madonna rises from its swanlike neck, while the hair decorates the lid with the preciosity of Cellini's goldwork. The features of the angels are similarly constructed, exchangeable like coins, being made even more masklike by the repetition, a device that increases rigidity, as Bergson has shown.

If the subject matter of *The Madonna with the Long Neck* is a sacred scene, then Burckhardt's denunciation of "insupportable affectation" is certainly justified. If, however, the conventional symbols are no more than a support for an interpretation of line, color, volume, and texture, then Burckhardt's denunciation is irrelevant. To meet this painting halfway—and surely this is the responsibility of every serious viewer—the religious conventions must be dismissed, and then the subject matter can be experienced properly as secular. The design of this delicate work, this "splendor of form shining on the proportionate parts of matter," ought to bring one to a better understanding and appreciation of the rhythmic qualities of line, the sinuous sensuousness of spiraling shapes, the fluidity of bulkless volumes, and the cooling, calming powers of certain textures and colors, but this heretical design, despite its lifting flow, will never waft you to a Christian Heaven on the wings of faith.

The Madonna with the Long Neck is such a magnificently secular work of art that the excommunication of the conventional symbols is rather easily accomplished, at least in our day. Abstract painting has opened our eyes to the intrinsic value of sensa, and *The Madonna with the Long*

Neck is a kind of abstract painting. In lesser works than Parmigianino's, however, such as Bronzino's *Christ in Limbo* (Plate 12), 1552, the quality of the work is so much poorer that the use of conventional symbols is a parody. Christ advances with an affected dancing step, his curled and perfumed face[27] almost indistinguishable from the man in profile immediately to the right and the man whose figure is cut by the frame. The aphrodisiac figure of Mary, posing between these two men, would better grace a poster of a Pigalle nightclub. All the bodies are over-muscular but unexercised and listless, a cold, contorted, claustrophobic display of strip-tease sensuality. Despite the inclusion of conventional symbols, I know of no better example of a work of art—if it is[28]—that is so clearly nonreligious.

In nonportraiture the Mannerists took the secular trend begun by Cimabue to its final conclusions. When they used conventional symbols at all, their treatment of them generally was either perfunctory or profane. There are exceptions, for example in some of the last works of Parmigianino's—such as the *Madonna with St. Stephen and John the Baptist*, 1540—where the conventional symbols are portrayed within a religious context of reverence. For the most part, however, religious feeling when it is portrayed is implicit and is found mainly in portraiture. The same Mannerists— for example, Parmigianino, Bronzino, Pontormo, Salviati, and Il Rosso—who usually used conventional symbols as props in nonportraiture, rarely used conventional symbols in portraiture and yet often portrayed an ultimate concern that implies *Being-as-transcendental*. It is as if their profane use of conventional symbols in glorifying the secular in nonportraiture found expiation in portraiture. The close-up face

27. More precisely, these facial features are a mask. For the distinctions between "face," "effigy," and "mask," see my "On Portraiture: Some Distinctions," *The Journal of Aesthetics and Art Criticism* 20 (Sept. 1961) : 61–72.
28. We should be careful about dismissing too quickly such works as nonart. See my "On Enjoying Decadence," *The Journal of Aesthetics and Art Criticism* 17 (June 1959) : 441–46.

of Parmigianino's *Young Prelate* (Plate 10), c. 1529, for example, seems to be experiencing the "vanity of vanities." The mild, magnificent eyes of this sensitive prelate seem to be gleaming replies and rebuttals to our questions, while his unavoidable gaze both meets us and withdraws. He seems accessible and yet diffident, as if shy or fearful of disclosing his thoughts, cautiously probing us while defending himself against our probing, and his lips seem about to part either in greeting or in a mumbled excuse for departure. Although the volume of his face is not exceptionally large, it appears so because it almost fills the frame. This helps bring our contact so close that we seem to perceive the beating of the pulse, while the outlines of the nose are blurred, as when we are overly close to an object, thrown further out of focus by the way his eyes draw our attention. The effect of immediacy and spontaneity is overwhelming. The prelate asserts his individuality by intruding into the present moment, just as when we meet an interesting person the uniqueness of his personality dominates; whereas later, as we reflect upon him, we begin to type him by fitting his personality into the framework of our preconceptions. It is as if Parmigianino had lain in ambush before his sitter, waiting and spying for a Joycean "epiphany." And what he caught was the smothered inquietude, the concern so profound that only the absence of *Being* seems to explain it. Such portraits as this,[29] despite the lack of conventional symbols, are far more religious than paintings such as *The Madonna with the Long Neck* (Plate 11) and *Christ in Limbo* (Plate 12), just as *Guernica* (Plate 18) is far more religious than the paintings of Heinrich Hofmann. But it is clearer and, in turn, more useful to describe works such as *The Young Prelate* and *Guernica* as no more than implicitly religious. Religious art without qualification must include not only the first but both the second and third levels of the depth dimension.

Only representational painting can be religious painting

---

29. For further examples, see my "Spiritual Asymmetry in Portraiture," *The British Journal of Aesthetics* 5 (Jan. 1965): 6–13.

without qualification. Abstractions, other things being equal, are more likely to open us to *Being* because they free our perception from both time and temporality. Thus abstractions are more extraordinary, more likely to cut us loose from our ontical habits. Moreover, abstractions interpret *Being* through the icon of permanency and sometimes a plausible case can be made that they portray religious feeling—for example, that ultimate concern is revealed in Gorky's *Agony,* reverence in Kandinsky's *Élan tranquille,* and peace in Malevitch's *White Square on a White Background.* The plausibility for such interpretations is increased when we remember that there is considerable consensus that representational paintings such as landscapes lacking any significant depiction of human beings may nevertheless portray religious feeling—for example, ultimate concern in Van Gogh's *Cypresses* (Plate 16), reverence in Cézanne's *Mte. Ste. Victoire* (Plate 15), and peace in Hobbema's *A Wooded Landscape* (Plate 13). But, in any case, since abstractions do not portray conventional symbols, what they can reveal about *Being* remains vague, and however profound, the interpretation is very narrowly confined. Abstractions cannot be more than implicitly religious. On the other hand the representational painter, because he can include conventional symbols, can interpret *Being* with much greater precision and breadth. The representational painter who is also a religious painter tends both to sensa and those codified meanings which man through the ages has used to relate himself and pay homage to the ground of his being. The abstract painter is a Shepherd of sensa; the religious painter is a Shepherd of symbols.

5

Literature and Immanent Recall

Literature—the verbal art that usually is read but can be heard—guides us to *Being* by helping us become aware of where we have already been. In the participative experience of anything, the present always dominates, for the given "thinks in us," and the given can do this only if it holds our attention in the vivid immediacy of the present. Yet because of the given's qualities and the way the given refers, the sense of the future or the past may coalesce more or less strongly with the present. Thus within the always controlling context of the intensive present, the sense of the future comes to the fore as we listen to music. The percepta of music, because they are presented successively, awaken in us the desire for tracing out the temporal curve that is coming. The possibilities ahead draw our attention to the future. On the other hand, the present so completely dominates our participation with paintings, especially abstractions, that both future and past, although not irrelevant, are kept at the fringe of our attention. The percepta of painting, because of the allurement of their sensuousness and their nonsuccessive presentation, draw us into an unusual unification with the "here-now." In our participation with literature, however, the inheritance of the past fills in the present with exceptional plenitude. On the one hand, the percepta of literature, *i.e.,* words, unless in the rare case that they are being heard rather than read, lack the power of the successive presentation of music. Thus the pull of the future is not so demanding. On the other hand, words rarely possess the sensuosity and, consequently, the attractiveness of the percepta of painting. Thus the push of the present is not so intense. Hence literature is able to bring the past into the present in such a way that what was initially more or less insignificant becomes significant. The unfocused becomes focused by means of words—as though the events that had existed before the words, sometimes long before, needed time for the words to arrive and give names to them. Before that lapse of time language was utilitarian, theoretical, or merely chatter, the noise of things. But now the naming of language embraces the event, and a miraculous metamorphosis takes place. Language becomes the dwelling place for the *Being* of past things to come to presence. This is the logos of language. The poet and the novelist by tending to words are Shepherds of the past.

"Language," as Friedrich Schlegel noted, "is the great collective memory of the human race." Words are haunted with meanings from the past. But when we sacrifice the present for the future, as so often in everyday experience, words degenerate into counters, things to be manipulated. The poet and the novelist, however, have piety toward words. They arrange them in such a way that the words reveal, if we attend, something of their past through how and what they designate. What they designate in part is something of the depth dimension of the things they name, and because of the vast scope and flexibility of language these things can be anything. Literature, in turn, makes it possible for the depth dimension of my past to be recuperated and comprehended, reestablishing between me and myself communications that seemingly had perished. By resurrecting the *Being* of my past, literature brings me back to an explicit awareness of both my spiritual continuity and my ontological roots. The superimposing of the *Being* of the past on the present forces my ego to come out in such a way that I recognize not only that I am something more than "I think therefore I am" but also that what is deepest in me is not of me. The opening up of my interior reality simultaneously opens up my awareness of exterior reality. Literature is double-edged. How literature sharpens our ontological sensitivities will be the subject of the first section of this chapter. How literature interprets *Being* will be the subject of the second.

I

The given of every work of art is a "mediated immediacy." What is given directly to our senses is the "immediacy," the physically given—in literature the look and sound and rhythm of words, the feel of the percepta and their embodied references. What is given indirectly is the "mediated," the imaginatively given—in literature the designative references of the words. The immediate and mediate are fused in our participation with a work of art because we get to the mediated only through sensitive attention to the immediate. The qualities and the embodied references of the words have intrinsic values that must be perceived if we are to fully understand the designations of the words. The language of literature resists—we encounter it. The language of non-literature is permeable—we see straight through it. The language of literature is a force rather than a transparency. In other words, translucent icons are at the center of a verbal work that is literature. In a verbal work that is nonliterature, translucent icons, if present at all, are peripheral. Sometimes in, for example, Plato's *Phaedrus.*
the place of the translucent icons is not easily determined, as
Literature has many species. In lyric poetry the qualities of the words, such as accent, tone, and texture, and their

embodied references, such as assonance, alliteration, and rhythm, generally are more translucent than, at the other extreme, prose fiction. In the first section of the Choric Song from Tennyson's "The Lotus-Eaters," for instance, the designations on one level refer to a river valley and its objects. The last four lines are:

> Here are cool mosses deep,
> And thro' the moss the ivies creep,
> And in the stream the long-leaved flowers weep,
> And from the craggy ledge the poppy hangs in sleep.

The languid texture of the words, especially the soft hush of the "o's" and "s's," the smoothness of the alliteration and assonance, the slow, regular iambic rhythm, the gradual lengthening of the lines, and the gentle tone of quietness form a translucent icon that, like a prism, colors the first level of designative meanings and bends them into the basic and unifying reference—the heavy sleepiness of sleep. That is why these lines cannot be explained by reference to the objects mentioned in them or paraphrased without essential loss of meaning, for an essential part of the meaning depends on the qualities of the words and their arrangements. The very texture of the words, like the sculptural relief of a print, are impressed into the designative meanings. In prose fiction this also is the case, although not quite so obviously. The immediate is less alluring than in lyric poetry, because, among other reasons, the range of designations is usually far wider and more complex. Our attention focuses more on the mediate than on the immediate because the mediate is carrying the main weight of meaning. Yet no fiction could be participated with if we saw straight through its words. Without some translucent control by the immediate, we would dominate. The given would not think in us but we would think about the given. Improper distance would be established—we would be spectators. To be insensitive to the short, hurried, chopped-up, aggressive qualities of the words and sentences in Hemingway's *To Have and Have Not* is to mis-understand much of what this language designates. In *The Sound and the Fury*, we understand Benjy's mental defi-ciencies not just by understanding the designation of the words that flow through his consciousness but by understand-ing the way they flow. The embodied references of a work of art are the focus of its form, and these embodied references fuse with the designative references, the focus of the content of a work of art. Form and content are phenomenologically indistinguishable. Artistic form is not a kind of envelope that contains its content.

Literature generally has less immediacy than the other arts because words generally are less sensuous and, in turn, less enticing than the percepta of the other arts. On the other hand, the unparalleled power and flexibility of words to designate permits literary works to reveal worlds with a breadth and specificity that no other art can begin to rival. In participating with literature, the subordination of the immediate to the mediate, compared to the other arts, re-sults in our imaginations being less strictly controlled. There is, consequently, more danger that we will not give ourselves to the given. The fact that a poem or a novel, unless it is being read to us, is largely at our disposal as to pace of read-ing increases this danger. Despite the necessary linearity of all linguistic expressions, the mind has time to look around. What saves us from this break in participation, if anything, is the way our past fills in and adds intensity of interest to the "imaginary construction"—the unity of words and their meanings that is the literary work as it is being actualized in our awareness. Memory provides the cement that binds the construction together.

All conscious experience is temporal, an awareness of at least the immediate future and the immediate past as in-herent in the present. Consciousness of a "now" is always a duration of a present that spreads forward and backward. Unlike the points of time that can be abstracted from dura-tions, consciousness, as William James puts it, is never a knife-edge but a saddle back "with a certain breadth of its own on which we sit perched, and from which we look into two directions. . . . The unit of composition of our perception . . . is a *duration,* with a bow and a stern, as it were— a rearward- and a forward-looking end. It is only as parts of this *duration-block* that the relation of succession of one end to the other is perceived."[1] And it is only *after* the duration, as James, Bergson, Husserl, Whitehead, Heidegger, and many others have pointed out, that these parts and their succession can be distinguished. I am listening to a tone. At the beginning of this duration the "now accent," the vivid immediacy, is A followed by B, C, and so forth. As the now accent shifts to B, the sounding of A is retained, echoing as just past, and C is anticipated as just coming. The A and C are felt as continuous, mixed in, with the B. In the succeeding phase of the duration, the now accent is on the C, with B fading off and A fading off even further. In the next phase, A may drop out entirely and, if so, A is no longer a part of the present duration. A, then, is no longer a part of the immediate past but becomes a part of the finished past, the past that no longer is retained. In this "running off phenomenon" as Husserl describes it, memory is "primary" as long as it holds the echoes of the immediate past within the present duration. Apparently for most of us, primary memory endures no longer than about twelve seconds.[2] However that may be, in a relatively short period of time the echoes of the A fade out completely from the now accent. The A can still be recalled, of course, but then the A comes back carrying the sense of the finished past. Furthermore, as James insists, "the reproduction of an event *after* it has once completely dropped out of the rearward end of the specious present [duration], is an entirely different psychic fact from its direct perception in the specious present as a thing immediately past."[3] The memory of the finished past is reproduc-

---

1. *The Principles of Psychology* (New York: H. Holt and Co., 1890) , 1: 609f.
2. *Ibid.,* pp. 612ff.
3. *Ibid.,* p. 630.

tive or "secondary," for instead of mere retention as in primary memory, the past must be brought back, "re-presented." In Husserlian terminology, secondary memory has a different "intention" from that of primary memory.[4] However, secondary memory is dependent upon primary memory, for without retention there would be nothing to recall. That does not mean that I am explicitly aware of the retention of primary memory. When I begin a sentence I do not say to myself that I have begun it, and yet I must retain that beginning or I would not be able to proceed. Primary memory involves only implicit awareness of the past. Secondary memory, on the other hand, is much more likely to be explicitly aware of the past as past. Both primary and secondary memory are involved in the participation with every work of art, of course, but with a literary work our secondary memory is activated in an extraordinary way. By bringing back the finished past involuntarily, literature opens up for us its particular path to *Being*.

Voluntary recall is a deliberate act in which we remember because it helps us with some present problem. I recall the date and place of my birth in order to fill out the passport form in order to arrange for my vacation. Voluntary recall is a practical memory, a vassal of the intelligence, referring back to the past in order to manipulate the present for the sake of the future. Thus K.'s memory in *The Castle* by Kafka is almost invariably voluntary, striving to recall anything that might help him get in contact with the Castle's authorities. Thus Jason in *The Sound and the Fury* remembers in order to scheme for better things to come. There is always a knowledge of the track of time in voluntary recall, of measurable events strung out in an irreversible order, of a clear disassociation of past from present from future. There is a sense of retrogression as we remember the past that can-

---

4. For an extended analysis of the differences between primary and secondary memory, see Edmund Husserl, *The Phenomenology of Internal Time Consciousness*, ed. Martin Heidegger, trans. James S. Churchill (Bloomington, Ind.: Indiana University Press, 1964), pp. 40–70.

not be again, a sense of progression as we imagine the future that is coming, and a sense of the fugitive present, unfulfilled because of our anticipations of the future. When forethought completely preoccupies our minds, as is usually the case, we are filled with restlessness. K. and Jason are in a constant lather because their past and present are meaningless except as a means to something better ahead. Launched only for the future, sailing ceaselessly beyond themselves, they are never satisfied because they are always preparing to be satisfied.

Involuntary recall is a nondeliberate act of consciousness in which something in the present, because of some resemblance or association, spontaneously triggers off a memory.[5] There are two basic kinds of involuntary recall—bifurcated and immanent. In bifurcated recall the evocation of the past excludes the present from the center of attention, the present serving as a springboard that, once used, is ignored. In immanent recall, however, the present remains in the center of attention, the past mingling in and merging with the present. In bifurcated recall the motion is centripetal, away from the present to the past. In immanent recall, conversely, the motion is centrifugal, the past being pulled back into the present. Immanent recall, unlike both voluntary recall and bifurcated recall, is an affective memory, for the past is "refelt" as if it were present. Immanent recall, unlike primary memory, does not retain the immediate past in the present but brings back the finished past into the present. The past is not represented as in bifurcated recall but "re-presented." Or, to put it another way, immanent recall makes a recollection feel like a perception.

When Proust, as he described it in *Remembrance of Things Past,* dipped a bit of madeleine cake into a cup of linden tea, he was on his way to the recapture of the past. Everything that took form and solidity had sprung from his cup of tea. Yet, since the memories stirred up, although involuntary, refused fusion with the cup of tea, the recall was bifurcated. On the other hand, hawthorns invariably excited

---

5. See James, *Principles of Psychology* 1: chap. 14 and 661ff.

in Proust involuntary memories that combined with the hawthorns, examples of immanent recall:

> I found the whole path throbbing with the fragrance of haw-thorn-blossom. The hedge resembled a series of chapels, whose walls were no longer visible under the mountains of flowers that were heaped upon their altars; while underneath, the sun cast a square of light upon the ground, as though it had shone in upon them through a window; the scent that swept out over me from them was as rich, and as circumscribed in its range, as though I had been standing before the Lady-altar, and the flowers, themselves adorned also, held out each its little bunch of glittering stamens with an air of inattention, fine, radiating "nerves" in the flamboyant style of architecture, like those which, in church, framed the stair to the rood-loft or closed the perpendicular tracery of the windows.[6]

And on and on, but as the images spread out, the hawthorns still remain in the center of Proust's vision, his memories of the church and other things interweaving with the flowers. Furthermore, we know, for Proust analyzed the phenomenon of immanent recall with remarkable acuity, that this recall was not a matter of "forcing metaphors" but depended upon the grace of chance. "It is a labour in vain to attempt to re-capture it [the past]: all the efforts of our intellect must prove futile. The past is hidden somewhere outside the realm, beyond the reach of intellect, in some material object (in the sensation which that material object will give us) which we do not suspect. And as for that object, it depends on chance whether we come upon it or not before we our-selves must die."[7]

In primary memory there is no more than an implicit awareness of the immediate past. Since the past is so close to the present and so involved with it, there is no explicit awareness of the past as past. In voluntary recall, on the other hand, there is explicit awareness of the past because our

---

6. *Swann's Way*, trans. C. K. Scott Moncrieff (New York: Random House, The Modern Library, 1928) , pp. 196f.
7. *Ibid.*, p. 61.

intention to recall clearly locates our memory as focused on the past. In involuntary recall of the bifurcated type, there is also explicit awareness of the past, for we sense the present as a springboard into the past which is clearly disassociated from the present. In involuntary recall of the immanent type, however, the awareness of the past as past is stronger than in primary memory, for the past that is called back is the finished past. On the other hand, the sense of the past is weaker than in bifurcated recall because the present stays in the center of our attention. In participating with music, the immanent recall of the designative references is entirely implicit. The awareness of the designative references, the structure of the feeling of tragic tenderness, for example, in the "Pie Jesu" section of Fauré's *Requiem,* immanently recalls the "feel" of that kind of emotion which I have experienced in the past. With great increase in awareness, I feel what I have felt before. But if I explicitly recalled those emotions or the situations that evoked them, the music would pass me by and my participation would be broken. In participating with paintings, the immanent recall of designative references is likely to be more explicit. The gaiety of color that sings in Booth's *April 2, 1960* (Plate II), for example, may immanently recall the "feel" of the felicities of many an April day. Moreover, even explicit memories of the emotions and even the settings that evoked them may mingle with those colors, for we can take all the time we want. Explicit recall does not break our participation with paintings as it does with music. Yet, generally, it is much more likely that explicit awareness of the past will occur with literature.

The designations of literature, in the first place, are far broader in scope than those of music and painting, and thus the possibilities for the reaches of reminiscence are far greater. In turn, our powers of memory and our need to use them are much more strongly activated. Second, in our participation with literature as compared with music, there is more time for our memories—both of the work and of our personal pasts that are relevant to the work—to become a part of the imaginary construction. The words of literature like the tones of music are presented successively, it is true, but this presentation is not so pressing. In reading most novels, for example, we are usually very much interested in what is going to happen, but we can take our time in getting there. And the sense of the present in participating with literature, although dominant, is also not so overwhelming as in the participation with painting, because words are not so sensuously enticing as colors, lines, light, and textures. Third, the vast majority of works of literature are presented in the past tense, inducing a mood of unhurried, meditative retrospection.[8] Thus as we proceed to build the imaginary construction, following the blueprint provided by the words, memories have a very favorable framework within which to return at least implicitly and sometimes explicitly.

Whether the immanent recall is explicit or not depends largely upon two basic factors—the repetition, if any, of the participation, and the degree of resemblance of the imaginary construction to our personal pasts. In the first reading of a poem or novel, our attention is usually so absorbed in anticipating and constructing that the immanent recall of our own past is largely implicit. In later readings, however, the demands upon our imaginations in actualizing the literary work are less urgent. Reconstruction is less demanding than construction. Thus more conscious energy is available for becoming explicitly aware of the memories surging up from the depths. The situation is analogous to our awareness of unrealized possibilities in participating with music. Until we have grasped the form of the music, a matter of at least one and usually several listenings, unrealized possibilities

8. On the role of tense in literature, see John Crowe Ransom, "The Tense of Poetry," in *The World's Body* (New York: Charles Scribner's Sons, 1938); Theodore Meyer Greene, *The Arts and the Art of Criticism* (Princeton: Princeton University Press, 1940), chap. 9, sec. 6; and Suzanne K. Langer, *Feeling and Form* (New York: Charles Scribner's Sons, 1953), pp. 264–66. Langer claims that the "primary illusion" of "poesis" is the creation of "virtual history," and literature proper presents that history in "the mode of memory."

are a vague massive foreground that act as a lure for feeling. In further listenings this foreground becomes increasingly differentiated (see above, chapter 3). With literature, as with all the arts, a nebulous foreground of unrealized possibilities also plays a role, and further readings bring this foreground into sharper focus. But with literature, unlike music, the past rather than the future, the background rather than the foreground, supplies the larger and far more important penumbral region. With rereadings this background becomes more luminous.

I first read Tolstoy's *Anna Karenina* many years ago, and my recent second reading was a very different experience. In my first reading I was mainly absorbed in what was going to happen to Anna and Vronsky. In my second reading, since I knew the ending and how it came about, more conscious energy was available for immanent recall both of events in the novel and in my own life. My antecedent knowledge of the plot in the second reading, however, does not entirely account for the more explicit role of immanent recall. *Anna Karenina,* I suspect, is a novel that cannot be fully appreciated by the very young. Their experiences are not closely indentifiable with Tolstoy's story. When the imaginary construction more closely resembles our past, immanent recall is almost always wider in scope and more explicit. Even on first reading, *The Catcher in the Rye* by Salinger brought forth for me exceptional explicit awareness of my past. Pencey Prep was modeled after Valley Forge Military Academy in Wayne, Pennsylvania, and Salinger had been there two years before me. The "phoniness" of such schools and of the Stradlaters, Ackleys, and Spencers were an integral part of my past also, hence immanent explicit memories packed into my participation much more vividly than the memories aroused by *Anna Karenina* even on second reading. Direct or relatively direct experience of the subject matter of a literary work, other things being equal, is likely to evoke more explicit recall than vicarious experience.

A literary work will make our experience participatory

only if the work significantly resembles, is iconic with, something from our past. Otherwise our imaginary constructing will be more like carrying out an engineering project than a participative experience. However, the iconic relation is not necessarily a close resemblance of fiction to historical fact, as the early chapters of *The Catcher in the Rye* are to me. The fiction need be iconic only in some significant respect with something of importance from our past, some analogy, however strange, with something deep within ourselves. Thus Orwell's *1984* for me is far more ahistorical than *The Catcher in the Rye*—in all likelihood this would not be the case for a refugee from totalitarianism—but *1984* also engages my participation because it mirrors with fantastic clarity where I think I may be going because of what has been. Céline's *Journey to the End of the Night,* on the other hand, fails to engage my participation because his depiction of man as animal, unlike Orwell's depiction of animal as man in *Animal Farm,* leaves very little of man. Céline's characters have only a slight resemblance to humanity as I have experienced it, and so his novel elicits for me very little immanent recall. In order to inform, a literary work must reform fact, but not to the point of losing all significant factual connection. The creator of literature does violence to facts, probes beneath their surface, in order to give us insight into the depth meanings of those facts. The proposition that near Philadelphia, Pennsylvania, there is a school named Pencey Prep is false. But Salinger's fiction about this imaginary school reveals, as no set of true propositions about schools such as Valley Forge Military Academy possibly can, the clandestine underside of such schools, "what makes them tick." Conversely, *Journey to the End of the Night,* although very skillfully composed, distorts facts so far that the illusion has only a scintilla of significant resemblance to reality. Coleridge's "Kubla Khan" and Bunyan's *Pilgrim's Progress* are far more fanciful than *Journey to the End of the Night,* and yet, in their much more roundabout way they maintain a significant resemblance to reality because they reveal something of the depth of that reality. Likewise, *The Catcher in the Rye* is a partial lie that informs, whereas *Journey to the End of the Night* comes so close to being a total lie that its form fails to inform. Salinger's violence to the facts, unlike Céline's, is a pious violence.

In a work of literature the events of life are simplified, and hence much more fully perceivable than the jumble of happenings in any person's actual history. In ordinary experience there is usually an invasion of irrelevant doings and divided interests and a congestion of too many objects beyond our power of assimilation. Everyday experience is usually dominated by negative prehensions because our resources of feeling are insufficient to meet and respond to all the imposing objects and events. Without the ability to ignore, we would simply break down. We have to manage ourselves in the world of things, and most of the time survival demands that we disregard many things and manipulate the rest. And so, for the most part, the significance of things passes us by. Yet at times we remember, and memory is the great organizer of consciousness. Memory tends to simplify and compose our past perceptions into more understandable units. Past experience as we remember it—unless that past experience was participative—usually takes on more form and character, shows us a little more of the qualities of a thing and its significance, more of a person's personality, for example, than vague looks and utterances. Memory not only may gain perspective on the past but normally tends to thresh out some of the irrelevancies of the past. That is why, incidentally, those who are presumably blessed with photographic memories actually carry a curse. The perspective of the nonphotographic memory, with its power to gather and foreshorten, enables us to make some sense out of what otherwise would remain mainly diffused and confused. A collection becomes a totality.

Yet even then this focusing power of memory, unless we are literary artists, is very limited. But with the help of literature, this limited power of perspective that memory provides is greatly magnified. In literature selection of the significant already has been made. Whatever is there, for the most part at least, is already significant—that is one of the reasons the work is literature—and it is not too much, as usually in life, to be comprehended. Thus Proust found in the novel not just the recapture of the past but the meaning of the past:

> The novelist's happy discovery was to think of substituting for those opaque sections, impenetrable by the human spirit, their equivalent in immaterial sections, things, that is, which the spirit can assimilate to itself. After which it matters not that the actions, the feelings of this new order of creatures appear to us in the guise of truth, since we have made them our own, since it is in ourselves that they are happening, that they are holding in thrall, while we turn over, feverishly, the pages of the book, our quickened breath and staring eyes. And once the novelist has brought us to that state, in which . . . every emotion is multiplied ten-fold, into which his book comes to disturb us as might a dream, but a dream more lucid, and of a more lasting impression, than those which come to us in sleep; why, then, for the space of an hour he sets free within us all the joys and sorrows in the world, a few of which, only, we should have to spend years of our actual life in getting to know, and the keenest, the most intense of which would never have been revealed to us because the slow course of their development stops our perception of them. It is the same in life; the heart changes, and that is our worst misfortune; but we learn of it only from reading or by imagination; for in reality its alteration, like that of certain natural phenomena, is so gradual that, even if we are able to distinguish, successively, each of its different states, we are still spared the actual sensation of change.[9]

The gift of the literary artist enables us to gain a further perspective on our past that supplements the perspective of memory. That is why the participative experience with a literary work is so illuminating. No psychological, sociological, or philosophical treatise can rival Ralph Ellison's *The Invisible Man,* for example, in revealing the situation of the Blacks in the United States in the early twentieth century.

9. *Swann's Way,* pp. 118f.

Positivists will deny this, of course, but their denial is inconsistent with the objectivity they so rigidly and passionately avow. Rather, the positivists protect their egos by denying what they cannot feel and therefore cannot understand.

The work of literature develops the new and the work of memory develops the old, but both proceed on parallel tracks. We recognize the imaginary construction of the literary work as a new world, as an illusion that never was and never will be. Yet this virtual world will evoke our intense response if it calls up an ensemble of experiences already lived, whose resonances prolong themselves within the new world. Then the new or present world and the old world firmly join together, for the present plunges its roots into the past and draws therefrom its strength. The past with its breadth gives depth to the present. The past comes in, furthermore, cleansed from necessity. The strain is over. The compulsions have been outlived. Immersed in *The Invisible Man,* for example, a white man immanently recalls his experiences with Black people without worrying about what he should do or say next, without the despotism of the fear and guilt that has clouded those relationships. Thus the past comes back purified, just as murky water, having run underground for awhile, emerges as clean spring water.

In this fusion of new and old, temporality is felt as dominating time. The sense of "once upon a time" is always there; and especially in the novel, at least until the work of Joyce, Proust, Faulkner, Gide, Beckett, and the "anti-novelists," there is usually also a fairly clear presentation of events as sequential. But the surging up of immanent recall dislocates and weakens our sense of chronological time even in "historical novels" such as Tolstoy's *War and Peace.* The feeling of temporality, especially of the union of past with present, throws our sense of time out of gear. By eliminating the sharp differences between what is presently perceived and constructed and what is remembered, the literary work creates in us a unity of present and past independent to some extent of chronological order. Here again the participative experience with a literary work is isomorphic with memory—both are more in temporality than in time. Our memories store experiences in such a way that affinities and associations based on analogies and contrasts are more relevant than time sequences. Similarly, even with novels that present strict chronologies, such as Richardson's *Pamela* and Dickens's *Great Expectations,* our immanent recalls, some of which may come from great distances, give us a feeling of being free to some extent from time. As reminiscences reverberate in and around, a multiplication develops within the framework of the imaginary construction in such a way that the distinction between present and past is weakened. Thus in our participation with a literary work there is usually some sense of the déjà vu, the already seen, especially when the immanent recall is explicit. We feel the originality and virtuality of the imaginary construction, feel that we have never been here before; and yet, paradoxically, we also feel, because of immanent recall, that we have been here before. Thus Coleridge in his sonnet "To John Thelwall":

> Oft o'er my brain does that strange rapture roll
> Which makes the present (while its brief fit lasts)
> Seem a mere semblance of some unknown past. . . .

It is this awareness of "once upon a time" and yet of being "outside time," the ambivalent feeling of both the past and yet the past as re-presented as present, that makes our participation with literature so extraordinary.

The imaginary construction attracts memories as the rod attracts lightning. Then the power of the past, like the heat and rays of a fire, rises from the depths, extending its warmth and splendor into the participative experience.

> Not the intense moment
> Isolated, with no before and after,
> But a lifetime burning in every moment. . . .
> T. S. Eliot, "East Coker"

This warmth may even loosen the inhibiting ice that blocks our repressions. Then the resistance so carefully built up out of hurt and fear and guilt breaks down, and then we are invaded with memories that rarely if ever had surfaced. The power of literature in bringing back the past, I suspect, may often exceed the power of the psychoanalysts. In any case, there is the feeling of exceptional intimacy with ourselves, so rare because of the everyday fear of self that will not let itself go. But the attraction of the imaginary construction, if we participate, makes us forget our fear and there is a letting go. We identify with the imaginary construction, and in doing so something of our "deep I," as Bergson named it, comes to presence. Our doubt about the integrity of our identity because of the feeling of vast voids in our spiritual continuity, the most terrorizing perhaps of all our doubts, is overcome to some extent. The immanent recall of the past fills in some of these voids. Fusion succeeds fission. We reassemble and come to rest with ourselves. And in this healing rest we sense that what is deepest in the "deep I" is not of us. We have been opened to *Being*.

II

Literature, because of the scope and flexibility of words, can bring back the depth dimension of anything. Any work of literature reveals the *Being* or depth dimension of something. A secular work, such as *The Catcher in the Rye,* does not interpret the reaction to the depth dimension awe-fully. *Being*-as-immanent is revealed but not *Being-as-transcendental,* and so the basis, the objective correlative, for the expression of awe is lacking. A work that is implicitly religious, such as *The Invisible Man,* interprets the reaction to the depth dimension awe-fully because *Being-as-transcendental* is suggested, but there is no explicit interpretation of that transcendency. As the "I" of *The Invisible Man* confronts the tragedies of reality, his concern becomes ultimate, suggesting as its correlative the depth dimension as a whole that somehow transcends the things in which it is immanent. But, like Picasso's *Guernica* (Plate 18), there is no explicit articulation of *Being-as-transcendental* as part of the content. Ellison makes no attempt to "say something" about *Being-as-transcendental,* except in a very secondary way through the character of Mary. A work that is explicitly religious, such as Bernanos's *The Diary of a Country Priest,* not only interprets the reaction to the depth dimension awe-fully but also explicitly interprets the transcendency of that depth dimension. In a secular work, to put it another way, *Being* is revealed but not as ultimately important. In a work that is implicitly religious, *Being* is revealed as ultimately important but the transcendency of *Being* that accounts for this ultimacy is not interpreted but only suggested. In a work that is explicitly religious, *Being* is revealed as ultimately important and the transcendency of *Being* that makes this importance possible is interpreted. That does not mean, however, that a work that is explicitly religious is necessarily better artistically than a work that is implicitly religious, or that either is necessarily better artistically than a secular work. Almost all critics agree that Tolstoy's *Anna Karenina* is artistically better than his *Resurrection.* Furthermore, and paradoxically, even the religious quality of a work may be stronger in a secular work than in either kind of religious work. A good case can be made, for example, that *The Catcher in the Rye* possesses more religious quality than *Resurrection* or even than *The Diary of a Country Priest.* Such would not be the case in art if "other things were equal," but these other things rarely are.

For *Being-as-transcendental* to be interpreted, symbols are necessarily a part of the means. When, furthermore, these symbols are conventional and traditional and are interpreted within an awe-full context, as in *The Diary of a Country Priest* and Eliot's *Four Quartets,* the symbols become religious symbols. Although all religious symbols are grounded in some iconic relation[10]—the purifying power of water, for instance, significantly resembles the purifying power of *Being*—the iconic symbolism alone is too illusive to function as a religious symbol. Thus the use of water for baptismal services requires the addition of conventional meanings, just as music with iconic symbols usually requires a program before it is useful in religious ceremonies. In order to pin down something of the iconic meaning clearly and distinctly so that it can be easily communicated and shared in a religious community, conventional meaning is imposed upon the iconic symbol.

Conventional symbols are either traditional, *i.e.*, a generally understood body of meanings, as in *The Diary of a Country Priest;* or nontraditional, as in Lawrence's *Lady Chatterley's Lover,* where sex organs and acts are used as symbols. Sometimes *Being-as-transcendental* seems to be interpreted without the use of symbols. Thus in the editorially omniscient and didactic passages in Hardy's *Tess of the D'Urbervilles,* the author uses such phrases as "the President of the Immortals" in place of "God."[11] But actually Hardy is referring not to *Being* but to a being. "The President of the Immortals" is a sign, not a symbol. Symbols are a necessary part of the means of interpreting *Being* without reducing the mystery of *Being* to a problem, *Being* to a being. However, the presence of symbols, iconic or conventional, in a work of art is no guarantee that the work is either implicitly or explicitly religious. Even the conventional and traditional symbol will function religiously only if it is within an awe-full context. All symbols point to *Being,* but only religious symbols point to *Being* awe-fully. A religious symbol is an outward, visible communication of an inward grace that functions within a religious com-

---

10. See, for example, Edwyn Bevan, *Symbolism and Belief* (New York: The Macmillan Co., 1938) , and Philip Wheelwright, *The Burning Fountain* (Bloomington, Ind.: Indiana University Press, 1954) .

11. In the 1892 Harper and Brothers edition, "Archsatirist" is used in place of "the President of the Immortals."

munity. Aristotle's "Prime Mover," like Hardy's "the President of the Immortals," is a sign, for it refers to a being, however supreme. A cross placed on the blackboard for demonstration purposes in a course on the Christian religion is a conventional symbol. A cross in the Roman catacombs is a religious symbol. Parmigianino's *The Madonna with the Long Neck* (Plate 11) contains conventional symbols. Cimabue's *Madonna Enthroned* (Plate 2) contains religious symbols. Religious symbols possess iconic and conventional elements; they are traditional; and they are within an awe-full context. Without religious symbols, there cannot be a language of the sacred.

All symbols originate from the need to express and retain in clear and consolidated perceptible forms man's insights about his participation with *Being* and its consequences. When a participative experience is strongly coercive, resulting in such religious feelings as ultimate concern, reverence, and peace, there is usually a desire not only to "say something" about *Being*, to try at least to corner its mystery, but also to show how this participation with *Being* affects or should affect our lives. Private religious feeling tends to express itself in communion with others. And, as Wach has demonstrated (see chapter 1 above), there are three basic forms of religious expression—theoretical, practical, and sociological. The artistic form of religious expression, in turn, is a synthesis that includes these basic forms as part of its subject matter. All of these forms of expression move the privacy of the coercive participative experience into the public domain. This is the beginning of any religion as an institution.

Iconic symbols alone are too subtle and provisional for institutional purposes. Stipulations must be added to the iconic foundation if the symbol is to become a religious symbol. Thus only conventional symbols are able to communicate the often very complicated and always mysterious ultimate meanings of participative experiences in simple and concentrated forms, easily intelligible to the unsophisticated.

Thus religious symbols are socially rooted and supported. Without communal acceptance, a symbol cannot become a religious symbol. Thus D. H. Lawrence's conventional symbols have not become religious symbols. If a conventional symbol is too difficult for most of the people of a religious community to comprehend to some extent, it will not become a religious symbol. On the other hand, the clarity of the religious symbol must not completely obscure the numinous character of its ultimate meanings. The religious symbol must carry the mystery of *Being* like a misty halo around a clearly delineated head. The religious symbol is a peculiar compound that includes, as in Michelangelo's *Pietà* in the Duomo of Florence, both clarity and ambivalence. If clarity is absent, the conventional symbol will be too esoteric for institutional purposes, as with most of the symbols in the poetry of William Butler Yeats. If ambivalence is absent, the conventional symbol will fail to suggest the mystery of its referent, as with the "symbols" used by the deistic John Toland in *Christianity not Mysterious* (1696). In the context of Toland's usage, what are usually symbols have become signs. Parts of a religious symbol must be clearly outlined by means of convention, but the religious symbol as a whole can never be circumscribed within definite boundaries. In the final analysis a symbol, whether religious or nonreligious, is bottomless, having depths that no soundings can plumb satisfactorily. That is why an exact conceptual statement of the total meaning of a symbol is impossible. Whatever you say about a symbol, unlike a sign, is ultimately inadequate. That is why a symbol, unlike a sign, cannot be exchanged.

Symbols are consolidations that are more or less self-sufficient. In order to lighten the presentation, I shall use "symbol," unless otherwise qualified, to mean conventional symbol. But it should be remembered that the stipulations of conventional symbols are always added to an iconic foundation. Symbols are shorthand expressions that point to something about *Being*. Thus the word *symbol* is derived from the Greek verb *symballein,* meaning "to bring together." Symbols unify and simplify a complex of beliefs and ideas often ambiguous and uncertain and always highly associative in meaning. In order to unify and simplify and, at the same time, be easily intelligible, symbols must be vividly perceptible. Thus symbols find their most natural habitat in the concrete embodiment of the visual image and, when presented verbally, symbols suggest sensuous figurations to our imaginations. But symbols in language, such as "God," are syntheses that, unlike symbols in the plastic media, invite unending analyses. Symbols as visual images lead into themselves, whereas symbols as words lead away from themselves. Symbols in language, even in literature, tend to be caught up in elaborations or explanations, or even, as in Dante and Dostoevski sometimes, in theological and philosophical systems. In this movement the *Gestalt* of the imaginary picture is weakened, sometimes to the point where the symbol disappears into a sign in a theology or philosophy or ideology. It is extremely difficult, in any case, to isolate any word or a few words in our comprehension, except as a child or foreigner learning a language in bits and pieces, because any word is very much a part of an intricate and wide web of linguistic interrelationships. A verbal sound or configuration that is not internally related to a syntax is not a word. A color also has internal relationships, the "syntax" of the color wheel, for example; but this syntax has limited scope and definite boundaries, and a color is likely to have more intrinsic value than a word. Thus a color tends to "pull in" its syntactical relationships, not only because the color syntax is more limited and in turn more manageable, but also because a color is more likely to stay at the center of our attention. A word, on the other hand, tends to get "stretched out" by the "pull" of its syntactical relationships. To think about a word inevitably gets us thinking about other words.

This tendency can be mitigated by various techniques such as repetition, as in "O My Luve's like a red, red rose" (Robert Burns) or "A rose is a rose is a rose is a rose" (Ger-

trude Stein) or "You know I know you know I know you
know" (Thom Gunn). Or a combination of means may be
used, as in the first four lines of John Donne's Sonnet Number XIV in the *Holy Sonnets:*

> BATTER my heart, three person'd God; for, you
> As yet but knocke, breathe, shine, and seeke to mend,
> That I may rise, and stand, o'erthrow mee, and bend
> Your force, to breake, blowe, burn and make me new.

The fourth line in particular—which includes the standard
ten syllables—alters the expected iambic pentameter rhythm
by the introduction of a spondaic foot. This focuses attention
on the violent verbs, each of which intensifies the corresponding verb of the second line—knocke-breake, breathe-
blowe, shine-burn. The violence of the fourth line is intensified further by the fact that the "b" alliteration of the verbs
is part of a pattern of "b" alliteration begun by "BATTER" in
the first line and continued by "breathe" in line two and
"bend" in line three. The fourth line is made even more
forceful by the use of monosyllables only, usually a more
emphatic expression, because of the slight pause required
between the words, than an expression using polysyllables.
The cumulative power of these devices is iconic with the
central designative meaning of the quatrain and the poem
as a whole—the violent request or even demand that God
provide the impetus to break the pattern of life that the
speaker has been pursuing so that he can be born anew in
the grace of God. All the meanings, with their extremely
tight interrelationships, converge around the symbol of the
"three person'd God," a somewhat strange and thus striking
way of referring to God as the Trinity.

Yet none of these literary devices, even in lyric poetry and
even when used with the consummate skill of a John Donne,
has achieved or is likely to achieve for the verbal symbol the
contractive power of the visual symbol. The "three person'd
God" of a painting, for example Masaccio's *Trinity*

(Plate 5), is also involved with many meanings, but Masaccio's visual symbol is likely to hold our attention more strongly than Donne's verbal symbol. The self-enclosing form of Masaccio's symbol, with its tightly interrelated lines, colors, and shadings, draws in the references more securely.

The symbol as image, in general, is much more likely to preserve its "shorthand" character, and thus its unique meaning function, than the symbol as word. Consequently, symbols are mainly the preserve of the image makers, the plastic artists, and especially the representational painter, whereas the extended elaboration of ultimate meanings is mainly the preserve of literary artists and those who use language more discursively and systematically, the theologians. It was quite natural for the Church Fathers, therefore, in a time of widespread illiteracy, to view the symbol as image as an educational device, while recognizing its dangers. Pope Gregory in the sixth century asserted, for example, with reference to the iconoclastic controversy, that "it is one thing to worship a picture and another to learn from the language of a picture what that is which ought to be worshipped. What those who can read learn by means of writing, that do the uneducated learn by looking at a picture. . . . That, therefore, ought not to have been destroyed which had been placed in the churches, not for worship, but solely for instructing the minds of the ignorant." But Gregory failed to note that since the symbol as word cannot be so concise as the symbol as image, the latter is also more likely to grasp the immediate attention even of the literate.

Since the extensive character of the syntax of language tends to dissolve the condensation of the verbal symbol, the conspicuous use of symbols in literature does not occur so often as in painting. Moreover, in twentieth-century literature the Judaic-Christian symbols—the only generally understood or traditional body of symbols pervasive throughout the Western world since the fall of the Roman Empire—if used at all are usually used as props, perfunctorily or peripherally. For example in Hemingway's *The Old Man and the Sea,* Santiago, after his ordeal with the shark, stretches out to sleep like Christ on the cross. Although this reference to a symbol plays its part, of course, it is not central in the content. The participator would miss very little if he missed this symbolic reference, because neither does the rest of the novel especially prepare for it nor the symbol add much to what preceded. Sometimes, furthermore, when traditional symbols belonging to a religious institution are used, as in William Carlos Williams's "Choral: The Pink Church," they are derided. In general, in the literature of this century such symbols are interpreted as of secondary importance, rarely being raised to the status of religious symbols because of the absence of awe-full contexts. In pre-contemporary times there are notable literary works, of course, in which institutionalized symbols are basic in the content—*The Divine Comedy, Paradise Lost, Moby Dick,* and *The Brothers Karamazov,* to mention just a few. And even in the contemporary period there are a few outstanding examples, such as Eliot's *Four Quartets,* W. H. Auden's *For The Time Being,* and Thomas Mann's novels about Joseph. Although contemporary writers like Lawrence and Yeats use symbols as much as, if not more than earlier writers, they tend to disregard or play down the importance of those symbols codified by religious institutional fiat.

At almost any time, except in societies organized like the Byzantine Empire, implicitly religious as well as secular literary works far outnumber the explicitly religious. In the religious dimension, literature is best equipped for the interpretation of either religious feeling, especially as lyric poetry, or what evokes religious feeling, especially as prose fiction, or, more usually, the interpretation of both religious feeling and its causes. The interpretation of *Being-as-transcendental* in prose fiction, even in so great a work as *The Brothers Karamazov,* tends to turn *Being* into a being because symbols in narrative presentation tend to fade into signs. In lyric poetry, the brevity of the form and the greater opportunities available for disrupting syntax and expectation make it

easier for the poet to maintain the self-enclosed, shorthand
character of the symbol, and thus keep the symbol from becoming a sign. Moreover, the greater opportunities for em-
phasizing words by means of visual placement make it possible for the poet to accent the perceptible quality of the
symbol. Thus George Herbert arranged the words of "The
Altar" in the following visual form:

```
A     broken    altar,   Lord,   Thy    servant    rears,
Made   of    a   heart   and   cémented   with     tears;
       Whose  parts  are  as  Thy  hand  did  frame;
       No  workman's  tool  hath  touched  the  same.
                    A       heart     alone
                    Is    such  .  a     stone
                    As      nothing    but
                    Thy    power   doth   cut.
                    Wherefore   each    part
                    Of     my    hard    heart
                    Meets    in    this    frame
                    To   praise   Thy   name;
       That   if   I   chance   to   hold   my   peace,
       These  stones  to  praise  Thee  may  not  cease.
Oh,    let    Thy   blessed    sacrifice    be    mine,
And    sanctify    this    altar    to    be    Thine.
```

Although this device of shaping the verse to look like a
symbol, drawing on the emblematic tradition, was popular
with some of the religious poets of the seventeenth century—
for instance George Herbert and Robert Herrick—since then
the device has fallen into disuse.[12] What we are more likely

---

12. Recently, in what is called "concrete poetry," there has been a revival of
    sorts of this seventeenth-century technique. A concrete poem usually
    interprets a photograph or painting which accompanies it, the visual
    image functioning as a kind of title. And sometimes, as with Herbert's
    "The Altar" and the shaped poems of Dylan Thomas's "Vision and
    Prayer," the verse looks like what the words mean. This mixed-media
    technique would seem to have interesting possibilities for preserving
    the religious character of the symbol, and, moreover, the use of pictures
    with poetry has strong roots in the West in the art of the Judaic-

to find in more recent religious poetry is the stress upon symbols produced by their unexpected visual placement or appearance. For example, in that magnificent poem of celebration by Gerald Manley Hopkins, "Pied Beauty," not only is the final line—"Praise him"—placed in an "understated" position, but our surprise is increased by the failure to capitalize "him." These "understatements" are so unexpected that paradoxically the symbolic character of "him" is heightened:

> GLORY be to God for dappled things—
>   For skies of couple-colour as a brinded cow;
>   For rose-moles all in stipple upon trout that swim;
> Fresh-firecoal chestnut-falls; finches' wings;
>   Landscape plotted and pieced—fold, fallow, and plough;
>   And áll trádes, their gear and tackle and trim.
>
>
> All things counter, original, spare, strange;
>   Whatever is fickle, freckled (who knows how?)
>   With swift, slow; sweet, sour; adazzle, dim;
> He fathers-forth whose beauty is past change:
>   Praise him.

The use of institutionalized symbols as central in the content of a work of art, nonliterary as well as literary, is possible but increasingly difficult at the present time because the traditional Judaic-Christian vision and its symbols for many if not most people are becoming meaningless. Moreover, no alternative frame of reference, no pervasive ideology of *Being* with a generally understood corpus of symbols has developed. As Karl Shapiro points out:

Christian tradition, for example *The Book of Kells*. Nevertheless, so far at least, the technique has been used almost exclusively for secular subject matter. See *Anthology of Concrete Poetry*, ed. Emmett Williams (New York: Something Else Press, 1967), and Thom and Ander Gunn, *Positives* (Chicago: University of Chicago Press, 1967).

> So various
> And multifoliate are our breeds of faith
> That we could furnish a herbarium
> With the American specimens alone.
> A choice anthology of a few of these
> Made its appearance just before the war;
> It is an album of philosophies
> Called *I Believe*. The essays it contains
> Have nothing in common but proximity.[13]

Nietzsche may have been a little premature in announcing the death of God, but for most of the Western world he would have been a true prophet in announcing the corollary —the death of Judaic-Christian symbolism. Place most of us behind those great windows of Chartres—their symbols, even if by chance we have read Henry Adams, are likely to be almost totally ignored in that amazing blaze of color. The symbolism does not seem important any more. The very fact that the symbols have to be explained is a witness to their loss of public power. How different it must have been for the men and women who planned and built those majestic monuments to their beliefs. "They had the Faith, and as they were, so did they work. Their achievement revealed God's truth, but without *doing it on purpose,* and because it was not done on purpose."[14] Even a nineteenth-century man like Adams could be in sympathy. But today we are likely to see that glass as if it were no more than a burning shimmering sheen. That is why that small minority of contemporary artists with intentions that are explicitly religious usually has tried to modify the institutionalized symbols, as in the case of Eliot, or derived its symbols from relatively unknown sources, as in the case of Yeats. As Nathan A. Scott, Jr., has remarked:

    . . . the particular tradition of Christian faith in which Eliot has

---

13. *Essay on Rime* (New York: Reynal and Hitchcock, 1945) , p. 63.
14. Jacques Maritain, *Art and Scholasticism,* trans. J. F. Scanlan (New York: Charles Scribner's Sons, 1946) , p. 52.

chosen to live—the tradition, say, of Origen and Dame Julian of Norwich and Jacob Boehme and St. John of the Cross—hardly strikes us as belonging to the great central tradition of Christian culture: it is very special and irregular, and its very reclamation by a contemporary Christian poet suggests that even his ortho- doxy will, in its attainment, represent something of the same kind of improvisation that has tended generally to characterize the philosophic and religious stratagems of the modern artist.[15]

Yeats, like Eliot, also had a "passion for the symbol," but for his sources Yeats turned to Celtic lore and to various esoteric mythologies with neo-Platonic overtones. In his *Autobiography* Yeats wrote: "I am very religious, and de- prived by Huxley and Tyndall, whom I detested, of the simple-minded religion of my childhood, I . . . made a new religion, almost an infallible church, of poetic tradition." He failed in creating a new religion, but that, of course, was not his purpose. Yeats was an artist, not a prophet, and he succeeded in explicitly interpreting *Being* in a highly original and illuminating way by bringing back a largely forgotten symbolism.

All living symbolism, according to Northrop Frye (follow- ing William Blake), can be no more than a variation upon one basic archetypal vision which functions as a timeless schema.[16] Thomas Mann, in his speech in Vienna in 1936 honoring the eightieth birthday of Freud, made a similar claim:

> . . . the myth is the foundation of life; it is the timeless schema, the pious formula into which life flows when it reproduces its traits out of the unconscious. Certainly when a writer has ac- quired the habit of regarding life as mythical and typical there comes a curious heightening of his artistic temper, a new re- freshment of his perceiving and shaping powers, which other-

---

15. "The Broken Center: A Definition of the Crisis of Values in Modern Literature," in *Symbolism in Religion and Literature,* ed. Rollo May (New York: G. Braziller, 1960), p. 192.
16. *Fearful Symmetry: A Study of William Blake* (Princeton: Princeton University Press, 1947). Frye apparently developed his theory inde- pendently of the somewhat similar theory of C. G. Jung.

wise occurs much later in life; for while in the life of the human race the mythical is an early and primitive stage, in the life of the individual it is a late and mature one. What is gained is an insight into the higher truth depicted in the actual; a smiling knowledge of the eternal, the ever-being and authentic; a knowledge of the schema in which and according to which the supposed individual lives, unaware, in his naive belief in himself as unique in space and time, of the extent to which his life is but formula and repetition and his path marked out for him by those who trod it before him.[17]

These are large claims. But there can be little doubt that the living symbol is enlivened by its past. The artist who invents symbols *ex nihilo* is unlikely to communicate, and a "private religious symbol" is a contradiction in terms. On the other hand, most contemporary artists—even those who have creedal commitments, such as T. S. Eliot, Graham Greene, W. H. Auden, Robert Lowell, and François Mauriac—must modify the traditional symbols passed on by family, custom, Church, and State because the unmodified symbols are no longer in harmony with their religious responses.

Whether any particular work of literature is correctly classified as secular or implicitly or explicitly religious raises issues that are quite illuminating. Eliot's *Four Quartets*, for instance, are clear-cut examples of poems that are explicitly religious. Within a tightly designed context expressing religious feeling, recurrent symbols, mostly traditional and Christian, form the basic theme that is central in the content—modern man's destruction by his time-obsessed ways and the possibility of redemption.

> Time past and time future
> Allow but a little consciousness.
> To be conscious is not to be in time. . . .
> "Burnt Norton"

Faulkner's *The Sound and the Fury,* including this same

---

17. *Essays of Three Decades*, trans. H. T. Lowe-Porter (New York: Alfred A. Knopf, 1965), p. 422.

theme as basic in its content and, like the *Quartets,* a great
work of art, also uses traditional symbols even more clearly
Christian within a context expressing religious feeling. But
The Sound and the Fury is not explicitly religious because
the pattern of Christian symbols is cross-cut by an equally
important secular pattern. The resulting conflict creates a
context so full of ambivalence and tension that the Christian symbols in their overall effect do not function as religious symbols. Whereas in the *Quartets* one basic and coherent religious view of reality prevails, in *The Sound and
the Fury* two basic views, one nonreligious and the other
religious, are in constant contention.[18]

The nonreligious view is revealed in the Quentin-Caddy-
Mr. Compson line of action dominated by *loss* of meaning,
and in the Jason-Miss Quentin line of action dominated by
absence of meaning. For the characters in both these lines of
action, reality is hostile and hopeless, ungraced by *Being.*
When *Being* is conceptualized, as by Quentin and Mr.
Compson, *Being* does not seem to be encountered. Thus
Being is reduced to a being. When *Being* is encountered, as
at times by Caddy, the participation is not sustained. When
Being is neither conceptualized nor encountered there is no
meaning at all, as with Jason and Miss Quentin, although
ironically, except for Jason at rare times, they do not know it.
Both these negative lines are accompanied by a skeptical or
stoical point of view, although unarticulated by any of the
characters except Mr. Compson, which helps interpret the
action. The religious view is revealed mainly in the Benjy-
Dilsey line of action in which the awe-full presence of *Being*
is manifest and sustained, and, as a result, meaning is dis-
covered and endures. For Benjy and Dilsey reality is fallen,
but graced, nevertheless, by *Being,* and thus is redeemable
through *Being.* This positive line, in turn, is accompanied

18. John W. Hunt in *William Faulkner: Art in Theological Tension* (Syracuse, N. Y.: Syracuse University Press, 1965) has worked out in detail
the conflicting Christian and Stoical viewpoints in Faulkner's major
works. I am much indebted to Hunt's analysis.

by traditional Christian symbolism that helps interpret the action.

Quentin's despair is so deep that all hope is cut off. He decapitates the future from time. Quentin presupposes his suicide, which will occur a few hours after he begins his inner monologue, as a fixed fact, like a solid mirror from which he can only look back into the past. Sartre observed that "Faulkner's vision of the world can be compared to that of a man sitting in an open car and looking backwards. At every moment, formless shadows, flickerings, faint tremblings and patches of light rise up on either side of him, and only afterwards, when he has a little perspective, do they become trees and men and cars."[19] This identification of Faulkner's vision of the world with the extremely narrow and obsessed one of Quentin's is mistaken—it is as if, among other things, Sartre had read neither Jason's nor Dilsey's (the last) section—but it is a brilliant description of how Quentin saw reality.

Time has become the sign of reality for Quentin. Time is fated, inexorable, for time has no open forward end, no possibilities, and thus no future. Man is doomed to be time-bound. "When the shadow of the sash appeared on the curtains," so begins Quentin's death day, "it was between seven and eight o'clock and then I was in time again, hearing the watch." Quentin tries every possible maneuver to escape time, even inventing incest with Caddy because its terrible significance presumably would lift them out of time: ". . . it was to isolate her out of the loud world so that it would have to flee us of necessity and then the sound of it would be as though it had never been." But like everything else this fantasy fails, and so now he tries to avoid listening to chimes and looking at watches. "I went to the dresser and took up the watch, with the face still down. I tapped the crystal on the corner of the dresser and caught the fragments of glass in my hand and put them into the ashtray and

---

19. *Literary and Philosophical Essays*, trans. Annette Michelson (New York: Criterion Books, 1955) , pp. 81f.

twisted the hands off and put them in the tray." But "the watch ticked on." And the chimes strike on. A poised gull over the Charles River and Gerald Bland's mechanical rowing become signs of the irresistible push-pull of time. "Constant speculation regarding the position of mechanical hands on an arbitrary dial which is a symptom of mind-function. Excrement Father said like sweating." "Time is dead as long as it is being clicked off by little wheels; only when the clock stops does time come to life." But for time to come to life, *i.e.*, for time to return to temporality, the future as open possibility would have to be taken into durations of present and past. And this Quentin cannot do because he has lost all hope. Nothing can heal. As with Meursault (until near the end) in Camus's *The Stranger,* everything, or almost everything, is meaningless. The meaning Quentin once had found in his conception of the aristocratic code of honor of the Southern tradition, a strange concoction centered on Caddy's chastity, is irredeemably lost. Even when he helps the little Italian girl, "little sister," the sympathy is only apparent. She is only another sign to Caddy and the past. His memories keep swarming back involuntarily but never immanently. "I am not is, I was." What is happening in the present is insignificant except as a stepping stone to the past. Quentin can participate with neither the present nor the past, for such participation would require their union. And this union is impossible because there is no future. Although the past has completely preempted Quentin's consciousness, he fails to understand its meaning. Lacking a future and unaware of the present, he has no perspective through which he could gain understanding and, in turn, transcendence of the past. With temporality shut off because the future is missing, the only escape from time for him, and this alone Quentin knows with Cartesian clarity, is suicide.

Unlike our way of knowing Quentin, we know Caddy only through the refracted views of others. But it is quite apparent that, although reckless, Caddy is a warm, sympathetic person, fully capable of the love her whining, neurasthenic mother lacks. Thus she becomes a substitute mother to Benjy. But her love is rarely reciprocated, except by Benjy; and Quentin, with his puritanical obsessions about sex, makes her feel dirty and guilty about her sexual indiscretions. Yet she seems to really love Dalton Ames: "Yes I hate him I would die for him I've already died for him I die for him over and over again." But Ames leaves her pregnant and Quentin's moralistic tauntings help break her courage to be. Her ontological sensitivities are not so quickly and totally destroyed as Quentin's, but, except for her daughter, Miss Quentin, she simply gives up. Apparently Caddy worked, by selling herself, and fought, only for her daughter, and at the end, in the Appendix added by Faulkner, we see her as a mistress of a Nazi. She knew meaning in life, not as Quentin did, by living in the illusion of a dead and distorted myth, but by living to some extent in the depth dimension of life. Thus her loss of meaning, despite Quentin's much greater intellectual range, is much more tragic.

Mr. Compson, the father and ineffectual lawyer, tries to escape time by means of a Stoical philosophy, fed by Latin authors and lightened by alcohol which, by naming the absurdity of reality, seems to give him some transcendence over it. Mr. Compson, except for Jason to a lesser extent, is the only character in the negative lines of action who stands aside occasionally and evaluates the action. His judgments, usually in the form of advice to the Hamlet-like Quentin, are seemingly as platitudinous as the admonishments of a Polonius. But the depth of Mr. Compson's melancholy makes them ring sincere. His conclusions are totally skeptical: ". . . a man is the sum of his misfortunes. One day you'd think misfortune would get tired, but then time is your misfortune."

Quentin, I give you the mausoleum of all hope and desire [his father's watch]; it's rather excruciating-ly apt that you will use it to gain the reducto absurdum of all human experience which can fit your individual needs no better than it fitted his or his father's. I give it to you not that you may remember time, but that you might forget it now and then for a moment and not spend all your breath trying to conquer it. Because no battle is ever won he said. They are not even fought. The field only reveals to man his own folly and despair, and victory is an illusion of philosophers and fools.

Time is a tomb filled with inevitable and irredeemable sorrows. But there is a loss of meaning in Mr. Compson, also, because his gentleness and kindness come from his tradition. He has not only a past but a sense of the past, and so Mr. Compson's way of life, as Quentin realized more than anyone else, is linked to a better time.

Jason, the businessman of the family who keeps the "flour barrel full," faces the future with utter contempt for the past and its traditions. Time is hostile not because it is a tomb but because there is not enough time to pursue his mean-spirited materialism. "Sane" and "normal," Jason finds meaning in life not by participation, as Caddy once did, nor in the traditions of the past, as Quentin and Mr. Compson once did, but in a total utilitarianism. And despite his never-ending failures, he never gives up on practicality. But Faulkner never lets us forget that Jason's ideal turns out to be sound and fury signifying nothing. Even Jason, with his frontier realism and sardonic sense of humor, sometimes reveals the truth to himself in his cynical observations, but his anxieties and a twisted courage carry him forward. Whereas Quentin cuts off the future, Jason cuts off the past. Jason has no base, no spiritual continuity: he is like a man with a broken compass, and so his progress is no progress at all but a frantic circling. Without the immanence of the past in the present, the future is a frenzied anticipation that cannot fulfill.

Miss Quentin, despite her justified hatred for Jason, follows his course. Unlike her mother, Miss Quentin lacks compassion. In those poignant scenes, so strangely juxtaposed in Benjy's consciousness, showing Caddy and Miss Quentin with their lovers in the swing, Caddy turns to Benjy: "I won't . . . I won't anymore, ever. Benjy. Benjy."

But Miss Quentin threatens to tell Dilsey: "You old crazy loon . . . I'm going to make her whip you good." Caddy is tragic, for she understands the difference between good and evil based on meanings she is losing. Her daughter is just pathetic, for she has found no meaning to lose.

Benjy, "de Lawd's chile" as Dilsey names him, is conscious only of the present. Benjy often involuntarily recalls the past, but it always comes back as the immediate rather than the finished past. For Quentin only the past was significant, for Jason only the future; for Benjy there is only the saddle-back present within the narrowest possible confines of consciousness. Nevertheless, this accent on the immediacy of the present ties him to things and he can participate. Thus meaning, limited as it is to a three-year old comprehension, is achieved and sustained. Its intensity is apparent—positive with such things as firelight and flowers and "Caddy smelling like trees"; negative when such things are missing or "Caddy smells like perfume." Benjy smells sickness, death, the imminence of catastrophe, and above all good and evil. Thus perhaps more than Quentin's moralizing, it is Benjy's reaction to Caddy's promiscuity, functioning like a moral mirror, that forces Caddy to face her guilt. Benjy invariably wails, with "the grave hopeless sound of all voiceless misery under the sun," when sorrow and evil are manifest. As Roskus phrases it, "He know lot more than folks thinks." With childlike innocence Benjy has sure senses for both good and evil because he has not been conditioned away from participation. He has a spiritual center because he "is open," in however restricted a way, to the given and lets it "be in him." Thus despite his idiocy he seems more human than his brothers. Few scenes in literature are more moving than the episode in which Benjy, at the age of eighteen, frightening some school girls because he mistakes them for Caddy, keeps repeating "I was trying to say." Furthermore, despite Benjy's pathos, his inability to project more than a tiny fragmentary world, and his self-centeredness, there is wisdom in his instincts because his ontological sensitivities are nearly always operative. Even though Benjy has not the slightest theoretical comprehension of how *Being* is behind the becoming, he points the way to redemption through his ability to participate.

Dilsey embodies the way. She lives completely in reality, as none of the others do, with love, fortitude, and humility. With a serenity based on "de power and de glory," she faces her problems with complete realism, utilizing the tools at hand. She always lives in the present as the time of opportunity, drawing in the possibilities of the future and the memories of the past in order to fulfill the "now." *Kairos*—the time of opportunity and fulfillment—is the redemptive time of God, and Dilsey is in harmony with that time or temporality rather than with the mechanical time of Quentin. Thus when all the others panic, Dilsey remains morally active. "I does de bes I kin." She not only fights the battle, unlike Mr. Compson, but wins it. Nothing can defeat her, even the final destruction of the family she loves, because she draws her strength to endure from *Being*. "I seed de beginnin, en now I sees de endin," she says, with reference to the decline and fall of the Compsons. But she sees all this within the perspective of "the Lawd's own time." She finds and preserves meaning, where all the others except Benjy fail, through her faith. God redeems. In his commentary on Dilsey in the Appendix Faulkner simply said: "They endured."

Faulkner, as has been frequently pointed out, supports the Benjy-Dilsey line of action with Christian symbolism. The "present action" of the novel begins with Jason's monologue on April 6, 1928, Good Friday, and ends in Dilsey's section on April 8, 1928, Easter Sunday. Since Benjy's thirty-third birthday falls on April 7, 1928, and since he is innocent, persecuted, and an apparently infallible although inarticulate judge of good and evil, the analogue with Christ is too obvious to be ignored. On the other hand, an identification of Benjy with Christ is blocked by Benjy's lack of mental capacity and physical dignity. The analogue is really irony. Moreover, it is much more in Dilsey's actions and thoughts, and in Faulkner's commentary upon them, that the Christian symbolism becomes embedded in the content. In church during Shegog's Easter sermon, "Dilsey sat bolt upright . . . crying rigidly and quietly in the annealment and the blood of the remembered Lamb." Almost every act of Dilsey is motivated by her Christian faith, and almost every thought of Dilsey is wrought in Biblical terms. When Caddy, for example, taunts her about her identity, Dilsey replies:

> My name been Dilsey since fore I could remember and it be Dilsey when they's long forgot me.
> How will they know it's Dilsey, when it's long forgot, Dilsey, Caddy said.
> It'll be in the Book, honey, Dilsey said. Writ out.
> Can you read it, Caddy said.
> Won't have to, Dilsey said. They'll read it for me. All I got to do is say Ise here.

Since Dilsey is the only successful human being in the novel, and since her achievement obviously depends upon her Christian faith, and since this faith is elaborated symbolically throughout but especially in the final culminating section, it would seem that *The Sound and the Fury* should be classified as explicitly religious. But such an interpretation ignores too much of what Faulkner created. Take, for example, the scene where Shegog, "dat big preacher fum Saint Looey," begins his Easter sermon:

> "Brethern and sisteren. . . . I got the recollection and the blood of the Lamb!" . . . . He tramped steadily back and forth . . . hunched, his hands clasped behind him. He was like a worn small rock whelmed by the successive waves of his voice. With his body he seemed to feed the voice that, succubus like, had fleshed its teeth in him. And the congregation seemed to watch with its own eyes while the voice consumed him, until he was nothing . . . and . . . his monkey face lifted and his whole attitude that of a serene, tortured crucifix that transcended its shabbiness and insignificance and made of it no moment. . . .

Since a succubus is a female demon thought to have sexual
intercourse with sleeping men, the animal-like imagery of
metamorphosis is hardly an attractive vehicle for an affirmative statement of the resurrection. Moreover, the episode of
Dilsey and her trip to church with Benjy Easter morning,
the only episode in which Christian doctrine comes sharply
to the foreground, occurs at the beginning of the final section. The following lengthy description of Jason's futile
pursuit of Miss Quentin is so melodramatically and comi-
cally portrayed that Dilsey and her church tend to fade
away in Jason's whirling landscape.

Christianity in general is rarely vital enough even to be
rejected, except for some of the uneducated blacks. For
Quentin, Christ is no more than an inanimate doll with
"sawdust flowing from what wound in what side that not
for me died not." In most of the story the religious view of
reality is simply ignored. Furthermore, even Dilsey's actions,
although clearly affirmative for her, are ultimately ineffectual for others. When Dilsey remarks as she begins the up-
bringing of Miss Quentin that she had raised them all, there
is at least some justice in Jason's reply: "And a damn fine
job you made of it." And even Dilsey seems to give in to
inexorable fate when Melissa Meek, the little librarian from
Jefferson, brings Caddy's picture with the Nazi to Memphis
for Dilsey to identify. Dilsey refuses even to look because
"My eyes aint any good anymore." Loss of meaning and
meaninglessness are so continually pervasive, and at the last
count Dilsey's heroism is so ineffectual that, rather than
embodying "the way," or so it can be reasonably argued,
Dilsey is more like a tragic chorus. In any case, the positive
theme of redemption is at least balanced by the negative
theme of doom. Mr. Compson's nihilism and Jason's cyni-
cism deny as much as Dilsey's faith affirms. And stoicism,
Faulkner seems to be finally saying, is as good an answer as
Christianity because it is far more realistic. The last scene
epitomizes the unresolved tension. Driving to the cemetery
with Benjy contentedly holding a flower upright in his fist,

Luster, Dilsey's swaggering and callous grandson, approaches the main square of Jefferson "where the Confederate soldier gazed with empty eyes beneath his marble hand into wind and weather." In order to impress some loitering Negroes, Luster turns Queenie to the left, and Benjy begins bellowing with mounting crescendoes as Jason tears across the square to strike Luster and Benjy and turn Queenie back to the right.

> Queenie moved again, her feet began to clop-clop steadily again, and at once Ben hushed. Luster looked quickly over his shoulder, then he drove on. The broken flower drooped over Ben's fist and his eyes were empty and blue and serene as cornice and façade flowed smoothly once more from left to right; post and tree, window and doorway, and signboard, each in its ordered place.

Benjy imposes his order on Jason. But it takes Jason to execute the order.

How different the affirmation of the last lines that close Eliot's last "Quartet":

> Quick now, here, now, always—
> A condition of complete simplicity
> (Costing not less than everything)
> And all shall be well and
> All manner of things shall be well
> When the tongues of flame are in-folded
> Into the crowned knot of fire
> And the fire and the rose are one.

The Sound and the Fury dramatizes the point that to be caught in time is either to lose meaning or have no meaning, and that in temporality we transcend time and gain and sustain meaning. The novel suggests, moreover, that in participation there may even be redemption. For only in the lives of Benjy and Dilsey is there any saving grace, and what distinguishes them from the others is their openness to the

depth dimension. But there is no firm affirmation because
the skeptical view plays its balancing role. The total impact
of *The Sound and the Fury,* nevertheless, is implicitly religious, for the effect of awe in front of the tragic mystery of
human existence has rarely been more powerfully rendered.

As we build the imaginary construction following Faulkner's blueprint, some of our past, because of all kinds of
associations and analogues, comes in immanently. Our immanent recall is all the more involved by the way the blueprint is presented. In Benjy's section his of dialogue and
scenes, often with no apparent connection, unroll in Benjy's
consciousness with little regard for chronological sequence.
These events as we first encounter them are minimally meaningful, except as we are lured on by the belief that they will
become much more meaningful. As we read on, these events
keep coming back, first in Quentin's monologue and then in
Jason's. Finally, in the omniscient author's section, they
come back for the last time in the third-person narration. As
we continue to construct, the earlier events are immanently
recalled and their meanings become cumulatively more explicit and significant. So it is in life, for the significance of
what happens now, unless we participate, is largely missed.
When the past returns immanently, then we can participate
with it far more deeply than when the past was the chaotic,
fugitive, everyday experience of the present. And then the
Being of the past is revealed. *The Sound and the Fury* is
formed in such a way that we are led to recall immanently
not just some of the events of our own past but most of the
past events in the novel. All literary artists guide us this way
to some extent, but, with such exceptions as Proust, Joyce,
and Eliot, very few have done it with the effectiveness of
Faulkner in *The Sound and the Fury.*

Why did Faulkner in *The Sound and the Fury,* and in his
other works as well,[20] stop short of a construction that was
explicitly religious, Christian or otherwise? An adequate

20. Including "The Bear," *Light in August,* and *A Fable.* See Hunt, *William
Faulkner: Art in Theological Tension.*

answer to this question would also help solve some of the puzzles of one of the greatest of all mysteries—the creative process of the artist. Despite the vast amount of research on this subject in recent years, we know very little indeed. But the previous analyses suggest a hypothesis that hopefully may shed a little light: an artist creates works that are explicitly religious only if the pressure of the presence of *Being* in his life is so coercive that *Being* becomes ultimately important. We must be cautious here, because this seems to suggest Buffon's dictum that "style is the man," whereas Mark Schorer's dictum that "style is the subject matter" is closer to the facts. The subject matter of a work of art controls the form (style) because the function of form is to inform its subject matter, to reveal the significance of the subject matter, to transform the subject matter into content. *Being* is part of the subject matter of all artists, for all artists are Shepherds of *Being*. But beings are the primary subject matter of artists who produce works that are secular or implicitly religious. For them *Being* is so embedded in things that the unity of *Being* or *Being-as-transcendental* is not interpreted. Thus *Being* does not stand out as ultimately important.

Every artist must have, as Eliot in his famous review of Joyce's *Ulysses* insisted, some means "of controlling or ordering, of giving a shape and a significance. . . ."[21] There must be some kind of comprehensive focus, a *Weltanschauung*, some way that enables the artist to select his subject matter and do it justice.[22] This *Weltanschauung* may be influenced by anything the artist experiences—the economic-political-sociological climate, the insights of others, especially artists, and so on—but these influences are subordinated, largely unconsciously, to the "constitutive matrix" that is formed by the artist's participative experiences. In these experiences

---

21. "Ulysses, Order, and Myth," in *Critiques and Essays on Modern Fiction*, ed. John W. Aldridge (New York: Ronald Press Co., 1952), p. 426.
22. See my "The Artist, Autobiography, and Thomas Wolfe," *The Bucknell Review* 5 (March 1955): 15–28.

Being "thinks in the artist," and it is from these experiences that the artist develops the primordial perspective that governs the projection of his world. The constitutive matrix is grounded in participations with *Being,* providing the presuppositions which single out the subject matter and guide its transformation. The constitutive matrix provides the "first principles" of the artist's creative process. Without these artistic "premises" grounded in *Being,* the most skillful techniques could produce only decoration.

When the pressure of *Being* on the artist's constitutive matrix is overwhelmingly coercive, his subject matter inevitably becomes not just *Being* as embedded in beings but *Being-as-transcendental,* as sacred. The religious artist cannot dismiss beings any more than the secular artist can dismiss *Being,* for beings and *Being,* although distinguishable, are inseparable, but for the religious artist *Being* becomes ultimately important. Thus the "passion for the symbol" of the religious artist, as in Yeats and Eliot, follows, because he must articulate *Being* as holy. He must not only point to *Being* awe-fully, as does the artist who is implicitly religious, but he must interpret something of the unity of *Being.* Without symbols it would be impossible to do this, for only the symbol, with its unique combination of clarity and vagueness, can both "say something" about *Being-as-transcendental* and still respect its mystery. If the theories of Frye, Jung, and Mann are correct, furthermore, the symbols are generated from the "timeless schema" itself—the *Being* component—within the constitutive matrix. Religious symbolism, in any case, is a "descending symbolism," for it is the pressure of *Being* in the constitutive matrix that controls, if it does not generate, the symbolism.

When the pressure of *Being* is not strongly coercive in the artist's life, *Being* is not welded into the constitutive matrix. Then the primordial perspective of the artist sees beings first, as the primary subject matter, and *Being* second, as the secondary subject matter. *Being* is revealed in his work of art, of course, but it is revealed as the background of the dominating surfaces of reality. *Being-as-immanent* is revealed, rather than *Being-as-transcendental*. There is no "passion for the symbol" in such an artist, because he lacks belief in the ultimate importance of *Being*. Symbols may be used, as in *The Sound and the Fury*, but they "ascend" from the depths of the ontical subject matter rather than "descend," as in the case of the later Eliot, from the constitutive matrix. The symbols are generated and controlled by the need to interpret the surface by means of the depth. The pointing to *Being* by means of symbols does not reveal *Being-as-transcendental* but helps reveal beings as something more than ontical. The symbols function more or less as devices, as more or less dispensable. Symbols used in this way do not become religious, and they will seem to partake of the "timeless schema" of symbolism only accidentally, if at all. And then it is quite appropriate, as in Kafka's *The Castle*, to use symbols that lack obvious connections with traditional symbolism.

Faulkner never experienced *Being* coercively enough to believe in *Being-as-transcendental*, *Being* as holy. Yet, unlike a secular novelist such as Salinger, he experienced *Being-as-immanent* coercively enough to use symbols in a way that pointed to the possibility of *Being* as holy. Eliot, on the other hand, experienced *Being* so coercively in his later life that his use of symbols in his later works leaves no doubt that *Being* is interpreted as holy. This does not mean that Eliot is a better artist than Faulkner or that Faulkner is a better artist than Salinger. It does mean that each of these artists shepherds *Being* in his own distinctive way.

6

Architecture and Sublimity

Space is the power of the positioned interrelationships of things. Space is not a mere collection of given things. Nor is space a mere imagined framework added to the sum of such given things, although since Newton—and despite Bergson, Einstein, and Whitehead—space is usually so conceived. Space is not a thing, and yet, because of the positioned interrelationships of things, space "spaces." Space has vitality. But in ordinary experience we pass by this power because we see the position of things only in order to use them. We abstract from the full concrete reality of space and see space only as a means. We *know* space, but because of the anaesthesia of practicality, we fail to *feel* space.

The painter does not command space; he only feigns it. The sculptor molds out into space, but he does not enfold an enclosed or inner space for our movement. The "holes" in the sculpture of Henry Moore are to be walked around, not into, whereas our passage through inner space is one of the conditions under which the solids and voids of architecture have their effect. Space is the material of the architect, the primeval cutter,[1] who carves apart an inner space from

1. This meaning is suggested by the Greek *architectōn*.

an outer space in such a way that both spaces become fully visible and, in turn, intrinsically valuable. Invisible air is rendered visible. Inside his building, space is filled with emergent forces. Outside his building, space becomes organized and focused. The enfolded inner space is anchored to the earth. The convergent outer space is oriented around the inner space. Thus light, rain, snow, mist, and night fall gracefully upon the cover protecting the inner space as if drawn by a channeled and purposeful gravity, as if these events of the outside belonged to the inside as much as the earth from which the building rises. Inner and outer space come together to the earth to form a centered and illuminated clearing. If we are nearby we tend to be drawn into this clearing, for unless we are ontically obsessed centered space has an overpowering dynamism that captures both our attention and our bodies. Centered space is vital and insists upon intruding itself. Centered space propels us out of the ordinary modes of experience in which space is used as a means. There is an inrush from the outside that is difficult to escape, that overwhelms and makes us acquiescent. We see and feel space not as a receptacle containing things but rather as a context empowered by the positioned interrelationships of things. Centered space intrudes as a force that is both "other" and imposing, as, even in our most harassed moments, we can hardly help feeling in such places as the Piazza before St. Peter's. Even when—as in Bramante's Tempietto in Rome—the inner space is very small and the outer space is hemmed in by nearby buildings that failed to follow Bramante's more spacious plan, the convergent outer space still seems immense because the power of what we see stretches our imaginations into the spaces that have been shut off. We feel incommensurate. We find ourselves in the presence of a power that seems beyond our control. We feel the sublimity of space.

No special training is required to feel this sublimity. Space is breathing-space, a part of the stuff of life—"il faut de l'espace pour être un homme" (E. E. Cummings, *Jot-*

tings) —and space exerts its power by pushing in upon us. Gravitational force is only one, but the most obvious, manifestation of this power, for gravity works continuously on every aspect of everything. Without some sensitivity to space we cannot survive. But because of life's exigencies, we learn to push things around in space. Insofar as this pushing succeeds easily and efficiently, and in a technological age such success becomes increasingly possible, space tends to become no more than a framework within which we manipulate the position of things. We become insensitive to the intrinsic value of the positioned interrelationships of things. We become explicitly conscious of space only when space frustrates us, and then only as an area within which we have to work. Space becomes a part of a problem. In our aggressiveness we enslave space to the point that we pass by the power of space. Then it takes either the embracing thrust of the great spaces of nature (and these spaces, such as in and around the Grand Canyon, are always centered to some significant extent) or the centered spaces of architecture to return us to an explicit awareness of the sublimity of space.

Architecture is the creative conservation of space. The architect sees the centers of space in nature, and builds to preserve what he has seen. The architect is confronted by a centered space which desires to be made through him into a work. This space of nature is no offspring of his soul but an appearance which steps up to him and demands protection. If the architect succeeds in carrying through this request, the power of the natural space streams forth through him and the work arises. The architect is the Shepherd of space. In turn, the paths around his shelter lead us away from our ordinary preoccupations demanding the utilization of space. We come to rest. Instead of our using up space, space takes possession of us with a ten-fingered grasp. In this extraordinary experience the sublimity of space opens us to *Being*.

On a hot summer's day some years ago, following the path of Henry Adams, I was attempting to drive from Mont St. Michel to Chartres in time to catch the setting sun through

the western rose. In my rushing anxiety—I had to be in Paris
the following day and I had never been to Chartres before—
I became oblivious of space except as providing landmarks
for my time-clocked progress. Thus I have no significant
memories of the towns and countrysides I hurried through.
Late that afternoon the two spires of Chartres, like two
strangely woven strands of rope let down from the heavens,
gradually came into focus. The blue dome of the sky also
became visible for the first time, centering as I approached
more and more firmly around the axis of those spires. The
surrounding fields and then the town, coming out now in
all their specificity, grew into tighter unity with the church
and the embrace of the sky. I recalled a passage from Aeschylus: "The pure sky desires to penetrate the earth, and the
earth is filled with love so that she longs for blissful unity
with the sky. The rain falling from the sky impregnates the
earth, so that she gives birth to plants and grain for beasts
and men." No one rushed in or out or around the church.
The space around seemed alive and dense with slow currents
all ultimately being pulled to and through the central portal.
Inside, the space, although spacious far beyond the scale of
practical human needs, seemed strangely compressed, full of
forces thrusting and counterthrusting in dynamic interrela-
tions. Slowly, in the cool silence inlaid with stone, I was
drawn down the long nave following the stately rhythms of
the columns. But my eyes also followed the vast vertical
stretches far up into the shifting shadows of the vaultings.
It was as if I were being borne aloft. Yet I continued down
the narrowing tunnel of the nave, but more and more slowly
as the pull of the space above held back the pull of the space
below. At the crossing of the transept the flaming reds of
the northern and southern roses transfixed my slowing pace,
and then I turned back at last to the western rose and the
three lancets beneath; a delirium of color, dominantly blue,
was pouring through. Earthbound in the crossing, the blaze
of the Without was merging with the Within. Radiant space
took complete possession of my senses—visual, tactile, audi-

tory, kinaesthetic, and even thermal. In the protective grace of this sheltering space, even the outer space which I had dismissed in the traffic of my driving converged around the center of this crossing. Instead of being "outside" things— my body, the church, the town, the fields, the sky, the sun— I was "inside" them, at one with them. The *Being* of these things had come to presence. I also became aware of a unity in the depth of these things, a transcendency as well as an immanency of *Being*. This housing of holiness in this strange land made me feel at home in the homeland.

Living space is the feeling of the positioning of things in the environment within which we move or imagine that we can move. Taking possession of space is our first gesture, and sensitivity to the position of other things is a prerequisite of life. Space infiltrates through all our senses. Each of our senses records the positioning of things, expressed in such terms as up-down, left-right, and near-far. This requires a reference system with a center. In the case of abstract perceptual space, as when we estimate distances visually, there is one center—the zero point located between the eyes. But with living space, since all the senses are involved, the whole body is a center. Furthermore, the body in relation to a place or places of most value, such as the home, form a configurational center. If we oversimplify, we can say that for the peasant his body and his farm, that place to which he most naturally belongs, constitute his configurational center—with the Roman it was Rome, with medieval man the church and castle, with a Babbitt the office, with a Sartre the café, and with a De Gaulle the nation. But for most men at almost any time, although probably more so in modern times, there are more than a couple of centers and often these are more or less confused and changing. In living space, in any case, places, principal directions, and distances arrange themselves around a configurational center.

The configurational center forms our personal inner space, to some extent private and protected. Outside space is more public and dangerous. The security of the home gradually lessens as we step out through the door into the yard into the immediate neighborhood, and then into more remote places. As we move onto the typical modern highway in northeastern United States, for example, the concrete cuts abusively into the earth and through the landscape as straight as possible with speed the only aim. The arteries of commerce pump efficiency, and there is no time for piety to space. Everyone passes hurriedly and aloof. There is no place for pedestrians or peace. Even the roadside rests, if any, for the fatigued driver are drowned in the whine of tires, and the necessities such as gas stations, restaurants, and motels are usually repetitious vulgarities that excite us to move on. Everyone from the hitchhiker to the other motorist is a threat. Only a police car or a severe accident is likely to slow us down. The machine takes over, and when we have reached our destination *on time,* the machine mentality is likely to maintain its clutch.

This desecration of outer space may even lead us to forget our inner space, the center that gives directionality and meaning to outer space. Then orientation with reference to intrinsic values is lacking. We become displaced persons, refugees from ourselves. Then living space, inner as well as outer, becomes used space. And then used space tends to become geometrical space, for the efficient use of used space requires precise placements. Space becomes a static schematic vacuum. The geometricians measure out coordinate systems whereby everything is related quantitatively. The centers now are entirely impersonal, for the basic characteristic of geometrical space is its homogeneity. No center and no direction in this democracy of places is preferred to another. When we, in turn, want to move through space most efficiently, geometrical space provides the map. To the degree that efficiency of movement dominates our concerns, living space becomes abstract space. Like the lumber barons of California ripping out the redwoods, we see straight through space. We still see things and the "between" of things, but only as means. Space itself—the power of the positional interrelationships of things—is ignored. Space becomes a waste-land.

A building that is not architecturally designed, although it encloses a convenient void, encourages us to ignore its space. And normally we will be blind to the building and its space as long as it serves its practical purposes. However, if the roof leaks or a wall breaks down, then we will see the building, but only as a damaged instrument. A building that is architecturally designed brings us back to living space by centering space. Such buildings raise to clarity preceding impressions that were obscure, confused, and inarticulate. The potentialities of power in the positioned interrelation-ships of things is captured and channeled. Our feeling for space is reawakened, and we become aware of the power of space as a given that dominates us. The sublimity of archi-tectural space opens us to *Being*.

Architecture interprets *Being* by structuring space in such a way that it significantly resembles the way *Being* empowers our existence—the place, projection, and source of our pos-sibilities. *Being* is that intangible matrix that makes our being possible. Architecture symbolizes, vaguely but surely, the coming to presence of the primordial power of *Being* in human experience. Architecture does this by revealing "earth," "world," and "region" as interrelated iconic sym-bols. Whereas pure music possesses an icon of the *Being* of human beings abstracted from things, architecture pos-sesses an icon of the *Being* of human beings interdependent with things. Pure music presents in its structure an objec-tive correlative of *Being* as temporality or process manifest-ing itself within human beings. Architecture presents, both structurally and qualitatively, an objective correlative of *Be-ing* as temporality or process manifesting itself within human beings and their environment.[2]

---

2. In a very beautiful description of a Greek temple, Heidegger suggests this iconicity between architecture and Being-in-the-World. "The Origin of the Work of Art," trans. Albert Hofstadter, *Philosophies of Art and Beauty*, eds. Albert Hofstadter and Richard Kuhns (New York: Random House, The Modern Library, 1964), pp. 669ff. But, as so often in Heideg-ger's work, the suggestion is not developed.

The earth as revealed by architecture is symbolic of *Being* as the securing agency that grounds the place of our existence, where we take our stand in the present, our center. In the crossing of Chartres I was completely centered and at a standstill, and thus I felt the attraction and support of the earth beneath me much more strongly than when I was on the outside. I became more explicitly aware of my place, my here and now, as being secured by a power over which I had no control and which seemed strangely "other." In most primitive cultures it is believed that man is born from the earth. And in many languages man is "the Earth-born." In countless myths Mother Earth is the bearer of man from birth to death. Of all things the expansive earth, with its germinal riches and vegetative fecundity, is the most natural symbol of security. Moreover, since the solidity of the earth encloses its depth in darkness, the earth is symbolic not only of the securing agency but also of the self-concealment of *Being*. No other thing exposes its surface more pervasively and yet hides its depth dimension more completely. The earth is closure in the midst of disclosure. If we dig below the surface, there is always a further depth in darkness that continues to escape our penetration. Thus the Earth Mother has a mysterious, nocturnal, even funerary aspect—she is also often a Goddess of Death. But, as Eliade points out, "even in respect of these negative aspects, one thing that must never be lost sight of, is that when the Earth becomes a goddess of Death, it is simply because she is felt to be the universal womb, the inexhaustible source of all creation."[3] Nothing in nature is more iconic with the securing agency and mystery of *Being* than the earth. Architecture accentuates this natural symbolism more than any other art.

A world or sky as revealed by architecture is symbolic of *Being* as the generating agency that enables us to project our possibilities and realize some of them. A horizon, always a necessary part of a world, is symbolic of the limitations that *Being* places upon our possibilities and realizations. The

3. Mircea Eliade, *Myths, Dreams and Mysteries,* trans. Philip Mairet (New York: Harper, 1961), p. 188.

light and heat of the sun are more iconic than anything else in nature with the generating agency of *Being*. Dante declared that "there is no visible thing in the world more worthy to serve as symbol of God than the Sun; which illuminates with visible life itself first and then all the celestial and mundane bodies." The energy of the moving sun brightens the sky which, in turn, opens up for us a spacious context within which we attempt to realize our possibilities. In total darkness we may be able to orient ourselves to the earth, but in order to move with direction, as do the blind, we must imagine space as open in some way, as a world enlightened with light even if our imaginations must provide that light. Total darkness, at least until we can envision a world, is terrifying. That is why, as the Preacher of Ecclesiastes proclaims, "the light is sweet, and a pleasant thing it is for the eyes to behold the sun." The "light of the living" is a common Hebrew phrase, and the Greek $\beta\lambda\acute{\epsilon}\pi\epsilon\iota\nu \ \phi\tilde{\omega}\varsigma$, "to behold light," is synonymous with the verb "to live." The light of the sky reveals the positioned interrelationships of things. The semi-spherical space of the sky with its limits provided by the horizon gives us a world within which we find ourselves. But a world is above all the context for activity. Thus a world stirs our imaginations to prehend possibilities. A world, with its suggestion of expectation, turns our faces to the future, just as the smile of the sun lures our eyes. Architecture organizes a world, usually far more tightly than nature, by centering that world on the earth by means of a building that reveals a region. By accentuating the natural iconicism of sunlight, sky, and horizon, architecture opens up a world that is symbolic of *Being* as the generating agency that empowers our projections into the future.

The "region" as revealed by architecture is symbolic of *Being* as the preserving agency that enables the past to be immanent in the present. The region is the cultural environment that supplied the values that guided the selection of the site and the shaping of the structure of a building. Medieval Christianity, feudalism, and scholasticism, for example, are part of the region of Chartres Cathedral, as Adams's *Mont St. Michel and Chartres* and Panofsky's *Gothic Architecture and Scholasticism* make clear. That cultural past, like all pasts, is no more. Yet what is now on the earth of Chartres would not be without that past, and that past makes its presence peculiarly felt in the present. Architecture brings out not only the presence of the past but the power of *Being* that makes this presence possible. With literature it is mainly a personal past that is immanently recalled, but with architecture it is mainly an impersonal past. Whereas literature is primarily a private art, architecture is primarily a public art. Through literature we feel the immanent recall of the past as more or less within our powers. The words are the catalysts, and then, or so it seems, our memories take over. With architecture, however, the past is more directly *in* the building, preserved in the way the materials have been formed. Whereas the immaterial flexibility of words, relatively speaking, allows them to take on new meanings that cover over the original meanings, materials such as stone ingrain the past in a way that resists masking. Even if erosion has erased most of the traces of the original forms, the patina of the erosive process leaves an indelible print. Thus the past as part of the given is much more tangibly present in architecture than in literature. This objectification or "regioning" of the past in a structure on the earth of the here and now leads us to remember—whereas literature may lead us to forget—that *Being* is the preserving agent, the power beyond our powers, that enables the past to coalesce with the present. The region is the source that shaped the present space of any work of architecture, just as our past is the source that shaped our present existence. But the traces of the past embedded in architecture make us aware, more than any other art or introspection, that the traces of the past in our memories are part of the process of *Being* which makes our human existence possible. Nothing made by man is more symbolic of the preserving agency of *Being* than architecture.

The earth is an icon of the present, a world of the future, and the regioning in a building, even one that is not architecture, of the past. But outside the realm of architecture these icons are usually not very vivid. Within the realm of architecture, however, they become vivid mainly because of their interdependence. The temporal phases these icons resemble are referred to each other as inseparable, and the effect of this ecstatic unity is of a vast power beyond our powers, of sublimity. Architecture opens us to *Being* in this way. But by also vivifying each of these icons, architecture transforms their vague resemblance to the temporal phases of *Being* into symbols that interpret *Being*.

We project our plans within a world limited by a horizon from the earth on which we stand. But how we stand, the source or region of our projections, is our past. The future represents the possibility and the past the basis of our lives in the present. In the open circle of future and past there exists no possibility which is not structured by the past, nor any realization which does not bring with it new possibilities. This ongoing circling is possible because of the present as the center. Around such a center as human existence, the future never shuts its doors and the past never assumes a final shape. Without the outer space or world of Chartres, the shaping of the inner space as determined by the region would not come to light. Without the region, there would be no shaping of the inner space and, in turn, no orientation of the outer around the inner space. Without the earth, there would be no centering of the inner and outer spaces. In our participating with architecture, past-present-future is felt as inseparable, and because we are led from outside to inside and around, interflowing images of reminiscence and premonition combine with our kinaesthetic feeling of the forces of space. As with music, we are caught up in temporality, although not quite so forcefully, because with architecture as with all the major plastic arts the order of perception is more under our control. Of all the works of man, however, only architecture strongly symbolizes the ecstatic unity of the temporal phases of *Being* in man as interdependent with his environment.

Music presents the structure of temporality, future-present-past as inherently interlinked, with the accent upon the future. Painting accents the present. Literature accents the past. Architecture, unlike pure music, presents the structure of temporality with things. And, unlike music, painting, and literature, architecture may accent any one of the three phases of temporality. All three, however, are always inseparably evident and, generally, are given relatively equal emphasis.

Architecture discloses the earth by drawing our attention to the building's site, to its submission to gravity, to its raw materials, or to its centrality in outer and inner space. Sites whose surrounding environment can be seen from great distances are especially favorable for helping a building bring out the earth. The site of the Parthenon, for example, is superior in this respect to the site of Chartres, because the Acropolis is a natural center that stands out prominently within a widespread concaved space. Thus the Parthenon is able to emphasize by continuity both the sheer heavy stoniness of the cliffs of the Acropolis and the gleaming whites of Athens, and by contrast the deep blue of the Mediterranean sky and sea and the grayish greens of the encompassing mountains that open out toward the weaving blue of the sea like the bent rims of a colossal flower. All of these elements of the earth would be present without the Parthenon, of course, but the Parthenon, whose columns from a distance push up like stamens, centers these elements more tightly so that their interrelationships add to the vividness of each. Together they form the ground from which the Parthenon slowly and majestically rises up and firmly returns.

The Parthenon is also exceptional in the way it manifests a gentle surrender to gravity. The horizontal rectangularity of the entablature follows evenly along the plain of the Acropolis with the steady beat of its supporting columns and quiets their upward thrust. Gravity is not only accepted but accentuated in this serene stability, and the hold of the earth is secure.

The site of Mont St. Michel can also be seen from great distances, especially from the sea, and the church, straining far up from the great rock cliffs, organizes a vast scene of sea, sand, shallow hills, and sky. But the spiny, lonely verticality of the church overwhelms the pull of the earth. We are lured to a world of light, whereas the Parthenon draws us back into the womb of the earth. Mont St. Michel discloses the earth, for both the earth and a world to be opened up require centering and thus each other, but the defiance of gravity weakens the securing sense of place. Mont St. Michel moves us around its walls with a dizzying effect, whereas the Parthenon moves us around slowly and securely so that our orientation is never in doubt. The significance of the earth is felt much more deeply at the Parthenon than at Mont St. Michel.

The complex of skyscrapers that composes Rockefeller Center (Plate 22) in New York City is an exceptional example of an architecture that allows for only a minimal submission to gravity. The surrounding buildings, unless we are high up in one nearby, block out the lower sections of the Center. If we are able to see the lower sections by getting in close, we are blocked from a clear and comprehensive view of the upper sections. Thus the relationships between the lower and upper sections are somewhat disintegrated, and there is a sense of these tapering towers, especially the R.C.A. Building, not only scraping but being suspended from the sky. The Lever House and the Union Carbide Building (Plate 27) not far away carry this feeling even further by placing their shaft-like boxes on stilts. These apparently weightless buildings mitigate but do not annihilate our feeling of the earth, for despite their arrow-like soaring we are aware of their base. Even at night, when the sides of these structures become dark curtains pierced by hundreds of square lights, we feel these lights, as opposed to the light of the stars, as

Plate 19   Giovanni Paolo Panini: *The Interior of the Pantheon* (c. 1740). 50½" x 39". Samuel H. Kress Collection. Courtesy The National Gallery of Art, Washington, D. C.

Plate 20 Anthemius of Tralles and Isidorous of Miletus: Hagia Sophia (532-63). Istanbul. Courtesy Turkish Information Office.

Plate 21   Richard Upjohn: Trinity Church (1839-46). Broadway at Wall Street, New York City. Photograph Eric Hass.

Plate 22 Collaboration of Reinhart and Hofmeister, Corbett, Harrison and MacMurray, and Hood and Fouilhoux: Rockefeller Center (1931-40). Fifth Avenue to Sixth Avenue, West 48th to 50th Streets, New York City. Courtesy Rockefeller Center, Incorporated.

Plate 23 Frank Lloyd Wright: Edgar J. Kaufmann House, "Falling Waters" (1936). Bear Run, Pennsylvania. Courtesy Western Pennsylvania Conservancy.

Plate 24 Le Corbusier: Notre-Dame-du-Haut (1950-55). Ronchamps, France. Courtesy Ezra Stoller © ESTO.

Plate 25 Henri Matisse: Chapel of the Rosary of the Dominican Nuns (1951). Vence, France. Courtesy the French Government Tourist Office.

Plate 26 Frank Lloyd Wright: Solomon R. Guggenheim Museum (1959). Fifth Avenue between 88th and 89th Streets, New York City. Courtesy Solomon R. Guggenheim Museum.

Plate 27 Skidmore, Owings, and Merrill: Union Carbide Building (1960). 270 Park Avenue, between 47th and 48th Streets. Courtesy the Union Carbide Corporation.

Plate 28 Cass Gilbert: Woolworth Building (1911-13). Broadway between Park Place and Barclay Street, New York City.

Plate 29 John Russell Pope: National Gallery of Art (1941). Seventh Street, Constitution Avenue, Fourth Street and Madison Drive, Washington, D. C. 1941. Courtesy The National Gallery of Art.

somehow grounded. Architecture in setting up a world always sets forth the earth, and vice versa.

When the medium of architecture is made up totally or in large part by unfinished materials furnished by nature, especially when they are from the site, these materials stand forth and also help to reveal the earthiness of the earth. In this respect stone, wood, and clay in a raw or relatively raw state are much more effective than steel, concrete, and glass. If the Parthenon had been made in concrete rather than in native Pentelic marble—the quarries can still be seen in the background—the Parthenon would not grow out of the soil so organically and some of the feeling of the earth would be dissipated. On the other hand, if the paint that originally covered most of the Parthenon had remained, the effect would be considerably less earthy than at present. Frank Lloyd Wright's Kaufman House (Plate 23) is an excellent example of the combined use of manufactured and raw materials that helps set forth the earth. The concrete and glass bring out by contrast the textures of stone and wood taken from the site, while the lacelike flow of the falling water is made even more graceful by its reflection in the smooth clear flow of concrete and glass. Like a wide-spreading plant, drawing the sunlight and rain to its good earth, this home seems to breathe within its homeland.

Finally, a building that is strongly centered, both in relation to its outer space and within its inner space, helps disclose the earth. Perhaps no building is more centered in its site than the Parthenon, but the weak centering of its inner space slackens somewhat the significance of the earth. There is no strong pull, as at Chartres, into the Parthenon, and when we get inside, the inner space, as we reconstruct it, is divided in such a way that no certain center can be felt. There is no place to come to an unequivocal standstill as at Chartres. Even Versailles, despite its seemingly never-ending partitions of inner space, brings us eventually to something of a center in the bedroom of Louis XIV. Yet this centering is made possible primarily by the view from the room that focuses both the pivotal position of the room in the building and the room's placement in a straight line to Paris in the far distance. Conversely, the inner space of Chartres, most of which from the crossing can be taken in with one sweep of the eye, achieves centrality without this kind of dependence upon outside orientation. Buildings such as the Parthenon and Versailles that divide the inner space with solid partitions invariably are weaker in inner centrality than buildings without such divisions. The endless boxes within boxes of the Union Carbide Building (Plate 27) negate any possibility of significant inner centering, adding to the unearthiness of this cage of steel.

Buildings whose inner space not only draws us to a privileged position but whose inner space or most of it can be seen from that privileged position evoke a feeling of powerful inner centeredness. This feeling is further enhanced when the expanses of inner space are more or less equidistant from the privileged position. Thus a Greek-cross building, such as Giuliano da Sangallo's S. Maria delle Carceri in Prato, is likely to center us in inner space more strongly than a Latin-cross building such as Chartres. If Bramante's and Michelangelo's Greek-cross plan for St. Peter's had been carried out, the centrality of the inner space would have been greatly enhanced. It does not follow, however, that all centrally planned buildings that open up all or almost all of the inner space will be strongly centered internally. San Vitale in Ravenna, for example, is basically an octagon, but the enfolded spaces are not clearly outlined and differentiated as in S. Maria delle Carceri. There is a floating and welling of space working out and up through the arcaded niches into the outer layers of the ambulatory and gallery that fade into semi-darkness. The dazzling colors of the varied marble slabs and the mosaics lining the piers and walls, unlike the somber static grays and whites of Sangallo's inner church, add to our sense of spatial uncertainty. We can easily discover the center of San Vitale if we so desire, but there is no directed movement to it because the indeterminacy of the surrounding spaces makes the feeling of the center insecure and insignificant. The unanchored restlessness of the interior of San Vitale belies its solid weighty exterior.

Buildings in the round, other things being equal, are the most internally centered of all. In the Pantheon (Plate 19) all inner space can be seen with a turn of the head, and the grand and clear symmetry of the enclosing shell draws us to the center of the circle, the privileged position, beneath the "eye" of the dome opening to a bit of the sky. Few buildings root us more firmly in the earth. The massive dome with its stony bluntness seems to be drawn down by the funneled and dimly spreading light falling through the "eye." This is a dome of destiny pressed tightly down on men. We are driven earthward in this crushing ambience. Even on the outside the Pantheon seems to be forcing down. In the circular interior of Wright's Guggenheim Museum (Plate 26) not all of the inner space can be seen from the privileged position, but the smoothly curving ramps that come down like a whirlpool make us feel the earth beneath as our only support. The Chapel of M. I. T. by Saarinen, also circular, accents the earth somewhat differently. The only natural light allowed to come inside falls upon pools of water that lie below the floor and around the perimeter of the drum, the light flickering up the undulating interior walls. Thus in a strange way it appears as if the light, like the water, were coming up from the earth. This helps draw the drum down into the ground. In buildings such as these we are made to feel the presence of the earth with exceptional force, especially in their centers. Whereas in buildings such as Mont St. Michel and Chartres mass is overcome, the weight lightened, and the downward motion thwarted, in buildings such as the Pantheon, the Chapel of M. I. T., and the Guggenheim Museum mass comes out heavily and pushing down.

The importance of a center, usually within a circle, as a privileged and even sacred position in relation to the earth, is common among the spatial arrangements of ancient cultures, for example, Stonehenge on the Salisbury Plain of England. And, according to Plutarch,[4] the first city of Rome was laid out by the Etruscans around a circular trench or *mundus,* over which was placed a great capstone. Around the *mundus* the Etruscans outlined a large circle for the walls which would enclose the city. Following a carefully prescribed ritual, a deep furrow was plowed along the circle and the plow was lifted from the ground wherever a gate was to appear. This circular plan was subdivided by two main cross-streets. The *cardo* ran north and south in imitation of the axis of the earth, while the *decumanus* ran east and west, dividing the city into four equal parts. These streets crossed at the site of the *mundus,* believed to be an entrance to the underworld, and the capstone was removed three times each year to allow the spirits passage between the world of the living and the world of the dead. The beliefs generating such planning and customs are as dead in Western civilization as Nietzsche's God, but if we are not ontologically obtuse, a powerful centering of space may help return *Being* to our awareness.

Architecture accentuates the natural iconicism of the earth —its resemblance to both security and self-concealment. The earth of architecture is set forth within a world by means of a regioning. Thus the earth of architecture becomes a symbol of *Being* as the securing and yet mysterious agency that grounds us in our present place, that makes the present possible within the context of future and past.

Architecture discloses a world by drawing our attention to the sky bounded by a horizon, accomplished by means of making a building appear high and centered within the sky or defying gravity or tightly integrating the light of outer with inner space. Negatively, architecture that accents a world deemphasizes the features that accent the earth. Thus the manufactured materials such as the steel and glass of the Union Carbide Building (Plate 27) help separate this build-

---

4. *Plutarch's Lives,* trans. John Dryden (New York: Random House, The Modern Library, 1932), p. 31.

ing from the earth. Positively, the most effective means at
the architect's disposal for accenting a world is turning his
structure toward the sky in such a way that the sky's horizon
forms a spacious context. Architecture is an art of bounding
as well as opening.

Even before buildings become architecture, primitive man
expresses this need for a world by centering himself in relation to the sky by means of an *axis mundi*. Eliade presents
many instances, for example among the nomadic Australians,
whose economy is still at the stage of food gathering and
small-game hunting:

> According to the traditions of an Arunta tribe, the Achilpa, in
> mythical times the divine being Numbakula cosmicized their
> future territory, created their Ancestor, and established their
> institutions. From the trunk of a gum tree Numbakula fash-
> ioned the sacred pole (*kauwa-auwa*) and, after anointing it
> with blood, climbed it and disappeared into the sky. This pole
> (the *axis mundi*) represents a cosmic axis, for it is around the
> sacred pole that territory becomes habitable, hence is trans-
> formed into a world. The sacred pole consequently plays an
> important role ritually. During their wanderings the Achilpa
> always carry it with them and choose the direction they are
> to take by the direction toward which it bends. This allows
> them, while being continually on the move, to be always in
> "their world" and, at the same time, in communication with
> the sky into which Numbakula vanished.
>
> For the pole to be broken denotes catastrophe; it is like "the
> end of the world," reversion to chaos. Spencer and Gillen report
> that once, when the pole was broken, "the entire clan were in
> consternation; they wandered about aimlessly for a time, and
> finally lay down on the ground together and waited for death to
> overtake them."[5]

When buildings accent a world, their turning to the sky
invariably suggests a kind of *axis mundi*. The perpendicu-
larity and centering of the Acropolis, for example, make it a
kind of natural *axis mundi* that would open up the sky to
some extent even if the Parthenon had never been built.

5. *The Sacred and the Profane,* trans. Willard R. Trask (New York: Harcourt, Brace, 1959) , pp. 32f.

But the flat plains around Chartres would rarely turn us to the sky without the spires of the Cathedral. At one time the spire of Trinity Church (Plate 21), 1839–46, in New York City, beautifully proportioned despite its lack of originality, and higher than the spires of Chartres, must have organized the sky. But now its thrust is impotent, because the outer space it once centered is swamped by skyscrapers. Buildings that stretch up far above the land and nearby structures, such as Mont St. Michel, Durham Cathedral, Chartres, and Rockefeller Center (Plate 22), not only direct our eye to the sky but act as a center that orders the sunlight in such a way that a world with a horizon comes into view. The sky both opens up and takes on limits. Such buildings reach up like an *axis mundi,* and the sky reaches down to meet them in mutual embrace. And we are blessed with an orienting center, and our motion is given direction and boundaries.

The more a building appears to defy gravity, the more it is likely to disclose the sky, for this defiance draws our eyes upward. The thrust against gravity is not simply a question of how high the building goes. Most of the skyscrapers of New York City, like the Woolworth Building (Plate 28), and unlike the Union Carbide Building (Plate 27), seem to finally stop not because they have reached a more or less perfect union with the sky but because the space used up had exhausted them. They hang lifelessly despite their great height. They seem to have just enough strength to stand upright but no power to transcend the rudimentary laws of statics. Gravity wins out after all. The up and the down frustrate each other, and their conflict dims the world that might have been. Chartres is not nearly so tall as the Woolworth Building, and yet it appears far taller. The stony logic of the press of Chartres's flying buttresses and the arched roof, towers, and spires that carry on their upward thrust seem to overcome the binding of the earth, just as the stone birds on Chartres's walls seem about to break their bonds and fly out into the world. The reach up is full of vital force and finally comes to rest comfortably and securely in

the bosom of the heavens. Mont St. Michel and Durham
Cathedral, mainly because of the advantages of their sites,
are even more impressive in this respect. But perhaps Bru-
nelleschi's dome of the Duomo of Florence is the most powerful structure ever built in seeming to defy gravity and
achieving height in relation to its site. The eight outside
ribs spring up to the cupola with tremendous energy, in part
because they repeat the spring of the mountains that encircle
Florence. The dome, visible from everywhere, appears to be
precisely centered in the Arno valley, precisely as high as it
should be in order to organize its sky. The world of Florence
begins and ends at the still point of this dome of aspiration.
On the other hand, Michelangelo's dome of St. Peter's, although grander in proportions and over fifty feet higher,
fails to organize the sky of Rome nearly so firmly, because
the hills of Rome do not lend themselves to centralized
organization.

When the light of outer space suffuses the light of inner
space, especially when the light from the outside seems to
dominate or draw the light from the inside, this also helps
accent a world. Inside Chartres the light is so majestic that
we cannot fail to imagine the light outside that is generating
the transfiguration inside. For a medieval man like Abbot
Suger, the effect was mystical:

> When the house of God, many colored as the radiance of
> precious jewels, called me from the cares of the world, then
> holy meditation led my mind to thoughts of piety, exalting my
> soul from the material to the immaterial, and I seemed to find
> myself, as it were, in some strange part of the universe which
> was neither wholly of the baseness of the earth, nor wholly of
> the serenity of heaven, but by the grace of God I seemed lifted
> in a mystic manner from this lower toward the upper sphere.

On the other hand, for a contemporary man with ontological sensitivity, the effect is more likely to be of *Being* as a
transcendental but also immanent power. The stained glass
is felt more as integrating us with rather than separating us

from a world. We sense the unity of inner with outer space by means of the light, the effect that Saarinen avoids in the Chapel of M.I.T. The upper chapel of Sainte-Chapelle in Paris, built by order of St. Louis, is an extraordinary example of how even a small building can accent a world by means of its stained glass. The inner space is so full of moving color energized by the sun, whose power changes with the hours and the seasons, that we image a great world outside even though we cannot see it directly and even though the structure of the building has little centralizing effect upon the sky. Unlike Sainte-Chapelle, Hagia Sophia in Constantinople (Plate 20) has no stained glass and its glass areas are completely dominated by the walls and dome. Yet the subtle placement of the little windows, especially around the perimeter of the dome, seems to draw the light of the inner space outside. Thus, unlike the Pantheon, the great masses of Hagia Sophia seem to rise. The dome floats gently, despite its diameter of 107 feet, and the great enfolded space beneath is absorbed into the even greater open space outside. We image a world.

Architecture sets forth the iconicism of a world—its resemblance to generation and activity. The sun's energy is the ultimate source of all life. The sun's light enables us to see the physical environment and guides our steps accordingly. "Arise, shine, for thy light is come" (Isaiah 60:1). The sky with its horizon provides a spacious context for our progress. The world of nature vaguely suggests the potentialities of the future. Architecture, however, tightly centers a world on the earth by means of a regioning. This unification vivifies the iconicity of a world to the future. Thus a world of architecture becomes symbolic of *Being* as the generating agency that makes the future possible within the context of present and past.

Architecture discloses a region by drawing our attention to the way the materials have been formed in separating an inner from an outer space. The structures of architecture

are part of the given, the directly present, but they refer back
to and interpret some of the fundamental values of the originating culture or society. Even the selection of the physical
environment of a building was influenced by the cultural
environment. Architecture is a peculiarly public art because
buildings generally have a social function and most buildings
require public funds. More than any other artist, the architect must consider his public. If he does not, very few of his
plans are likely to materialize. The essential values of contemporary society are a part of any artist's subject matter,
part of what he must interpret in his work, and this is
especially so with the architect. Even if the architect reacts
against these values, as all great architectural innovators are
likely to do, the values he reacts against are suggested. The
structures of architecture disclose some of the basic attitudes
of a culture—the region—as qualified by the architect's personality.

The way the architect is influenced by his region has been
given many explanations. According to Walter Abell, the
region, or what he calls the state of mind of a society, influences the architect directly. The historical and social circumstances generate in the minds of the members of a culture
psychosocial tensions and latent imagery. The architect, one
of the most sensitive members of a society, releases this tension and condenses this imagery in his art. The psyche of the
artist, elucidated by Abell by means of psychoanalytic
theory and social psychology, creates the basic forms of art;
but this psyche is controlled by the state of mind of the
artist's society which, in turn, is controlled by the historical
and social circumstances of which it is a part.

Art is a symbolical projection of collective psychic tensions. . . .
Within the organism of a culture, the artist functions as a kind
of preconsciousness, providing a zone of infiltration through
which the obscure stirrings of collective intuition can emerge
into collective consciousness. The artist is the personal trans-
former within whose sensitivity a collective psychic charge,

latent in society, condenses into a cultural image. He is in short the dreamer . . . of the collective dream.[6]

Whereas Abell stresses the unconscious tensions of the social state of mind that influence the architect's regioning of a society's values, Erwin Panofsky stresses the artist's mental habits, conscious as well as unconscious, that act as principles that guide the architect's regioning. For example:

> We can observe [between about 1130 and 1270] . . . a connection between Gothic art and Scholasticism which is more concrete than a mere "parallelism" and yet more general than those individual (and very important) "influences" which are inevitably exerted on painters, sculptors, or architects by erudite advisors. In contrast to a mere parallelism, the connection which I have in mind is a genuine cause-and-effect relation; but in contrast to an individual influence, this cause-and-effect relation comes about by diffusion rather than by direct impact. It comes about by the spreading of what may be called, for want of a better term, a mental habit—reducing this overworked cliché to its precise Scholastic sense as a "principle that regulates the act." . . . Such mental habits are at work in all and every civilization.[7]

Whatever the explanation, and Abell's and Panofsky's are two of the best,[8] the structures of architecture reflect and interpret some of the fundamental values of the society of the architect. Yet even as these structures are settling, the society changes. Thus the regioning of architecture, while keeping the past immanent in the present, takes on more and more the aura of the past, especially if the originating values are no longer viable or easily understandable. The Tomb of the Pulcella (Young Girl) in Tarquinia was built about the same time as the Parthenon, but because we have much more

---

6. *The Collective Dream in Art* (Cambridge, Mass.: Harvard University Press, 1957), p. 328.
7. *Gothic Architecture and Scholasticism* (Latrobe, Pa.: Archabbey Press, 1951), pp. 20f.
8. For an evaluation of these and other explanations, see my "The Sociological Imperative of Stylistic Development," *Bucknell Review* 11 (Dec. 1963): 54–80.

rapport with Greek than with Etruscan values, the tomb seems far older.

Anything that now exists but has a past may function as a sign of the past, but the regioning of architecture interprets the past. The structures of architecture not only preserve the past more carefully than most things, for most architects build buildings to last, but these structures enlighten that past. They inform about the region. The architect did the forming, of course, but from beginning to end that forming, insofar as it succeeded artistically, brought forth, along with the earth and a world, a region. Thus architectural structures are weighted with the past—a past, furthermore, that is more public than private. The past is preserved in the structures as part of the given of architecture, and this preservation appears as beyond our personal powers. With literature the past appears as more within us, as under the control of our memories, whereas with architecture the past appears as more outside us. This regioning on the earth within a world brings the past into ecstatic unity with the present and future. The structures of architecture, by disclosing a region, are symbolic of the preserving power of *Being* that makes possible the immanency of any past in the present.

The stronger the informing of the structures of architecture, the more the accent on the region's immanence in the present. Every stone of the Parthenon, in the way it was cut and fitted, tells us something about the values of the Age of Pericles—for example, the emphasis upon moderation and harmony, the importance of mathematical measurement and yet its subordination to man's aesthetic needs, the respect for the "thingliness" of things, the eminence of man and his rationality, the immanence rather than the absoluteness of the sacred. The weaker the informing of the structures, the weaker the disclosure of the region, and, in turn, the feeling of the past as immanent in the present because of the preserving power of *Being*. The Tomb of the Pulcella impresses us as very ancient, but the Tomb's structures are not so informing as the Parthenon's, probably, in part, because of our profound ignorance about Etruscan culture. In any case, the Tomb does not symbolize for us the preserving power of Being so strongly as the Parthenon. The past weighs on the Tomb, whereas the past enlightens the Parthenon. The Tomb, much more than the Parthenon, illustrates Hegel's remark: "The statues set up are now corpses in stone whence the animating soul has flown, while the hymns of praise are words from which all belief has gone. The tables of the gods are bereft of spiritual food and drink, and from his games and festivals man no more receives the joyful sense of his unity with the divine Being."[9]

Chartres is an example of forceful regioning. The structures reveal and interpret three principal regional sources: the special importance of Mary, to whom the cathedral is dedicated; the cathedral school, one of the most important centers of learning in Europe in the twelfth and thirteenth centuries; and the value preferences of the main patrons—the royal family, the lesser nobility, and the local guilds. The windows of the 175 surviving panels and the sculpture, including over 2000 carved figures, were a Bible in glass and stone for the illiterate, but they also were a visual encyclopedia for the literate. From these structures the iconographer can trace almost every fundamental facet of the originating region of Chartres—the conception of the history of mankind from Adam and Eve to the Last Judgment; the story of Christ from his ancestors to his Ascension; church history; ancient lore and contemporary history; the latest scientific knowledge; the curriculum of the cathedral school as divided into the Trivium and the Quadrivium; the hierarchy of the nobility and the guilds; the code of chivalry and manners; and the hopes and fears of the time. But, furthermore, the participator also becomes aware of a region that believed God to be absolute but the Virgin to be both divine and immanent, not just a Heavenly Queen but also a mother. For,

---

9. *The Phenomenology of Mind*, trans. J. B. Baillie (London: George Allen and Unwin, 1931) , p. 753.

as Henry Adams insisted: "You had better stop here, once for all, unless you are willing to feel that Chartres was made what is was, not by the artist, but by the Virgin." Even if we disagree with Adams, we understand, at least to some extent, Mary's special position within the context of awe aroused by God as "Wholly Other." The architecture of Chartres does many things, but above all, its structures preserve that awe. Something of the region of the Chartres that was comes into the present intensity with overwhelming impact. And then we can understand something about the feelings of such medieval men as Abbot Haimon of Normandy who, after visiting Chartres, wrote to his brother monks in Tutbury, England:

> Who has ever heard tell, in times past, that powerful princes of the world, that men brought up in honor and wealth, that nobles, men and women, have bent their proud and haughty necks to the harness of carts, and that, like beasts of burden, they have dragged to the abode of Christ these waggons, loaded with wines, grains, oil, stone, wood, and all that is necessary for the wants of life, or for the construction of the church ... ? When they have reached the church, they arrange the waggons about it like a spiritual camp, and during the whole night they cele-brate the watch by hymns and canticles. On each waggon they light tapers and lamps; they place there the infirm and sick, and bring them the precious relics of the Saints for their relief.

The clearing of this holy hearth creates on this earth a world into which a region flares. The present-future-past come forth in ecstatic unity.

The National Gallery of Art (Plate 29) in Washington, D. C., on the other hand, is an example of weak regioning. Combining the portico of the Temple of Diana and the dome of the Pantheon with vast wings that stretch out to a total length of 785 feet, this huge neoclassic building, despite the very expensive materials and the great engineering skill that went into its making, reveals practically nothing about its region except the imitative conservatism of its designers and the wealth and conservatism of its patrons. In the 1930s, when the Gallery was planned, mainly by John Russell Pope, the United States had risen from its worst depression and was beginning to face, as potentially the most powerful nation in the world, the crisis of the coming Second World War. At the Dedication of the Gallery in March 1941, President Roosevelt concluded his address:

> Seventy-eight years ago, in the third year of the war between the States, men and women gathered here in the capitol of a divided nation, here in Washington, to see the bronze goddess of liberty set upon its top.
> It had been an expensive, a laborious business, diverting money and labor from the prosecution of the war and certain critics . . . found much to criticize. . . . But the President of the United States, whose name was Lincoln, when he heard those criticisms, answered: "If people see the Capitol going on it is a sign that we intend this Union shall go on."
> We may borrow the words for our own. We, too, intend the Union to go on. We intend it shall go on, carrying with it the great tradition of the human spirit which created it.
> The dedication of this gallery to a living past and to a greater and more richly living future is the measure of the earnestness of our intention that the freedom of the human spirit shall go on too.

Brave words by a brave president. But what living past does the architecture of this building disclose? And in what way does this building bring forth the freedom of the human spirit that shall go on? The Gallery reveals rather the taste—derived from Jefferson's belief that the beautiful in architecture had been forever established in Roman masterpieces—that has bound the architecture of Washington to pale imitations of what had once been a living art. Nothing of the thrusting optimism of the United States, its ceaseless and ingenious ferment, its power and pragmatism comes out. Even the superb technology of this country is masked. Thus the engineering excellence of the steel structure is covered up, as if there were something shameful about the steel that had helped make the United States prosperous. Even the immense dome gets lost in the mass of marble, and so the building spreads out without centering the outer space. Instead, the Gallery awkwardly imposes its clumsy bulk into the graceful open ensemble of the Mall as planned by L'Enfant. Even the function of the building is hidden. The exterior tells us nothing about the use or even the structuring of the inner space. The building could have been constructed for just about any purpose that requires great inner dimensions. Even a "draw" by the inner into the outer space is lacking, surely an adjunct that a museum of art should provide. Indeed, the forty granite steps of mighty spread which mount up from the Mall to the main entrance, like the terror-inspiring stairways to the Mayan sacrificial platforms, tend to weaken the visitor or drive him away. If he persists and survives, the pictures mercifully take over his attention, although their display is rarely felicitous. The architecture, if it can be called that, goes unnoticed. The regioning is so weak that neither the earth nor a world comes into focus. Since no past becomes immanent in the given of this inert Gargantuan pile, the past and present and future fail to come forth as temporality. The breath of process that makes life possible is suffocated by the dead weight of the past. Unimaginatively conceived, the National Gallery of Art was still-born.

The architect carves space apart in such a way that the power of process is made visible and tangible by being enclosed within a boundary. All beautiful buildings possess an icon of temporality. Even secular buildings, such as the Union Carbide Building (Plate 27), reveal *Being-as-immanent*. But their revelations of the ontological dimension lack an awe-full context because their structures basically inform about ontical values. Thus despite the sublimity of the Union Carbide Building, its structures reveal more of the power of man's technology than of *Being-as-transcendental*. The power of *Being* is domesticated. The sublimity of buildings that are implicitly religious, on the other hand, remains more overpowering. Rockefeller Center (Plate 22) from the outside, for example, is not so surely secular as the Union Carbide Building. The sublimity of the Center is more "other" because its aura of offices is not so evident as around the Union Carbide Building. But, in contrast with the other arts, works that are implicitly religious are rare in architecture. Buildings usually are either secular or explicitly religious. The architect who does not interpret secular values as his primary subject matter is likely to feel the power of centered space as something more than merely immanent. Nothing in nature is more sublime than centered space, and for the architect this kind of space is for safekeeping. As he tries to protect and preserve centered space, its power tends to lead him to iconic and conventional symbolizations. The rolling roof of Le Corbusier's Chapel of Notre Dame du Haut (Plate 24) at Ronchamp, which twists up as if in agony and sweeping appeal, suggests ultimate concern; the dim flickering luminosity of the perfectly balanced interior of Saarinen's Chapel of M. I. T. suggests reverence; and the fresh radiant simplicity of Matisse's Chapel of the Rosary (Plate 25) at Vence suggests peace. These iconic symbols are effective and yet, like all iconic symbols, vague. The power of space demands further articulation. Conventional symbols such as the cross, socially rooted and supported and integrally involved with liturgical requirements, are needed to focus further the mysterious ultimate meanings of centered space. The architect may not necessarily have a "passion for the conventional symbol," but even more than patrons, *Being* may coerce him into their use. Then the architect consecrates space and creates a church.

When the architect shepherds space religiously, his shelter becomes the House of *Being*. Then most of the other religious works of art have their most suitable abode. Then the languages of the sacred can communicate in harmony. Our time has lost this unity. But our time discloses, as perhaps no other time, the utter futility of life that has forgotten *Being*. Dietrich Bonhoeffer, in one of his last letters from the Nazi prison of Tegel, noted that "now that it has become of age, the world is more Godless, and perhaps it is for that very reason nearer to God than ever before." We could not feel so homeless unless there were a home. We are patients who can be cured only if we acknowledge our sickness. And then in our care for *Being* is our cure. Our artists, secular as well as religious, not only reveal our despair but in the depths of that darkness open paths back to *Being*. If we take one of those paths, and if we listen to the sacred language along the way, *Being* may again grace our destinies.

Selected Bibliography

BOOKS

Abell, Walter. *Representation and Form*. New York: Charles Scribner's Sons, 1936.

——. *The Collective Dream in Art*. Cambridge, Mass.: Harvard University Press, 1957.

Adams, Henry. *Mont St. Michel and Chartres*. Boston and New York: Houghton Mifflin Co., 1933.

Aldrich, Virgil. *Philosophy of Art*. Englewood Cliffs, N.J.: Prentice-Hall, Inc., 1963.

Altizer, Thomas J. J. *Mircea Eliade and the Dialectic of the Sacred*. Philadelphia: Westminster Press, 1963.

—— and Hamilton, William. *Radical Theology and the Death of God*. Indianapolis: Bobbs-Merrill, 1966.

——. ed. *Toward a New Christianity: Readings in the Death of God Theology*. New York: Harcourt, Brace and World, 1967.

——. *The Descent into Hell*. Philadelphia and New York: J. B. Lippincott Co., 1970.

Arnheim, Rudolf. *Art and Visual Perception*. Berkeley and Los Angeles: University of California Press, 1954.

Auden, W. H. *The Collected Poetry of W. H. Auden*. New York: Random House, 1945.

Ayer, A. J. *Language, Truth and Logic.* London: V. Gollancz Ltd., 1936.

Barrett, William. "Art and Being." In *Art and Philosophy,* edited by Sidney Hook. New York: New York University Press, 1966.

Beardsley, Monroe. *Aesthetics: Problems in the Philosophy of Criticism.* New York: Harcourt, Brace, 1958.

————. *Aesthetics from Classical Greece to the Present.* New York: The Macmillan Co., 1966.

Beckett, Samuel. *Proust.* New York: Grove Press, 1931.

Bell, Clive. *Art.* London: Chatto and Windus, 1914.

Bellow, Saul. *Herzog.* New York: Viking Press, 1964.

Berdyaev, Nicolas. *Slavery and Freedom.* Translated by R. M. French. London: Geoffrey Bles: The Centenary Press, 1944.

Berenson, Bernard. *The Florentine Painters of the Renaissance.* New York: G. P. Putnam's Sons, 1909.

————. *Aesthetics and History.* Garden City, N.Y.: Doubleday and Co., 1953.

Bevan, Edwin. *Symbolism and Belief.* New York: The Macmillan Co., 1938.

Buber, Martin. *Between Man and Man.* Translated by Ronald Gregor Smith. Boston: Beacon Press, 1955.

Bugbee, Henry G., Jr. *The Inward Morning.* State College, Pa.: Bald Eagle Press, 1958.

Bunyan, John. *The Pilgrim's Progress.* New York: E. P. Dutton and Co., 1906.

Céline, Louis-Ferdinand. *Journey to the End of the Night.* Translated by John H. P. Marks. New York: Little, Brown, and Co., 1934.

Cohen, Morris. *A Preface to Logic.* New York: H. Holt and Co., 1944.

Cohen, Selma Jean. "A Prolegomenon to an Aesthetics of Dance." In *Aesthetic Inquiry: Essays on Art Criticism and the Philosophy of Art,* edited by Monroe Beardsley and Herbert M. Schueller. Belmont, California: Dickenson Publishing Co., 1967.

Coleridge, Samuel Taylor. *The Complete Works of Samuel Taylor Coleridge.* 7 vols., edited by W. G. T. Shedd. New York: Harper and Brothers, 1853.

Collingwood, R. G. *The Principles of Art.* New York: Oxford University Press, 1958.

Croce, Benedetto. *Aesthetics.* Translated by D. Ainslie. London: Macmillan and Co., 1922.

Dewey, John. *Art as Experience.* New York: Minton, Balch, and Co., 1934.

——. *A Common Faith.* New Haven: Yale University Press, 1934.

Dezallier d'Argeuville, Antoine Joseph. *Abgégé de la vie des plus fameux peintres.* 4 vols. Paris: De Bure L'aîné, 1745.

Dickens, Charles. *Great Expectations.* New York: E. P. Dutton and Co., 1907.

Dixon, John W., Jr. *Nature and Grace in Art.* Chapel Hill, N. C.: University of North Carolina Press, 1964.

Donne, John. *The Complete Poetry and Selected Prose of John Donne.* Edited by Charles M. Coffin. New York: Random House, The Modern Library, 1952.

Dostoevsky, Fyodor. *The Brothers Karamazov.* Translated by Constance Garnett. New York: Random House, The Modern Library, 1929.

Dufrenne, Mikel. "The Aesthetic Object and the Technical Object." In *Aesthetic Inquiry: Essays on Art Criticism and the Philosophy of Art,* edited by Monroe Beardsley and Herbert M. Schueller. Belmont, Calif.: Dickenson Publishing Co., 1967.

Duhem, Pierre. *The Aim and Structure of Physical Theory.* Translated by Philip P. Weiner. New York: Atheneum Publishers, 1962.

Durkheim, Émile. *The Elementary Forms of the Religious Life.* Translated by J. W. Swain. Glencoe, Illinois: Free Press, 1947.

Edie, James M., ed. *An Invitation to Phenomenology.* Chicago: Quadrangle Books, 1965.

Einstein, Albert. *Comment je vois le monde.* Traduit par le Colonel Cros. Paris: E. Flammamarion, 1934.

Eliade, Mircea. *Yoga: Immortality and Freedom.* Translated by Willard R. Trask. New York: Pantheon Books, 1958.

————. "Methodological Remarks on the Study of Religious Symbolism." In *The History of Religions,* edited by Mircea Eliade and Joseph M. Kitagawa. Chicago: University of Chicago Press, 1959.

————. *The Sacred and the Profane.* Translated by Willard R. Trask. New York: Harcourt, Brace and Co., 1959.

————. *Myths, Dreams and Mysteries.* Translated by Philip Mairet. New York: Harper, 1961.

Eliot, T. S. *Four Quartets.* New York: Harcourt, Brace and Co., 1943.

————. "Ulysses, Order, and Myth." In *Critiques and Essays on Modern Fiction,* edited by John W. Aldridge. New York: Ronald Press Co., 1952.

Ellison, Ralph. *Invisible Man.* New York: Random House, 1947.

Elton, William, ed. *Aesthetics and Language.* New York: Philosophical Library, Inc., 1954.

Eversole, Finley. *Christian Faith and the Contemporary Arts.* New York and Nashville: Abingdon Press, 1962.

Faulkner, William. *The Sound and the Fury.* New York: Random House, The Modern Library, 1946.

Focillon, Henri. *The Life of Forms in Art.* Translated by Charles Beecher Hogan and George Kubler. 2nd English ed., enlarged. New York: George Wittenborn, Inc., 1948.

Fraser, J. T., ed. *The Voices of Time: A Cooperative Survey of Man's Views of Time as Expressed by the Sciences and by the Humanities.* New York: George Braziller, 1966.

Frye, Northrup. *Fearful Symmetry: A Study of William Blake.* Princeton: Princeton University Press, 1947.

Gadamer, Hans-Georg. *Wahrheit und Methode.* Tübingen: Niemeyer, 1960.

Goethe, J. W. von. *Conversations of Goethe with Eckermann.* Translated by John Oxenford. London: J. M. Dent and Sons, 1930.

Greene, Theodore Meyer. *The Arts and the Art of Criticism.* Princeton: Princeton University Press, 1940.

————. *Moral, Aesthetic, and Religious Insight.* New Brunswick, New Jersey: Rutgers University Press, 1957.

Gunn, Thom and Ander. *Positives.* Chicago: University of Chicago Press, 1967.

Gurney, Edmund. *The Power of Sound.* London: Smith, Elder and Co., 1880.

Hanslick, Eduard. *The Beautiful in Music.* Translated by Gustav Cohen. New York: The Liberal Arts Press, 1957.

Hardy, Thomas. *Tess of the D'Urbervilles.* New York: Random House, The Modern Library, 1932.

Hartshorne, Charles and Weiss, Paul, eds. *Collected Papers of Charles Sanders Peirce.* Cambridge, Mass.: Harvard University Press, 1931–35.

Hartshorne, Charles. *The Philosophy and Psychology of Sensation.* Chicago: The University of Chicago Press, 1934.

————. *Man's Vision of God.* Chicago and New York: Willet, Clark and Co., 1941.

————. *The Divine Relativity.* New Haven: Yale University Press, 1948.

————. *Reality as Social Process.* Glencoe, Ill.: Free Press, 1953.

Hazleton, Roger. *A Theological Approach to Art.* Nashville and New York: Abingdon Press, 1967.

Hegel, G. W. F. *The Phenomenology of Mind.* Translated by J. B. Baillie. London: George Allen and Unwin, 1931.

Heidegger, Martin. *Kant und das Problem der Metaphysik.* Bonn: F. Cohen, 1929.

————. *Über den Humanismus.* Frankfurt a.M.: Klostermann, 1946.

————. *Holzwege.* Frankfurt a.M.: Klostermann, 1950.

————. *Erläuterungen zur Hölderlins Dichtung.* Frankfurt a.M.: Klostermann, 1951.

————. *Vorträge und Aufsätze.* Pfullingen: Neske, 1954.

————. *Vom Wesen des Grundes.* Frankfurt a.M.: Klostermann, 1955.

————. *Hebel der Hausfreund.* Pfullingen: Neske, 1957.

————. *Unterwegs zur Sprache.* Pfullingen: Neske, 1959.

————. *Nietzsche.* 2 vols. Pfullingen: Neske, 1961.

————. *Was Heisst Denken?* Tübingen: Niemeyer, 1961.

————. *Being and Time.* Translated by John Macquarrie and Edward Robinson. New York: Harper and Row, 1962.

————. "The Origin of the Work of Art." Translated by Albert Hofstadter. In *Philosophies of Art and Beauty,* edited by Albert Hofstadter and Richard Kuhns. New York: Random House, The Modern Library, 1964.

————. "Remembrance of the Poet." Translated by Douglas Scott. In *Existence and Being.* Chicago: Henry Regnery Co., A Gateway Edition, 1965.

————. "What is Metaphysics?" Translated by R. F. C. Hull and Alan Crick. In *Existence and Being.* Chicago: Henry Regnery Co., A Gateway Edition, 1965.

————. *Discourse on Thinking.* Translated by John M. Anderson and E. Hans Freund. New York: Harper and Row, 1966.

————. *Die Kunst und der Raum.* St. Gallen: Erker, 1969.

Hemingway, Ernest. *To Have and Have Not.* New York: Charles Scribner's Sons, 1937.

————. *The Old Man and the Sea.* New York: Charles Scribner's Sons, 1952.

Herbert, George. "The Altar." In *The Works of George Herbert.* Edited by F. E. Hutchinson. Oxford: Clarendon Press, 1941.

Hopkins, Gerard Manley. "Pied Beauty." In *Poems of Gerard Manley Hopkins,* 3rd ed., edited by W. H. Gardner. New York and London: Oxford University Press, 1948.

Hopper, Stanley Romaine, ed. *Spiritual Problems in Contemporary Literature.* The Institute for Religious and Social Studies. New York and London: Harper and Brothers, 1952.

Hungerland, Isabel C. *Poetic Discourse.* Berkeley: University of California Press, 1958.

Hunt, John W. *William Faulkner: Art in Theological Tension.* Syracuse, New York: Syracuse University Press, 1965.

Hunter, Sam. *Modern American Painting and Sculpture.* New York: Dell Publishing Company, Laurel Edition, 1964.

Husserl, Edmund. *Ideas.* Translated by W. R. Boyce Gibson. New York: Collier Books, 1962.

————. *The Phenomenology of Internal Time Consciousness.* Edited by Martin Heidegger. Translated by James S. Churchill. Bloomington, Ind.: Indiana University Press, 1964.

Ingarden, Roman. *Das Literarische Kunstwerk.* Halle: Niemeyer, 1931.

————. *Untersuchungen zur Ontologie der Kunst.* Tübingen: Niemeyer, 1962.

James, William. *The Principles of Psychology.* 2 vols. New York: H. Holt and Co., 1890.

————. *The Will to Believe.* New York: Longmans, Green, and Co., 1921.

————. *The Varieties of Religious Experience.* New York: Random House, The Modern Library, 1936.

Janis, Sidney. *Abstract and Surrealist Art in America.* New York: Reynal and Hitchcock, 1944.

Jaspers, Karl. *Man in the Modern Age.* Translated by Eden and Cedar Paul. London: Routledge and K. Paul, 1951.

Kaelin, Eugene F. "Notes Toward an Understanding of Heidegger's Aesthetics." In *Phenomenology and Existentialism,* edited by E. N. Lee and M. Mandelbaum. Baltimore: The Johns Hopkins University Press, 1967.

————. *Art and Existence: A Phenomenological Aesthetics.* Lewisburg, Pa.: Bucknell University Press, 1970.

Kafka, Franz. *The Castle.* Translated by Edwin and Willa Muir. New York: Alfred A. Knopf, 1951.

Kaufmann, Walter, ed. *Existentialism from Dostoevski to Sartre.* Cleveland: The World Publishing Company, Meridian Books, 1964.

Kepes, Gyorgy. *Language of Vision.* Chicago: Paul Theobald, 1944.

Kierkegaard, Søren. *Fear and Trembling.* Translated by Walter Lowrie. Princeton: Princeton University Press, 1941.

————. *The Sickness Unto Death*. Translated by Walter Lowrie. Princeton: Princeton University Press, 1941.

Kline, George L., ed. *Alfred North Whitehead: Essays on His Philosophy*. Englewood Cliffs, New Jersey: Prentice-Hall Inc., 1963.

Langer, Susanne K. *Philosophy in a New Key*. Cambridge, Mass.: Harvard University Press, 1942.

————. *Feeling and Form*. New York: Charles Scribner's Sons, 1953.

————. *Problems of Art*. New York: Charles Scribner's Sons, 1957.

Lawler, Justus George. *The Christian Image: Studies in Religious Art and Poetry*. Pittsburgh, Pa.: Duquesne University Press, 1966.

Lawrence, D. H. *Lady Chatterley's Lover*. New York: Grove Press, 1959.

————. *Paintings of D. H. Lawrence*. Edited by Mervyn Levy. New York: Viking Press, 1964.

Lewis, H. D. *Morals and Revelation*. London: George Allen and Unwin, 1951.

Mann, Thomas. *Essays of Three Decades*. Translated by H. T. Lowe-Porter. New York: Alfred A. Knopf, 1965.

Marcel, Gabriel. "On the Ontological Mystery." Translated by Manya Harari. In *The Philosophy of Existence*. Reprinted by arrangement with the Philosophical Library, Inc. Freeport, N.Y.: Books for Libraries Press, 1948.

Margolis, Joseph. *Philosophy Looks at the Arts*. New York: Charles Scribner's Sons, 1962.

————. *The Language of Art and Art Criticism*. Detroit: Wayne State University Press, 1965.

Maritain, Jacques. *Art and Scholasticism*. Translated by J. F. Scanlan. New York: Charles Scribner's Sons, 1946.

————. *Creative Intuition in Art and Poetry*. New York: Pantheon Books, 1953.

Meiss, Millard. *Giotto and Assisi*. New York: New York University Press, 1960.

Merleau-Ponty, Maurice. *Phenomenology of Perception*. Translated by Colin Smith. London: Humanities Press, 1962.

———. *Signs*. Translated by R. C. McCleary. Evanston, Ill.: The Northwestern University Press, 1964.

———. *The Primacy of Perception and Other Essays*. Edited by J. Edie. Evanston, Ill.: The Northwestern University Press, 1964.

———. *The Visible and the Invisible*. Translated by A. Lingis. Evanston, Ill.: The Northwestern University Press, 1968.

Meyer, Leonard B. *Emotion and Meaning in Music*. Chicago: The University of Chicago Press, 1956.

Morris, Charles. *Foundations of a Theory of Signs*. In *International Encyclopedia of Unified Science*. Vol. 1, No. 2. Chicago: The University of Chicago Press, 1938.

Müller-Vollmer, Kurt. *Towards a Phenomenological Theory of Literature: A Study of Wilhelm Dilthey's Poetik*. The Hague: Mouton and Co., 1963.

Murdoch, Iris. *The Bell*. New York: The Viking Press, Avon Books, 1966.

Natanson, Maurice. *Literature, Philosophy and the Social Sciences*. The Hague: Martinus Nijhoff, 1962.

Nietzsche, Friedrich Wilhelm. *The Genealogy of Morals*. Translated by Horace B. Samuel. New York: Boni and Liveright, Inc., 1918.

———. *The Joyful Wisdom*. Translated by Thomas Common. 2nd ed. London: T. N. Foulis, 1918.

Orwell, George. *Animal Farm*. New York: Harcourt, Brace and Co., 1946.

———. *Nineteen Eighty-Four*. New York: Harcourt, Brace and Co., 1949.

Otto, Rudolf. *The Idea of the Holy*. Translated by John W. Harvey. London: Oxford University Press, 1928.

Panofsky, Erwin. *Gothic Architecture and Scholasticism*. Latrobe, Pa.: Archabbey Press, 1951.

Pascal, Blaise. *Pensées*. New York: Random House, The Modern Library, 1941.

Pepper, Stephen C. *Principles of Art Appreciation.* New York: Harcourt, Brace and Co., 1949.

Plutarch. *Plutarch's Lives.* Translated by John Dryden. New York: Random House, The Modern Library, 1932.

Polanyi, Michael. *Personal Knowledge.* Chicago: University of Chicago Press, 1958.

Pratt, Carroll C. *The Meaning of Music.* New York: McGraw-Hill, 1931.

Proust, Marcel. *Swann's Way.* Translated by C. K. Scott Moncrieff. New York: Random House, The Modern Library, 1928.

Ransom, John Crow. "The Tense of Poetry." In *The World's Body.* New York: Charles Scribner's Sons, 1938.

Read, Herbert. *Icon and Idea.* Cambridge, Mass.: Harvard University Press, 1955.

Rebay, Hilla. "Value of Non-Objectivity." In *Solomon R. Guggenheim Collection of Non-Objective Paintings.* New York: Solomon R. Guggenheim Foundation, 1938.

Reid, Louis Arnaud. *A Study in Aesthetics.* London: George Allen and Unwin, 1931.

————. *Meaning in the Arts.* London: George Allen and Unwin, 1969.

Richardson, Samuel. *Pamela.* London: J. M. Dent and Sons, 1914.

Richardson, William J. *Heidegger: Through Phenomenology to Thought.* The Hague: M. Nijhoff, 1963.

Rickey, George. "The Morphology of Movement: A Study of Kinetic Art." In *The Nature and Art of Motion,* edited by Gyorgy Kepes. New York: G. Braziller, 1965.

Robinson, James M. and Cobb, John B., Jr., eds. *The Later Heidegger and Theology.* New York: Harper and Row, 1963.

Rudner, Richard. "On Semiotic Aesthetics." In *Aesthetic Inquiry: Essays on Art Criticism and the Philosophy of Art,* edited by Monroe Beardsley and Herbert M. Schueller. Belmont, California: Dickenson Publishing Co., 1967.

Saint-Exupéry, Antoine de. *Wind, Sand and Stars.* Translated by Lewis Galantière. New York: Reynal and Hitchcock, 1939.

Salinger, J. D. *The Catcher in the Rye*. Boston: Little, Brown and Co., 1951.

Sartre, Jean-Paul. *The Psychology of Imagination*. New York: Philosophical Library, Inc., 1948.

――――. *Nausea*. Translated by Lloyd Alexander. Norfolk, Conn.: New Directions, 1949.

――――. *Literary and Philosophical Essays*. Translated by Annette Michelson. New York: Criterion Books, 1955.

――――. *Being and Nothingness*. Translated by Hazel E. Barnes. New York: Philosophical Library, Inc., 1956.

Scheler, Max. *On the Eternal in Man*. Translated by Bernard Noble. London: SCM Press, 1960.

Schelling, Friedrich Wilhelm Joseph von. "Systems des transcendentalen Idealismus." In *Friedrich Wilhelm Joseph von Schellings Sammtliche Werke*. Vol. 7, edited by K. F. A. Schelling. Stuttgart and Augsburg: J. G. Cotta, 1860.

Schleiermacher, F. E. D. *On Religion*. Translated by John Oman. New York: Harper and Brothers, 1958.

Schopenhauer, Arthur. *The World as Will and Idea*. 3 vols. Translated by R. B. Haldane and J. Kemp. London: Routledge and Kegan Paul, 1957.

Scott, Nathan A., Jr. "The Broken Center: A Definition of the Crisis of Values in Modern Literature." In *Symbolism in Religion and Literature*, edited by Rollo May. New York: G. Braziller, 1960.

Seuphor, Michel. *The Spiritual Mission of Art*. New York: Galerie Chalette, 1960.

Shapiro, Karl. *Essay on Rime*. New York: Reynal and Hitchcock, 1945.

Sherbourne, Donald W. *A Whiteheadian Aesthetic*. New Haven: Yale University Press, 1961.

Souriau, Étienne. "Time in the Plastic Arts." In *Reflections on Art*, edited by Susanne K. Langer. New York: Oxford University Press, 1961.

Stace, W. T. *Mysticism and Philosophy*. Philadelphia: J. B. Lippincott Co., 1960.

Stravinsky, Igor. *Stravinsky: An Autobiography*. New York: Simon and Schuster, 1936.

Suzuki, Daisetz T. *The Essentials of Zen Buddhism*. Edited by Bernard Phillips. London: Rider and Co., 1963.

Temple, William. *Nature, Man and God*. London: Macmillan and Co., 1935.

Tennyson, Alfred Lord. *The Poems of Tennyson*. Edited by Alfred Ricks. London and Harlow: Longmans, Green and Co., 1969.

Tillich, Paul. "The World Situation." In *The Christian Answer*, edited by Henry P. Van Dusen. New York: Scribner, 1945.

————. *Systematic Theology*. Vol. I. Chicago: University of Chicago Press, 1951.

————. *Systematic Theology*. Vol. 2. Chicago: University of Chicago Press, 1957.

————. *Systematic Theology*. Vol. 3. Chicago: University of Chicago Press, 1963.

————. *The Courage to Be*. New Haven: Yale University Press, 1952.

————, (with Theodore M. Greene). "Authentic Religious Art." In *Masterpieces of Religious Art*. Chicago: The Art Institute of Chicago, 1954.

————. *Love, Power, and Justice: Ontological Analyses and Ethical Applications*. New York and London: Oxford University Press, 1954.

————. "Theology and Symbolism." In *Religious Symbolism*, edited by F. Ernest Johnson. New York: Harper, 1955.

————. "Existentialist Aspects of Modern Art." In *Christianity and Existentialism*, edited by Carl Michalson. New York: Scribners, 1956.

Tolstoy, Leo. *Anna Karenina*. Translated by Constance Garnett. New York: Random House, 1939.

————. *Resurrection*. Translated by Louise Maude. London: Oxford University Press, 1939.

————. *War and Peace*. Translated by Louise and Aylmer Maude. New York: Simon and Schuster, 1942.

Twain, Mark. *The Favorite Works of Mark Twain.* Garden City, N.Y.: Garden City Publishing Co., 1939.

Urban, W. M. *Language and Reality.* London: George Allen and Unwin, 1951.

Van der Leeuw, Gerardus. *Religion in Essence and Manifestation.* Translated by J. E. Turner. London: George Allen and Unwin, 1938.

————. *Sacred and Profane Beauty: The Holy in Art.* Translated by David E. Green. New York: Rinehart and Winston, 1963.

Vasari, Giorgio. *Lives of the Most Eminent Painters, Sculptors, and Artists.* Translated by Gaston Duc Devere. London: Macmillan and Co., 1912.

Vivas, Eliseo. *Creation and Discovery.* New York: The Noonday Press, 1955.

————. *D. H. Lawrence: The Failure and Triumph of Art.* Evanston, Ill.: Northwestern University Press, 1960.

————. *The Artistic Transaction and Essays on Theory of Literature.* Columbus: Ohio State University Press, 1963.

Wach, Joachim. *Types of Religious Experience.* Chicago: University of Chicago Press, 1951.

————. *The Comparative Study of Religions.* Edited by Joseph M. Kitawaga. New York: Columbia University Press, 1958.

Weiss, Paul. *Religion and Art.* Milwaukee, Wis.: Marquette University Press, 1963.

————. *The God We Seek.* Carbondale, Ill.: Southern Illinois University Press, 1964.

Wheelwright, Philip. *The Burning Fountain.* Bloomington, Ind.: Indiana University Press, 1954.

Whitehead, Alfred North. *Science and the Modern World.* New York: The Macmillan Co., 1925.

————. *Religion in the Making.* New York: The Macmillan Co., 1926.

————. *Symbolism, Its Meaning and Effect.* New York: The Macmillan Co., 1927.

————. *The Aims of Education and Other Essays.* New York: The Macmillan Co., 1929.

————. *Process and Reality.* New York: The Macmillan Co., 1929.

————. *The Function of Reason.* Princeton: Princeton University Press, 1929.

————. *Adventures of Ideas.* New York: The Macmillan Co., 1933.

————. *Modes of Thought.* New York: The Macmillan Co., 1938.

————. *The Philosophy of Alfred North Whitehead.* Edited by Paul A. Schilpp. 2nd ed. New York: Tudor Publishing Company for The Library of Living Philosophers, 1951.

————. *Dialogues of Alfred North Whitehead.* As recorded by Lucien Price. Boston: Little, Brown and Company, 1954.

Wieman, Henry Nelson. *Religious Experience and Scientific Method.* New York: The Macmillan Co., 1926.

Wilder, Amos. *Modern Poetry and the Christian Tradition: A Study in the Relation of Christianity to Culture.* New York: Charles Scribner's Sons, 1952.

Williams, Emmett, ed. *Anthology of Concrete Poetry.* New York: Something Else Press, 1967.

Williams, William Carlos. "Choral: The Pink Church." In *Modern American Poetry,* edited by B. Rajan. London: Dennis Hobson, 1950.

Wittgenstein, Ludwig. *Tractatus Logico-Philosophicus.* London: K. Paul, Trench, Trubner and Co., 1922.

————. *Philosophical Investigations.* Translated by G. E. M. Anscombe. New York: The Macmillan Company, 1953.

Yeats, William Butler. *Autobiography.* New York: The Macmillan Company, 1933.

ARTICLES

Ashmore, Jerome. "The Old and the New in Non-Objective Painting." *The Journal of Aesthetics and Art Criticism* 9 (June 1951) : 294–300.

———. "Some Differences Between Abstract and Non-Objective Painting." *The Journal of Aesthetics and Art Criticism* 13 (June 1955) : 486–95.

Colm, Hanna. "Healing as Participation." *Psychiatry* 16 (May 1953) : 99–111.

Dillenberger, John. "Tillich's Use of the Concept 'Being'." In *Christianity And Crisis* 13 (March 1953) : 30 f.

Isenberg, Arnold. "The Esthetic Function of Language." *The Journal of Philosophy* 46 (1949) : 5–20.

Loomer, Bernard M. "Tillich's Theology of Correlation." *The Journal of Religion* 36 (July 1956) : 150–56.

Macquarrie, John. "Feeling and Understanding." *Theology* 58 (May 1955) : 179–85.

Martin, F. David. "The Artist, Autobiography, and Thomas Wolfe." *The Bucknell Review* 5 (March 1955) : 15–28.

———. "Unrealized Possibility in the Aesthetic Experience." *The Journal of Philosophy* 52 (July 1955) : 393–400.

———. "On the Supposed Incompatibility of Expressionism and Formalism." *The Journal of Aesthetics and Art Criticism* 15 (Sept. 1956) : 96–99.

———. "On Enjoying Decadence." *The Journal of Aesthetics and Art Criticism* 17 (June 1959) : 441–46.

———. "On Portraiture: Some Distinctions." *The Journal of Aesthetics and Art Criticism* 20 (Sept. 1961) : 61–72.

———. "The Imperatives of Stylistic Development: Psychological and Formal." *Bucknell Review* 11 (March 1963) : 53–70.

———. "The Sociological Imperative of Stylistic Development." *Bucknell Review* 11 (Dec. 1963) : 54–80.

———. "Spiritual Asymmetry in Portraiture." *The British Journal of Aesthetics* 5 (Jan. 1965) : 6–13.

———. "Naming Paintings." *The Art Journal* 25 (Spring 1966) : 252–56.

———. "The Power of Music and Whitehead's Theory of Perception." *The Journal of Aesthetics and Art Criticism* 25 (Spring 1967) : 313–22.

———. "The Aesthetic in Religious Experience." *Religious Studies* 4 (October 1968) : 1–24.

———. "Heidegger's Thinking Being and Whitehead's Theory of Perception." *Bucknell Review* 27 (May 1969) : 79–102.

———. "The Persistent Presence of Abstract Painting." *The Journal of Aesthetics and Art Criticism* 28 (Fall 1969) : 23–31.

Matisse, Henri. *La Grande Revue* (Dec. 25, 1908).

Meyer, Leonard B. "Some Remarks on Value and Greatness in Music." *The Journal of Aesthetics and Art Criticism* 17 (June 1959) : 486–500.

Morris, Charles. "Esthetics and the Theory of Signs." *The Journal of Unified Science* 8 (June 1938) : 131–50.

Ortega y Gasset, José. "The Dehumanization of Art." *Symposium* I, edited by J. Burnham and P. Wheelwright. (April 1930) : 194–205.

Price, Kingsley. "Is a Work of Art a Symbol?" *The Journal of Philosophy* 50 (1953) : 485–503.

Robinson, Daniel S. "Tillich and Marcel: Theistic Existentialists." *Personalist* 34 (Summer 1953) : 237–50.

Rochberg, George. "The New Image of Music." *Perspectives of New Music* 2 (1963) : 1–10.

Sontag, Susan. "Notes on 'camp'." *Partisan Review* 21 (Fall 1964) : 515–30.

Sweeney, James Johnson. "New Directions in Painting." *The Journal of Aesthetics and Art Criticism* 18 (March 1960) : 368–77.

Tillich, Paul. "The Religious Symbol." *Journal of Liberal Religion* 2 (Summer 1940) : 13–33.

———. "Flight to Atheism." *The Protestant* 4 (March 1943) : 43–48.

————. "Existential Philosophy." *The Journal of the History of Ideas* 5 (January 1944) : 44–70.

————. "The Two Types of Philosophy of Religion." *Union Seminary Quarterly Review* 1 (May 1946) : 3–13.

————. "Religious Symbols and Our Knowledge of God." *The Christian Scholar* 38 (Sept. 1955) : 189–97.

————. "Theology and Architecture." *Architectural Forum* 103 (December 1955) : 131–36.

————. "Art and Ultimate Reality." A Lecture at the Museum of Modern Art in *Dimensions* (Feb. 17, 1959).

Tolnay, Charles de. "The Autobiographic Aspect of Fra Filippo Lippi's Virgins." *Gazette des Beaux-Arts* 39 (1952).

Tomas, Vincent. "Aesthetic Vision." *Philosophical Review* 68 (1959) : 52–67.

Trilling, Lionel. "The Two Environments." *Encounter* 25 (July 1965) : 3–13.

Vivas, Eliseo. "A Definition of the Aesthetic Experience." *The Journal of Philosophy* 34 (Nov. 1937) : 628–34.

————. "What is a Poem?" *Sewanee Review* 62 (1954) : 578–97.

Wallis, Mieczyslaw. "The Origin and Foundations of Non-Objective Painting." *The Journal of Aesthetics and Art Criticism* 19 (Fall 1960) : 61–71.

Weitz, Morris. "The Role of Theory in Aesthetics." *The Journal of Aesthetics and Art Criticism* 15 (September 1956) : 27–35.

Wylie, Ruth. "Musimatics: A View from the Mainland." *The Journal of Aesthetics and Art Criticism* 24 (Winter 1965) : 287–94.

Index

Abell, Walter: painting and plastic values, 153n; artist and collective dream, 249–50

Acton Collection: mentioned, 51

Adams, Henry: Chartres, and symbols, 211, on region of, 236–37, 253

Aeschylus: on sky and earth, 231

aesthetic experience: and *Being*, 53; discussed, 58–62; fusion in, 97. *See also* Participative experience; Spectator experience

aesthetic object: defined, 58; science as, 60; as natural or artistic, 60; as decoration, 60–61

Alfred, William: *Hogan's Goat*, mentioned, 49

Angelico, Fra: historical placement, 174–75

Aquinas, Saint Thomas: on corporeal metaphors, 166

architecture: and sublimity, 91, 229–30, 234, 238, 255–56; and process and presentational immediacy, 148, 156; and space, 228–34, 239–48, 255; and *Being*, 232, 234–39, 244, 247–48, 251, 255–56; and process, 234–39, 248, 251, 253, 255; and iconic symbols, 234–38, 244, 248, 255–56; and earth, 235–44, 246, 248, 251, 253, 255; and world or sky, 235–36, 238, 240–41, 244–48, 251, 253, 255;

and region, 236–38, 244, 248–53, 255; as public art, 237, 249–51; media of, 237, 239, 241, 248

Aristotle: Prime Mover as a being, 203

Arnolfo di Cambio: and Giotto, 171

Arp, Jean (originally Hans): *Mountain, Table, Anchor, Navel* as abstract, 140–41; abstractions and eternity, 152

artist: and subject matter, 61, 195; and *Being*, 66–69, 112, 225–27, 256–57; and inexhaustibility, 66; and ontical reality, 67; receptive creativity of, 67, 230; constructive creativity of, 67; and ontological sensitivity, 68; as secular, 69, 213; as religious, 69, 213, 225–27; abstract painter as Shepherd of sensa, 139, 182; and presentational immediacy, 145; representational painter as Shepherd of symbols, 182; and *Weltanschauung*, 225; constitutive matrix of, 225–27; architect, as primeval cutter, 228–29, as Shepherd of space, 230, 256; and contemporary values, 249–50; and mental habits, 250

art, work of: explicated, 60–62; media of, 66, 96; and participative experience, 65–67, 91, 98;

275

Index